Get the eBook FREE!

(PDF, ePub, Kindle, and liveBook all included)

We believe that once you buy a book from us, you should be able to read it in any format we have available. To get electronic versions of this book at no additional cost to you, purchase and then register this book at the Manning website.

Go to https://www.manning.com/freebook and follow the instructions to complete your pBook registration.

That's it!
Thanks from Manning!

How Large Language Models Work

How Large Language Models Work

EDWARD RAFF

DREW FARRIS

STELLA BIDERMAN

MANNING

SHELTER ISLAND

For online information and ordering of this and other Manning books, please visit www.manning.com. The publisher offers discounts on this book when ordered in quantity.

For more information, please contact

    Special Sales Department
    Manning Publications Co.
    20 Baldwin Road
    PO Box 761
    Shelter Island, NY 11964
    Email: orders@manning.com

Manning Publications Co.
20 Baldwin Road
PO Box 761
Shelter Island, NY 11964

Development editor:	Frances Lefkowitz
Technical editor:	Shreesha Jagadeesh
Review editors:	Aleksandar Dragosavljevic, Radmila Ercegovac
Production editor:	Andy Marinkovich
Copy editor:	Alisa Larson
Proofreader:	Melody Dolab
Typesetter:	Ammar Taha Mohamedy
Cover designer:	Marija Tudor

ISBN 9781633437081
Printed in the United States of America

brief contents

contents

The skeleton of this book began to come together in the late 2010s when we saw several significant advancements in the field of artificial intelligence (AI) that we knew could soon lead to a breakthrough. The convergence of new types of computer hardware, the availability of vast amounts of data, and the growth of neural networks were rapidly converging to a tipping point where it was now possible for machine learning algorithms to accurately capture nuances of language and meaning at a surprising level of fidelity. With the right combination of breakthroughs, we knew this would enable an entirely new class of applications. We conducted research, built prototypes, had conversations with our colleagues, clients, and families, and sought to tell the story of how these advancements could change the world and the underlying techniques that made that possible.

Then, at the end of November 2022, OpenAI released ChatGPT, and suddenly, this potential became a reality. By putting this technology into the hands of the public, anyone could gain firsthand experience by interacting with a chatbot powered by a large language model (LLM). As with any new technology, there was a lot of speculation as to what could possibly allow ChatGPT to interact with great fidelity and produce such high-quality output. We saw that, based on interactions with ChatGPT, people often assumed that there was more behind the curtain than truly existed, sometimes believing that we were truly on the cusp of general AI that could do anything. We found that our conversations shifted to what could practically be achieved using applications of LLMs, managing expectations, characterizing risks, validating behaviors, and negotiating the path between what's realistic and what's not safe or responsible to attempt.

Fast forward to 2025, and we're now firmly ensconced in the era of generative and agentic AI. We have seen a massive proliferation of models, applications, and capabilities and an explosion in the types of data we can work with. Each major vendor has a technology offering that incorporates an LLM, whether they are chatbots to talk to or agents that review our writing, help us write computer programs, or generate images. Many of these are controversial, leading to new conversations about data use and causing us to rethink our assumptions about the relationship between technology and creativity. Regardless, there are core principles that enable these applications, and our goal with this book is to describe these in a way that's accessible to readers from all walks of life.

Whether you're a CEO, a machine learning engineer, a casual coder, or just the average person seeking to use this technology, we hope you'll find something useful in this book that explains the algorithms and techniques that make LLMs work. It is a collection of our experiences working in the field of natural language processing, machine learning, and algorithmic research, where we set out to share our knowledge in a manner that is accessible to nearly everyone. Along the way, we will dispel some of the mystery, explain the limitations, and explore the implications of this fascinating new technology. We hope you'll join us on this voyage.

acknowledgments

This book would not be possible without the support of many of our colleagues, collaborators, and countless researchers in the field of artificial intelligence who have chosen to share their explorations of this technology.

We thank our colleagues at Booz Allen Hamilton for their support of this work, including John Larson, Steve Escaravage, Justin Neroda, Catherine Ordun, Jessica Reinhart, and Katrina Jacobs. Andre Nguyen and Matt Keating deserve special recognition for the many conversations on the nature of large language models and ways to think about their safety.

We also want to thank the outstanding staff at Manning Publications, including Frances Lefkowitz, our development editor, and Shreesha Jagadeesh, our technical editor, who both asked the hard questions and shaped and improved the book in so many ways by providing thoughtful feedback. We also thank Andy Waldron, our acquisitions editor; Rebecca Rinehart, our development manager; and Aira Ducic, who led marketing for this book.

We also acknowledge Melissa Ice and Radmila Ercegovac, who orchestrated the reviews throughout the writing process, and all of the anonymous reviewers who provided excellent feedback to make this book what it is today.

We owe a special debt to everyone who shepherded this book through the production effort with much patience, including Aleksandar Dragosavljevic and Andy Marinkovich, as well as Alisa Larson for editing and Melody Dolab for the final proofread. Sam Wood and Marija Tudor led the production of our cover, and Azra Dedic led the production of our graphics and figures.

To all the reviewers: Abdullah Al Imran, Adrian M. Rossi, Allan Makura, Ankit Virmani, Bhagvan Kommadi, Cristina-Ioana Casapu, David Cronkite, David Yakobovitch, Doug Puenner, Doyle Turner, Emanuele Piccinelli, Federico Grasso, Florian

Braun, Georg Sommer, George Onofrei, Girish Ahankari, Harsh Ranjan, Holger Voges, Ivan A. Fernandez, Jaganadh Gopinadhan, Jeremy Zeidner, John R. Donoghue, John Guthrie, Jose Morales, Kartik Dutta, Kelvin Chappell, Louis Luangkesorn, Mark Graham, Mattia Zoccarato, Matt Sarmiento, Mikael Dautrey, Mike Taylor, Mostofa Adib Shakib, Neeraj Gupta, Oliver Korten, Raj G, Sashank Dara, Simeon Leyzerzon, Simone Sguazza, Slavomir Furman, Sudharshan Tumkunta, Tony Holdroyd, Vincent Joseph, and Walter Alexander Mata López, your suggestions helped make this a better book.

We also want to thank Al Krinker, a former colleague at Booz Allen Hamilton and our first editor at Manning Publications, who helped us get started in the early days of this work.

Finally, and most importantly, we want to thank our families and friends who supported and encouraged us through many nights and weekends working on this book.

about this book

How Large Language Models Work is the culmination of countless hours of research, explorations, conversations, and building and evaluating large language models and the systems that use them to solve problems. It is a distillation of years of working in the fields of machine learning, natural language processing, and software engineering that we, the authors, bring to the table. It's important to us to share what we've learned and break down the complexities of the field into a straightforward conversation that presents foundational details on how LLMs work and builds from there to cover topics that are not widely understood. We seek to dispel some myths and shed light on the realities along the way.

This book does not describe how to implement LLMs like ChatGPT using code. Instead, it covers the foundational concepts that make LLMs operate, as well as the opportunities and limitations of this technology. We'll provide you with an understanding of how the underlying algorithms operate. As a result, you'll better understand why LLMs are implemented the way they are and how LLMs can be used to solve a variety of problems. Our goal is to translate years of LLM research into something understandable for someone new to the field.

To do this, we'll start with the basics to build a foundational understanding of the inner workings of LLMs and then transition to more advanced topics, including adjacent considerations that go beyond LLM operation. Along the way, we'll tackle misconceptions, limitations, and the ethical implications of building and using LLMs, as well as the many ways LLMs can be effectively deployed as technical solutions for challenging problems.

Who should read this book?

This book is intended for a variety of readers, including those who have just started working with LLMs, experienced software developers, and data scientists, as well as technical leadership, decision makers, and executives in the C-suite, who face the challenge of developing strategies for incorporating LLMs and generative AI into their businesses. Our goal in writing this book was to create a work that is both accessible and compelling for a broad audience, presenting LLMs in a nontrivial manner.

Perhaps you've previously encountered machine learning, either as a student or hobbyist who took an introduction to machine learning course, but you lack a strong foundation in the field. Perhaps you're someone who has used tools like OpenAI's ChatGPT, Google's Gemini, Anthropic's Claude, or Microsoft's Copilot for work or play and are curious about how these tools generate their results. Regardless of your background or experience, we believe there's something for you in this book.

Once you're done, you'll know

- How LLMs process human language data and identify the tasks that may fail when using an LLM
- How data flows through an LLM, the role of transformers and attention, how they operate at a high level, why they are important, and how they relate to other machine learning algorithms
- How LLMs are trained on data, including the concepts of parameters, gradient descent, pretraining, and why model size is critical
- How to choose a deployment strategy for LLMs in your applications and business
- How to identify tasks and scenarios that LLMs can't realistically solve
- The dangers and ethical concerns of using and building LLMs and where it is appropriate or inappropriate to use them

How this book is organized: A roadmap

In this book, we'll start with the basics of how LLMs process human language, the algorithms that make them possible, and how they learn from data. From there, we'll explore how LLM technology can be applied to tasks beyond text and wrap up with a discussion of LLMs' use and the implications of this technology.

Chapter 1 provides a high-level understanding of LLMs and generative AI in plain language. We explore the differences between how humans and machines work with language and begin to peel back the surface of what makes LLMs so capable, introducing their limitations and potential concerns when using them.

Chapters 2 to 5 delve deep into what's going on under the hood, focusing on the mechanics rather than the math. In chapter 2, we explain how large language models process text so that they can work with it before diving into the internals of how the things we enter into an LLM ultimately lead to the generative output they produce in chapter 3. Chapter 4 discusses how all of this is possible, the process of training an

LLM on incredible amounts of text, and why this training can fail to produce the expected outcomes. Chapter 5 describes how we can control and constrain an LLM and its outputs for specific applications.

Chapter 6 looks beyond working with languages and explores the use of LLMs for software development, formal mathematics, and beyond, including text, images, audio, and video.

Now that we've covered the mechanics, chapters 7 to 9 introduce the considerations behind using LLMs in real-world applications. First, we tackle many of the misconceptions, limits, and capabilities of LLMs in chapter 7. In chapter 8, we discuss different scenarios for designing solutions that use LLMs and identify situations where the obvious choices may not be the best options. Any discussion of LLM use wouldn't be complete without covering the ethical implications of building and using LLMs, which we cover in chapter 9. Do LLMs pose an existential risk to humanity? What are the ethics and implications of training on as much data as we can scrape from the internet? Join us on this journey, and you'll discover that along the way, you've become equipped with the knowledge you need for critical thinking about this compelling new technology.

Throughout the book, you'll find many references to other sources of information that go deeper into different aspects of LLMs that we cover. We collect all of these in a references section at the end of the book, providing easy access to the entire list of resources in one place. We encourage you to continue exploring LLMs by visiting these sources and delving deeper into topics that best align with your interests.

liveBook discussion forum

Purchase of *How Large Language Models Work* includes free access to liveBook, Manning's online reading platform. Using liveBook's exclusive discussion features, you can attach comments to the book globally or to specific sections or paragraphs. It's easy to make notes for yourself, ask and answer questions, and receive help from the authors and other users. To access the forum, go to https://livebook.manning.com/book/how-large-language-models-work/discussion.

Manning's commitment to our readers is to provide a venue where a meaningful dialogue between individual readers and between readers and the authors can take place. It's not a commitment to any specific amount of participation on the part of the authors, whose contribution to the forum remains voluntary (and unpaid). We suggest you try asking the authors some challenging questions lest their interest stray! The forum and archives of the previous discussions will be accessible from the publisher's website as long as the book is in print.

about the authors

EDWARD RAFF is a Director of Emerging AI at Booz Allen Hamilton, where he leads the machine learning research team. He has worked in healthcare, natural language processing, computer vision, and cybersecurity, as well as fundamental AI/ML research. The author of *Inside Deep Learning*, Dr. Raff has over 100 published research articles at the top artificial intelligence conferences. He is the author of the Java Statistical Analysis Tool library, a Senior Member of the Association for the Advancement of Artificial Intelligence, and twice chaired the Conference on Applied Machine Learning and Information Technology and the AI for Cyber Security workshop. Dr. Raff's work has been deployed and used by antivirus companies worldwide.

DREW FARRIS is a Principal at Booz Allen Hamilton. He specializes in artificial intelligence and machine learning, with over 14 years of experience building advanced analytics for public sector clients. Before joining Booz Allen, Drew worked with academic research teams and startups on information retrieval, natural language processing, and large-scale data management platforms. He has co-authored several publications, including Booz Allen's *Field Guide to Data Science* and *Machine Intelligence Primer*, and the Jolt Award-winning book *Taming Text* on computational text processing. Drew is also a member of the Apache Software Foundation and has contributed to open source projects like Apache Mahout, Lucene, and Solr.

STELLA BIDERMAN is a machine learning researcher at Booz Allen Hamilton and the executive director of the nonprofit research center EleutherAI. She is a leading advocate for open source artificial intelligence and has trained many of the world's most powerful open source artificial intelligence algorithms. She has a master's degree in computer science from the Georgia Institute of Technology and degrees in Mathematics and Philosophy from the University of Chicago.

about the cover illustration

The figure on the cover of *How Large Language Models Work*, captioned "Charles de Cleves, Count of Rethel," and dated 1852, is from the European Libraries collection, courtesy of the Lyon Public Library.

In those days, it was easy to identify where people lived and what their trade or station in life was just by their dress. Manning celebrates the inventiveness and initiative of the computer business with book covers based on the rich diversity of regional culture centuries ago, brought back to life by pictures from collections such as this one.

Big picture: What are LLMs?

The hype around terms such as machine learning (ML), deep learning (DL), and artificial intelligence (AI) has reached record levels. Much of the initial public exposure to these terms was driven by a product called ChatGPT, a form of generative AI built by a company called OpenAI. We now see generative AI offerings such as Gemini from Google, Copilot from Microsoft, Llama from Meta, Claude from Anthropic, and newcomers like DeepSeek in the daily news. Seemingly overnight, the ability of computers to talk, learn, and perform complex tasks has taken a dramatic leap forward. New generative AI companies are forming, and existing firms are publicly investing billions of dollars in the field. The technology in this space is evolving at a maddening pace.

1

This book aims to help you make sense of this new world by dispelling the mystery behind what makes ChatGPT and related technologies work. We will cover the knowledge necessary to understand their inner workings and how the components (data and algorithms) stack together to create the tools we use. We'll also discuss various cases where this technology can form the cornerstone of a broader system and others where systems based on large language models (LLMs) may be a poor choice.

After reading this book, you'll understand what generative AI like ChatGPT really *is*, what it can and can't do, and, importantly, the "why" behind its limitations. With this knowledge, you'll be a more effective consumer of this family of technology, whether as a user, a software developer, or a business decision maker in organizations deciding whether and, if so, how to incorporate it into your products or operations. This foundation will also serve as a launchpad for deeper study into the field by providing knowledge that will allow you to understand in-depth research and other works.

1.1 Generative AI in context

First, we need to get more specific about what we are discussing when we talk about LLMs, GPTs, and the various tools that rely on them. The GPT in ChatGPT stands for *Generative Pretrained Transformer.* Each of these words bears a particular meaning in the context of ChatGPT. We'll dedicate future chapters to discussing what *pretrained* and *transformer* mean, but we start here by discussing what *generative* means in this context.

AI chatbots like ChatGPT are a form of *generative* AI. Broadly, generative AI is software capable of creating, or generating, various media (e.g., text, images, audio, and video) based on data it has observed in the past and influenced by what people consider to be pleasing and accurate output. For example, if ChatGPT is prompted with "Write a haiku about snow falling on pines," it will use all of the data it was trained with about haikus, snow, pines, and other forms of poetry to generate a novel haiku as shown in figure 1.1

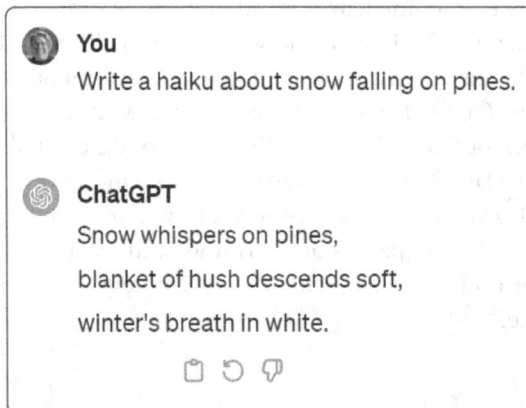

> **You**
> Write a haiku about snow falling on pines.
>
> **ChatGPT**
> Snow whispers on pines,
> blanket of hush descends soft,
> winter's breath in white.
>
> 📄 ↺ 👎

Figure 1.1   A simple haiku generated by ChatGPT

Fundamentally, these systems are machine learning models that *generate* new output, so generative AI is an appropriate description. Some possible inputs and outputs are demonstrated in figure 1.2. While ChatGPT deals primarily with text as input and output, it also has more experimental support for different data types, such as audio and images. However, from our definition, you can imagine that many different kinds of algorithms and tasks fall into the description of generative AI.

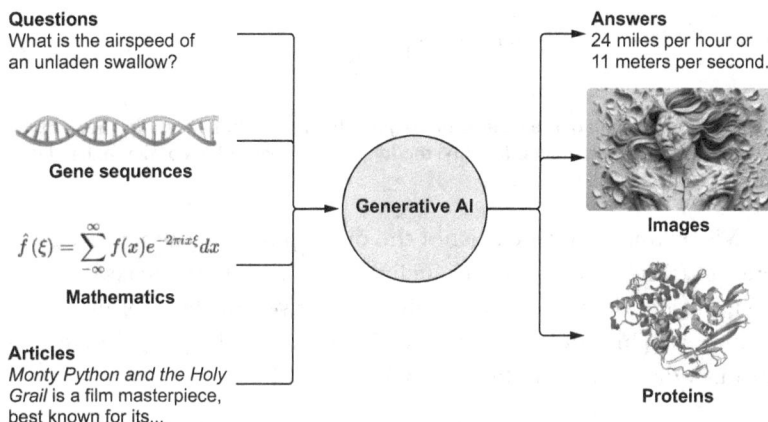

Questions
What is the airspeed of
an unladen swallow?

Gene sequences

$$\hat{f}(\xi) = \sum_{-\infty}^{\infty} f(x)e^{-2\pi i x \xi} dx$$

Mathematics

Articles
*Monty Python and the Holy
Grail* is a film masterpiece,
best known for its...

Generative AI

Answers
24 miles per hour or
11 meters per second.

Images

Proteins

Figure 1.2 Generative AI takes some input (numbers, text, images) and produces a new output (usually text or images). Any combination of input or output options is possible, and the nature of the output depends on what the algorithm was trained for. It could be to add detail, rewrite something to be shorter, extrapolate missing portions, and more.

Going a level deeper, ChatGPT is dealing with human text, and so it would also be fair to call it a model of human language—or a *language model* if you are a cool person who does work in the field known as *natural language processing* (NLP). The field of NLP intersects both computer science and linguistics and explores the technology that helps computers understand, manipulate, and create human language. Some of the first efforts in the field of NLP emerged in the 1940s when researchers hoped to build machines that could automatically translate between languages. As a result, NLP and language models have been around for a very long time. So what makes the new generative AI tools different? The most salient difference is that ChatGPT and similar algorithms are much larger than what people have historically built and are trained on much greater amounts of data.

For this reason, the name *large language models* (LLMs) has become quite popular to describe GPT and similar types of machine learning models. GPT describes a specific type of LLM developed by OpenAI, and other companies use similar technologies to build their own LLMs and AI chatbots. More broadly, LLMs are machine learning models trained on large amounts of linguistic data.

A diagram of these relationships can be seen in figure 1.3. ChatGPT, Copilot, Claude, and Gemini are some of the products that operate via text and are built using LLMs. LLMs use techniques from AI and NLP. The primary component of an LLM is a transformer, which we will explain in detail in chapter 3.

Some examples of generative AI include

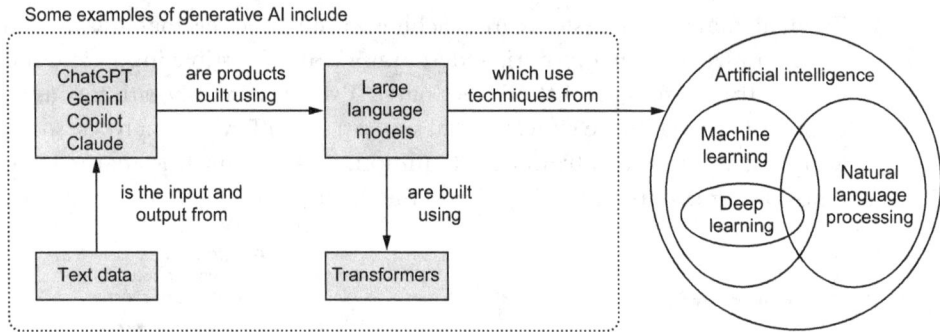

Figure 1.3   A high-level map of the various terms you'll become familiar with and how they relate. Generative AI is a description of functionality: the function of generating content and using techniques from AI to accomplish that goal.

> **NOTE**   Vision and language are not the only options for generative AI. Audio generation (think text-to-speech, such as when your GPS speaks out the street names), playing board games like chess, and even protein folding have used generative AI. This book will stick mostly to text and language since those are the primary data types employed by GPTs and LLMs.

As the name *large* implies, these models are not small. ChatGPT specifically is rumored [1] to contain 1.76 trillion parameters that are used to dictate the way it behaves. Each parameter is typically stored as a floating point number (a number with a decimal point) that uses 4 bytes for storage. That means the model itself takes 7 terabytes to hold in memory. This size is larger than most people's computers could fit in RAM, let alone inside the most powerful graphics processing units (GPUs) with 80 gigabytes of memory. GPUs are special-purpose hardware components that excel in performing the mathematical operations that make LLMs possible. Currently, many GPUs are required when making LLMs, so we are already discussing a lot of computational infrastructure and complexity over multiple machines to build an LLM. In contrast, more run-of-the-mill language models would be 2 GB or less in most cases—over 5,000× smaller, a much more reasonable size when considering building and using such a model on more standard hardware.

Optimizing LLMs

Many researchers are investigating ways to make LLMs consume less memory. Sometimes, this includes techniques that require less than 4 bytes to store a parameter utilizing a method called "mixed-precision" [2]. This approach stores some LLM parameters using 2 bytes or fewer and presents a tradeoff between accuracy and memory efficiency. In the end, the effect on accuracy is often negligible. This optimization is one of many that researchers make to make LLMs more resource efficient.

GPU alternatives

While GPUs are currently the most frequently used hardware to train LLMs, they aren't the only option available. Increasingly, companies are developing special-purpose hardware that offers general advantages for training machine learning models. For example, in 2018, Google made its Tensor Processing Unit (TPU) [3] available for public use as a part of the Google Cloud Platform (GCP). While TPUs generally have less computing capacity than GPUs, their specialized architecture allows them to perform better than GPUs for specific machine learning tasks.

1.2 What you will learn

Throughout this book, we will explain how LLMs work and equip you with the vocabulary needed to understand them. Once you've finished reading, you will have a conversational understanding of what an LLM is and the critical steps involved in its operation. Additionally, you will have some perspective on what an LLM reasonably can do, especially the considerations related to deploying or using one. We will discuss salient points about the fundamental limitations of LLMs and provide tips on how to design around them or when LLMs and, more broadly, generative AI should be avoided entirely.

Keep in mind that the details of how transformers are combined to build ChatGPT, Claude, or Gemini are nuanced, and this book primarily focuses on what all of these systems have in common. In fact, we can't know some of the actual differences between these LLMs because although commercial LLM providers have shared a great deal of information about their models, they have not shared some pieces of information, likely considered trade secrets.

Due to the effect that transformer-based LLMs will have on the world, we're purposely focusing on a wide audience for this book. Programmers of all backgrounds, executives, managers, sales staff, artists, writers, publishers, and many more will have to interact with or have their jobs affected by LLMs over the coming years. So we are going to assume you, dear reader, have a minimal coding background but are familiar with the basic constructs of coding: logic, functions, and maybe even some data structures. You also do not need to be a mathematician; we will show you a bit of math where it is helpful, but it will be optional in building an understanding of how LLMs work.

This approach means that very little code will be presented in this book. If you want to dive directly into building and using an LLM, other books in the Manning catalog, such as Sebastian Raschka's *Build a Large Language Model from Scratch* (2024) or Edward Raff's *Inside Deep Learning* (2022), will complement the material presented here. However, if you want to understand why the LLM you are using has unusual outputs, how your team might be able to use an LLM, or where to avoid using an LLM, or if you have a colleague with little machine learning background who needs to get conversationally competent, this is the book you and your colleague need.

In particular, the first part of this book focuses on what LLMs do: their inputs and outputs, converting inputs to outputs, and how we constrain the nature of those outputs. In the second part, we focus on what humans do: how people interact with technology and what risks this creates for using generative AI. Similarly, we'll discuss some ethical considerations that arise when using and building LLMs.

> **Training LLMs is expensive**
>
> Training an LLM is not realistically possible for most people; it is a $\geq \$100,000$ investment at a minimum and would be a $100 million effort to try to compete with OpenAI. At the same time, the resources available for training LLMs are constantly evolving. As a result, instead of walking you through what training an LLM looks like today, we focus on content with a longer shelf life—helpful knowledge that we believe will be valid years from now instead of example code that could be out of date in just a few months.

1.3 Introducing how LLMs work

Generative AI (GAI or GenAI) is poised to change how we produce and interact with information. The introduction of ChatGPT in November 2022 highlighted the capabilities of modern AI and fascinated a significant portion of the world. Currently, you can sign up for free at https://chat.openai.com/ to try it out.

If you enter the text prompt "Summarize the following text in two sentences," followed by all of the introductory text from this chapter, you will get something similar to the following.

"The recent surge in attention towards artificial intelligence, particularly large language models (LLMs) like ChatGPT from OpenAI, has highlighted their vast capabilities in natural language processing. This book aims to provide readers with a conversational understanding of LLMs, their operational intricacies, potential applications, limitations, and the ethical considerations surrounding their use while assuming only a basic familiarity with coding concepts and minimal mathematical background. That's pretty impressive, and to a casual audience, it may seem like this capability has come out of nowhere."

When you visit OpenAI's website and sign up for ChatGPT, you may notice an option similar to that shown in figure 1.4. As the name GPT-4 implies, Open AI is, as of this writing, working on its fourth generation of GPT models. LLMs like GPT-4 are a well-established area of ML research in creating algorithms that can synthesize and react to information and produce outputs that appear human generated. This ability unlocks several areas of interaction between people and machines that previously existed only in science fiction. The strength of the language representation encoded into ChatGPT enables convincing dialog, instruction following, summary generation, question answering, content creation, and many more applications. Indeed, it is likely that many possible applications of this technology do not yet exist because our gut reaction is to think of our current problems rather than new capabilities or products that could exist.

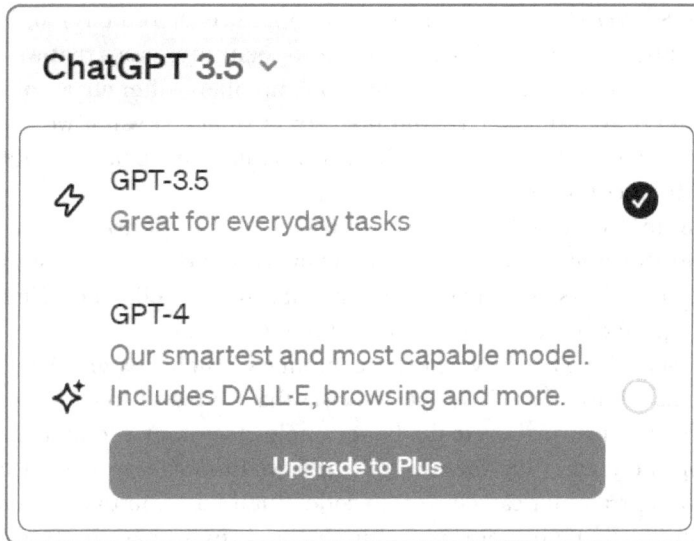

Figure 1.4 When you sign up for OpenAI's ChatGPT, you have two options: the GPT-3.5 model, which you can use for free, or the GPT-4 model, which costs money.

The critical factor for you, the reader, is that this technology did not come out of nowhere but is the result of steady progress over the past decade of dramatic year-over-year improvements in machine learning. Consequently, we already know quite a lot about how LLMs work and the ways that they can fail.

We are assuming a minimal background so that you can give this book to your friends and family. (One of the authors is hopeful that they can give this book to their mother, who is very proud of them even if she does not know precisely what their job is.) As a result, we need to cover a potentially large gap in the background before we dive in. This first chapter aims to give you that background so the next chapter can begin the process of answering this question: How on earth did a computer summarize the introduction of this book?

1.4 What is intelligence, anyway?

Artificial intelligence is an excellent name from a marketing perspective, although it was originally used as the name for an entire field of academic research. This practice has led to a subtle problem that gives people a false mental model of how AI works. We are going to try to avoid reinforcing this model. To explain why, we will discuss why artificial intelligence is not such a great name. We can demonstrate this easily by considering a simple question: What is intelligence?

You might think that something like an intelligence quotient (IQ) test would help us answer that question. IQ tests have a strong correlation with numerous outcomes like school performance, but they do not give us an objective definition of intelligence. Studies show that some amount of nature (hereditary) and nurture (environment) affect a person's IQ. It should also seem suspicious that we can boil down intelligence into something as simple as one number—after all, we often scold people for being only "book smart" but not "street smart." Even if we knew what intelligence was, what would make it artificial? Does intelligence have manufactured flavorings and food colorings?

The bottom line is that IQ tests measure your ability to perform a finite set of capabilities, mostly some specific types of logic puzzles under time constraints, but they don't help us understand the fundamental nature of intelligence. The truth is that there is no perfect understanding of what intelligence is.

The field of AI has long been trying to get computers, which are rigid, deterministic, rule-following machines, to perform specific tasks that humans can do but can't give precise definitions or instructions to do. For example, if we want a computer to count to 1,000 and print out every number divisible by 5, we can write detailed instructions that almost any programmer can convert to code. But if I ask you to write a program that attempts to detect if an arbitrary picture has a cat in it, that's quite a different challenge. You need to somehow precisely define what a cat is and then all the minutia of how to detect one. How exactly do we write code to find and differentiate between cat whiskers and dog whiskers? How do we successfully recognize a cat when it does not have whiskers? When it comes down to it, it isn't easy to do.

However, because AI and ML have focused on these hard-to-specify tasks that humans can perform, describing AI and ML algorithms using analogies has become especially common. To get a computer to detect cats, we provide thousands upon thousands of examples of images that are cats and images that are not cats. We then run one of many various algorithms with a specific, detailed, mathematical process for differentiating cats from the rest of the world. But in the technical vocabulary, we call this process *learning*. When the model fails to detect a cat in a new image because it is a lion and lions were not in the original list of cats, we often say that the model didn't *understand* lions.

Indeed, whenever we try to explain something to friends, we often use analogies to shared concepts that we are both familiar with. Because AI and ML are broadly focused on replicating human abilities to perform tasks, the analogies often use language that implies the literal cognitive functions of a human. As LLMs demonstrate capabilities at a level close to what humans can do, these analogies become more troublesome than helpful because people read too deeply into them and begin to believe that they mean more than they do.

For this reason, we will be careful with our analogies and caution the reader about following any analogies too far. Some terms, like *learning*, are technical jargon worth understanding, but we want you to be on your guard about what they might imply.

In some cases, analogies are still helpful in this book, but we will try to be explicit about the boundaries of how to interpret such analogies.

1.5　*How humans and machines represent language differently*

What does it mean to represent language? We humans implicitly start to learn how to represent language shortly after birth through interaction with others and the world around us. We proceed through formal education to develop an understanding of the components, underlying structures, and rules that govern language and its use. Our internal representation of language has been studied extensively. While some laws of language have been uncovered, many are still up for debate. ChatGPT's internal representation of language is based on portions of this knowledge. It is enabled using the concepts of *artificial neural networks*, also known as deep learning (another dangerous analogy), which are combinations of data structures and algorithms that are patterned loosely after human brain structures. However, our understanding of the ways the mind works is incomplete. While the neural networks that power LLMs are a mere simplification of the human brain structure, their power lies in their ability to capture and encode language in a useful way to generate language and interact with people.

> **NOTE**　Abstractions of the brain's structure have proven useful across many domains. Neural networks have demonstrated incredible progress in language, vision, learning, and pattern recognition. The convergence of advancements in neural machine learning algorithms, the extreme proliferation of digital data, and an explosion of computer hardware, such as GPUs, have led to the advancements that make ChatGPT possible today.

The critical detail to take from this discussion is that you, as a human, have an innate understanding of language you have learned over time. Your learning and use of language are interactive. Through evolution, we all seem to have relatively consistent ways of learning and communicating with each other. To find out more about this concept, look into the theory of universal grammar introduced by linguist Noam Chomsky. Unlike people, LLMs have a representation of language that is learned via a static process. When you have a conversation with Claude or ChatGPT, it mechanically participates in a dialog with you despite having never been in a conversation before.

The representation of language an LLM learns can be high quality, but it is not error-free. It is manipulable in that we can alter the behavior of LLMs in specific ways to limit what they are aware of or what they produce. Understanding that LLMs represent language using relationships inferred from examples helps us maintain realistic expectations. If you are going to use an LLM, how dangerous is it if it is wrong? How can you work with the representation of language to build a product or avoid a bad outcome? These are some of the high-level concerns we will discuss throughout this book.

1.6   *Generative Pretrained Transformers and friends*

The terminology *Generative Pretrained Transformer* was invented by OpenAI to talk about a new type of model they introduced in 2018 that incorporates a type of neural network component known as a transformer. While the original GPT model (GPT-1) is no longer used, the core underlying ideas of pretraining and transformers have become core pillars of the recent revolution in generative AI and tools like Claude, Gemini, Llama, and Copilot.

It is also essential to recognize that these GPT-based AI tools are only one example of an expansive domain of algorithmic research and application of LLMs. Outside of the release of ChatGPT, we have observed an incredible proliferation of LLMs. Some LLMs, like those released by EleutherAI and the BigScience Research Workshop, are freely available to the public to advance research and explore applications. Corporations like Meta, Microsoft, and Google, as we've mentioned, have released other LLMs with more restrictive licensing terms. Publicly available LLMs that anyone can use to build an application or system, sometimes called *foundation models*, have created a vibrant community of researchers, hobbyists, and companies exploring the applications, limitations, and opportunities LLMs and generative AI create. The concepts we teach in this book apply nearly uniformly to all LLMs. Each of these produce output using structures similar, if not identical, to those found in ChatGPT.

It may seem impossible for one book to contain a general summary applicable to many models. However, it is possible for a few reasons, one of the most important being that we will not go to the level of depth necessary to code an LLM yourself from scratch. Naturally, there are parts of ChatGPT and other commercial LLMs that remain trade secrets. As a result, our scope and descriptions are intentionally generalized to the most common aspects of all generative LLMs today.

The second reason we can give such a broadly applicable summary is the nature of LLMs. While it's true that many tweaks can be made to how they are built and operate, researchers in the field consistently find that the details that matter the most are the following:

- How large is the model, and can you make it larger?
- How much data was used to build the model, and can you get more?

These points can be frustrating for researchers who like to think they have vital insights or designs that meaningfully improve how these LLMs work and operate because, in many cases, the same improvement could be obtained just as easily by "making it bigger" or building a model with more data or more parameters instead. Increasing the size of both the models and the data pools is a crucial component of many ethical concerns around using and building LLMs, which we will discuss in chapter 9.

1.7   *Why LLMs perform so well*

We discuss the details of how LLMs work in the coming chapters, but it is also worth sharing here a key lesson learned by researching ML algorithms. For many years, getting better performance from your algorithm for whatever task you were trying to do often meant getting clever about designing your algorithm. You would study your problem, the data, and the math and attempt to derive valuable truths about the world that you could then encode into your algorithm. If you did a good job, your performance improved, you required less data, and all was good in the world. Many classic deep learning algorithms you may hear about, like convolutional neural networks (CNNs) and long short-term memory (LSTM) networks, are, at a high level, the result of people thinking hard and getting clever. Even simpler "shallow" ML algorithms, such as XGBoost, that do not rely on neural networks or deep learning were created using clever algorithm design.

LLMs demonstrate a more recent trend. Instead of getting clever about the algorithm, they keep it simple and implement a *naive* algorithm that simply captures relationships between pieces of information. In many ways, LLMs have fewer beliefs about the world forcibly baked into the algorithm. Fundamentally, this provides more flexibility. How could this be a good idea if I told you the opposite approach was how people improved algorithms? The difference is that LLMs and similar techniques are just bigger, massively so. They are trained on far more data and with far more ability to capture more relationships between more words in more sentences; this brute-force approach appears to have outpaced classic ML methods in performance. This idea is illustrated in figure 1.5.

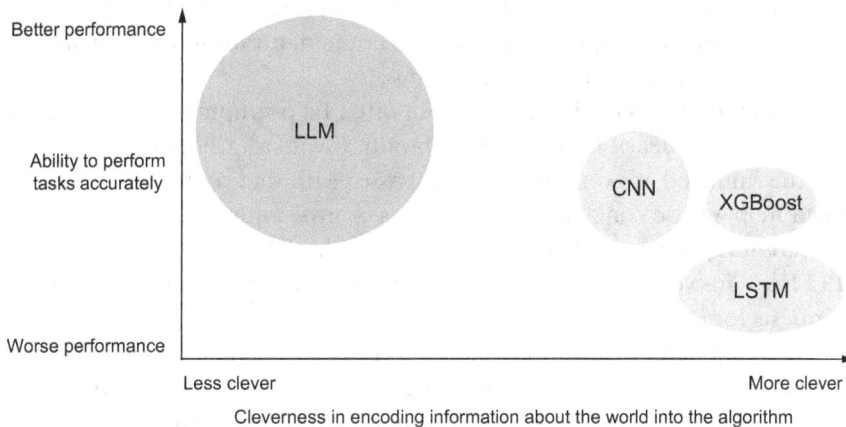

Figure 1.5 **If the cleverness of an algorithm is based on how much information you encode into the design, older techniques often increase performance by being cleverer than their predecessors. As reflected by the size of the circles, LLMs have mostly chosen a "dumber" approach of using more data and parameters and imposing minimal constraints on what the algorithm can learn.**

As we have already stated, bigger is not better by every metric. These models are currently a logistical and computational challenge to deploy. Many real-world constraints, including response time, power draw, battery drain, and maintainability, are all negatively affected. So it is only a narrow definition of "performance" by which LLMs have improved.

Still, the lesson on the value of "going bigger" over "getting clever" is worth considering. Sometimes, in your design of a machine learning solution, even if you are using an LLM, the best answer may be "Let's just go get a lot more data."

1.8 LLMs in action: The good, bad, and scary

Throughout this book, we will give examples of how LLMs can fail, often in hilarious or silly ways. The point of these illustrations isn't to say that LLMs are incapable of performing a task. With changes to the input, setup, or random luck, you can often get LLMs to work better.

The point of such illustrations is to show you how LLMs can fail, often on things so simple that a child can do them better. As you read through this book and interact with LLMs yourself, these illustrations should give you pause and lead you to the thought, "If I use ChatGPT for a hard task, but it fails on easy ones, am I setting myself up for failure?" The answer may often be an emphatic *yes*! Using LLMs safely requires a degree of skepticism or doubt about the outputs, work to verify and validate correctness, and the ability to adapt accordingly. If you use an LLM for a task you cannot do yourself, you risk exposing yourself to errant results you can't verify personally. We will continually weave this point and how to deal with it into the conversation as we discuss how to use LLMs more throughout the book.

It is easy to imagine many ways that LLMs can potentially make our lives easier when it does work—answering all your emails, summarizing long documents, and explaining new concepts. What does not come naturally to many is how things can go wrong and quickly become dangerous.

This kind of adversarial thinking can often be prompted with an initial example: say you want to learn how to make a bomb. If you ask ChatGPT that question, you get the sanitized answer, "Sorry, I can't assist with that request. If you're in crisis or need help, please contact local authorities or professionals who can help." However, researchers have recently shown how to get ChatGPT and many other commercial LLMs to answer the question without hesitation, among many other dangerous requests for information [4].

One might argue that if someone is so clever as to figure out how to trick the LLM, they could probably get whatever dangerous information they want from another source. This is likely true, but at the same time, it fails to account for the scale of automation in LLMs and generative AI tools. No AI or ML algorithm is perfect, and if millions of people ask questions, LLMs might produce a dangerous response 0.01% of the time. ChatGPT has over 100 million users [5], so that is 10,000 dangerous responses. The problem worsens when you consider what a malicious actor might begin to automate. We will discuss this problem further in the second half of the book.

We look forward to your joining us in exploring how LLMs work. In the end, you'll have a detailed understanding of many things to consider when employing LLMs' revolutionary capabilities in your business or daily life.

Summary

- ChatGPT is a type of large language model, which is itself in the larger family of generative AI/ML. Generative models produce new output, and LLMs are unique in the quality of their output but are extremely costly to make and use.
- LLMs are loosely patterned after an incomplete understanding of human brain function and language learning. This is used as inspiration in design, but it does not mean the models have the same abilities or weaknesses as humans.
- Intelligence is a multifaceted and hard-to-quantify concept, making it difficult to say whether LLMs are intelligent. It is easier to think about LLMs and their potential use in terms of capabilities and reliability.
- Human language must be converted to and from an LLM's internal representation. How this representation is formed will change what an LLM learns and influence how you can build solutions using LLMs.

Tokenizers: How large language models see the world

This chapter covers

- Creating tokens from sentences
- Controlling vocabulary size with normalization
- Avoiding risks in tokenization
- Tokenization strategies to remove ambiguity

As discussed in chapter 1, in the world of artificial intelligence, it is often helpful to find analogies to human learning to explain how machines "learn." How you read and understand sentences is a complex process that changes as you get older and involves multiple sequential and concurrent cognitive processes [1]. Large language models (LLMs), however, use simpler processes than human cognitive processes. They employ algorithms based on neural networks to capture the relationships between words in large amounts of data and then use this information about relationships to interpret and generate sentences.

Our discussion of how these algorithms work will begin with their input: sentences of text. In this chapter, we explore how the LLM processes these sentences to become inputs for the model. Just as language is critical for how you think and process information, the inputs to an LLM are crucial in influencing what kinds of concepts and tasks LLMs can perform.

2.1 Tokens as numeric representations

It may seem obvious that LLMs should process sentences, but to fully understand, we must be more specific. As we talk about how LLMs work, you will see that textual sentences are unnatural for the neural network algorithms that power LLMs because neural networks fundamentally employ numbers to do their work. As shown in figure 2.1, the algorithms employed by LLMs must convert human text into a numeric representation before working with it. *Tokens* are the representations that LLMs use to break text into pieces that can be encoded as numbers.

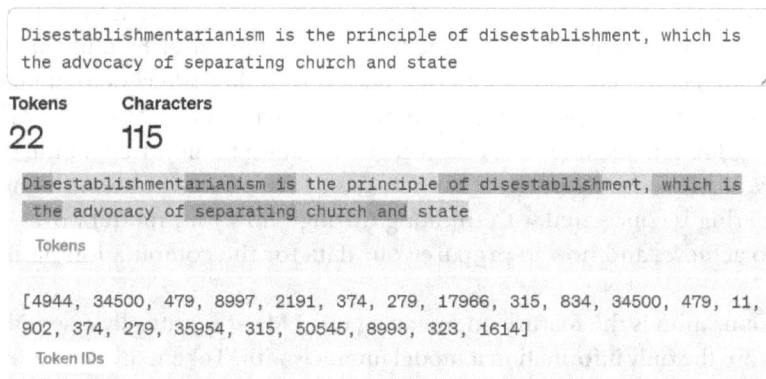

> Disestablishmentarianism is the principle of disestablishment, which is
> the advocacy of separating church and state

Tokens   **Characters**
22   **115**

Disestablishmentarianism is the principle of disestablishment, which is the advocacy of separating church and state

Tokens

[4944, 34500, 479, 8997, 2191, 374, 279, 17966, 315, 834, 34500, 479, 11, 902, 374, 279, 35954, 315, 50545, 8993, 323, 1614]

Token IDs

Figure 2.1 To understand text, LLMs must break text into tokens. Each unique token has a numeric identifier associated with it.

You can think of tokens as the smallest unit of text an LLM processes—an "atom," if you will, the smallest part from which all other things are built. So what are the atoms of text? Consider this: As you read this book, what are the smallest building blocks that your brain uses to process meaning? Two natural answers are *letters* and *words*. It is very tempting to define letters as the atom since words are made of letters, but do you consciously read every letter in every word? For most people, the answer is "no." (If you are dyslexic like one of the co-authors of this book, this is a bizarre question. But cognitive processing is complex and not fully understood; please bear with us on the analogies!) You look at the more prominent words and word parts. In fbct, yoy cn probbly unrestand ths sentnce ever through we diddt sue th ryght cpellng or l3ttrs. People unconsciously use parts of words to process text, and LLMs are built using the same principle.

In this chapter, you will learn how the process of converting text to tokens works. First, we will discuss tokens in more detail; then, we will discuss the procedures used to decide how sentences are turned into tokens.

2.2 Language models see only tokens

By adulthood, most English-speaking people know around 30,000 words [2]. GPT-3, the LLM that initially powered ChatGPT, has a vocabulary of 50,257 tokens [3]. These tokens are not words but parts of words referred to as *subwords,* a representation that is somewhere between words and letters. Intuitively, a token captures language's *minimum meaningful semantic unit.* For example, the word schoolhouse will often get broken into two tokens, school and house, and the word thoughtful as thought and ful. This is useful for recognizing frequent words and having the subwords to interpret new words we have never seen before. People often use a similar technique, called semantic decomposition, to understand words they've never seen before. We intuitively break new words into constituent parts to grasp their meaning based on words we already understand.

Feature engineering is the process of converting your data to a form that is more convenient to your algorithm and the task you want to solve. To build an algorithm that can detect the language of a given text, you could write code that takes text as input and outputs the percentage of times each character occurs. For example, if é appears a lot in a document, you have a good feature to indicate that the document is more likely to be Spanish or French than Russian or Chinese. Sound feature engineering is concerned with thinking through how your model works, what you want to achieve, and how to prepare your data for the combination of model and goal.

Tokenization is the feature engineering of LLMs; it is critically essential because tokens are the only information a model interacts with. Tokens are seen as individual, abstract *things* that are not inherently connected. The relationships are learned through observation of data.

Looking back at figure 2.1, it is evident that the tokens for Dis and dis are related, the only difference being that one starts with a capital D. However, you can see that the model assigns the identifier 4944 to Dis and the identifier 834 to dis. That is, the model doesn't inherently see any connection between the tokens representing Dis and dis, even if we, as humans, see an obvious connection. The model doesn't even *see* Dis or dis. For an LLM to process tokens, we must convert those tokens into numbers so that the model will see the numbers 4944 and 834. Importantly, the model doesn't have any direct way to know that these tokens are related.

A token is a mapping from a subword to a unique numeric representation. In turn, *tokenization* is the process of converting a full-text string into a sequence of tokens. If you have used machine learning libraries before (especially any natural language processing [NLP] tools), you are probably familiar with some of the simpler forms of tokenization. For example, a simple tokenization process breaks a text into tokens by splitting a text based on spaces. However, this approach limits our abilities to create subwords or process languages that don't use whitespace to delimit words, such as Chinese.

2.2.1   *The tokenization process*

The generic process that tokenization follows is shown in figure 2.2 with four key steps:

1 *Receiving the text to process*—This means obtaining text input as a `string` data type (a collection of letters, digits, or symbols) from a user, the internet, or whatever source that has the text you want.

2 *Transforming the string*—This often involves changing the string in some useful way, such as converting uppercase characters into lowercase. This could also be done for security reasons (e.g., the text came from a user, and we need to remove anything that might look like some malicious input) or to eliminate irrelevant variations in the text to help the algorithm learn better. This process is known as *normalization.*

3 *Breaking the string into tokens*—Once a string is available, it needs to be separated into a sequence of discrete substrings; these are the tokens found in the larger string. This is referred to as *segmentation.*

4 *Mapping each token to a unique identifier*—The unique identifier is usually an integer number, which produces output that the LLM can understand.

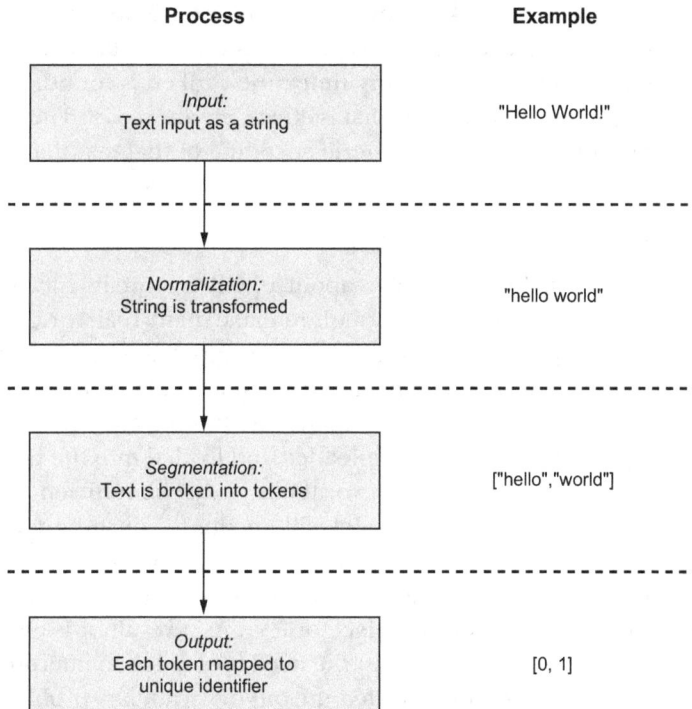

Process	Example
Input: Text input as a string	"Hello World!"
Normalization: String is transformed	"hello world"
Segmentation: Text is broken into tokens	["hello","world"]
Output: Each token mapped to unique identifier	[0, 1]

Figure 2.2 Generically, tokenization involves processing input to produce numeric identifiers for tokens.

The first and last parts of this process have little room for choice or different behavior. First, you need input to process; last, you need a numeric identifier for each token to store and retrieve the information you will associate with that token. The two middle steps, normalization and segmentation, are where you can choose what happens.

The last step of the tokenization process is where the vocabulary is built. The *vocabulary* of a model is the total number of unique tokens that are seen during training when we give the algorithm data to learn from. It almost always takes a large amount of data to build a rich vocabulary with many unique tokens.

Choosing the vocabulary for a model involves a series of trade-offs: the larger the vocabulary, the more information your model can process successfully. Consider a one-year-old child with a vocabulary of maybe a few dozen words. This child will not be a very effective communicator (but that's okay; they have lots of time to learn). So a more extensive vocabulary not only helps the model understand more things, but it also makes the model larger. If you have a vocabulary that's too large, you may make the model slower due to the number of computations required to use it, or the model may consume an excessive amount of memory or disk storage, which makes it more difficult to transfer or share to other machines—for example, when deploying it as a part of a software application.

You build the model's vocabulary by processing the training data and identifying tokens. Each time you see a new token, you give it a unique identifier based on the number of unique tokens you've seen. This process is often as simple as storing a counter set to 0 and incrementing it every time a new token is found. Once the process is complete, you have a tokenizer that is effectively an *encoder*. The tokenizer can receive text as input and return a numeric encoding of that text that the LLM algorithms can use as its output.

2.2.2 *Controlling vocabulary size in tokenization*

GPT-NeoX, a publicly available LLM, takes about 10 GB to store its vocabulary on disk. That is a lot of data, already large enough to make many real-world use cases challenging from the perspective of data storage and computation. It is so large that storing it on a micro-SD card would be prohibitively slow, making use on a mobile phone or some game consoles a significant challenge. It is big enough that it can't be streamed in real time and must be downloaded and loaded into the processor's RAM to perform tokenization. However, a vocabulary must be sufficiently large to represent all words and subwords the model will encounter during training and use. Suppose a model encounters a word that is not in its vocabulary and cannot be represented by combining subwords in its vocabulary. In that case, the model cannot capture information about that piece of text. As a result, it is essential to weigh concerns about vocabulary size against the need for models to interpret a wide variety of content. In NLP, this is often called the out-of-vocabulary problem, when we encounter words we can't represent using the tokens available to the model.

Vocabulary size is one factor contributing to an LLM's size, so discussing methods and tradeoffs for controlling vocabulary size is vital. In this section, we will describe how changing the tokenization process's behavior can influence vocabulary size and affect model capabilities and accuracy.

Process

Example

Input:
Text input as a string

"Hello World!"

Normalization:
String is transformed

"hello world"

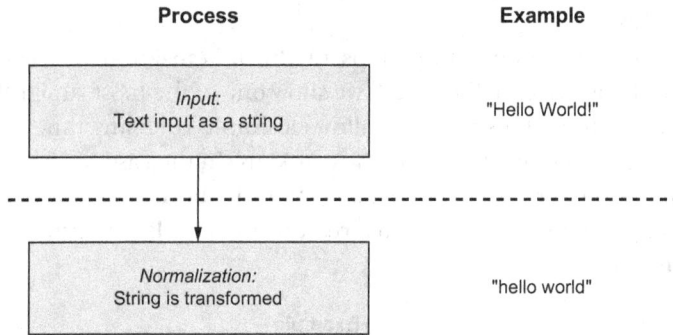

Figure 2.3 **The normalization process commonly involves changing text to remove uppercase characters and punctuation.**

In figure 2.3, we focus on the second transformation step, normalization, which converts the uppercase characters "H" and "W" to lowercase and removes punctuation. These common normalization steps originate from classical NLP pipelines and are still sometimes done in modern deep learning approaches today. They have the immediately desirable effect of reducing the size of the vocabulary. Instead of needing to represent "Hello" and "hello" as two separate tokens, they get mapped to one unique token. This mapping makes an enormous difference because every word that starts a sentence and gets capitalized would potentially duplicate a word in the vocabulary with a capitalized version. Such normalization can also help with various typos and misspellings.

For example, while writing this book, we typed "LLMs," "LLms," and "llms," and made various other mixed-case typos. Converting each character to lowercase in each variation resolves all these typos into a single, simple form, so we get a smaller vocabulary and decrease ambiguity.

However, converting text to lowercase doesn't always decrease ambiguity. Consider "Bill" and "bill." In the first situation, capitalization is vital for understanding that "Bill" is probably someone's name, and "bill" is more likely a unit of money (or one of the other definitions of "bill"). Capitalization is crucial not only for understanding the meaning of the text but also for understanding the errors in the text. Consider again all the various ways we miscapitalized "LLMs" in this book. A high-quality AI algorithm would be able to recognize that we made a typo and correct it! ChatGPT is capable of this and thus requires capitalization in the model. So there is an important tradeoff between vocabulary size and potential model accuracy to consider.

In classical NLP and even not-that-old deep learning models like BERT (a predecessor to the LLMs that power ChatGPT), the ability of an algorithm to recognize typos and fix them was extremely limited outside of solutions designed explicitly for that purpose. For this reason, much of the work that used to go into engineering a robust normalization step has been discarded for LLMs today. A more extensive vocabulary is desirable to produce more capable models that can learn to understand mistakes.

2.2.3   *Tokenization in detail*

The normalization and segmentation steps in the tokenization process largely determine the vocabulary size. In figure 2.4, we show one of the most straightforward strategies for tokenization. This strategy follows a simple rule: any time a space is seen in the text, split the larger string into those tokens. In the case of "hello world," it is as easy as calling `"hello world".split(" ")` in Python. This is a reasonable approach to take; it is how we, as humans, read sentences. But it also adds some subtle complexity.

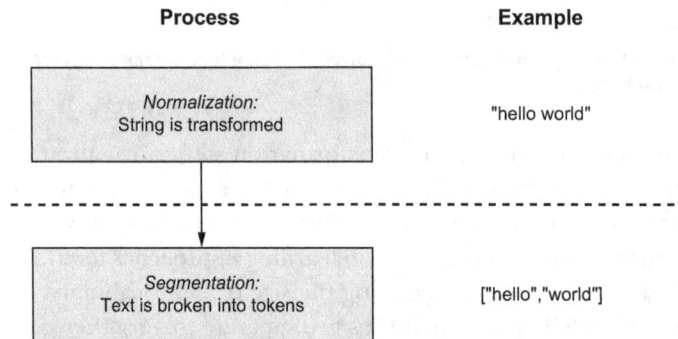

Process   **Example**

Normalization:
String is transformed   "hello world"

- -

Segmentation:
Text is broken into tokens   ["hello","world"]

Figure 2.4   The segmentation process breaks normalized text into words or tokens so that each can be processed independently.

What happens when you have punctuation in your text? If we use our white space rule to convert the string "hello, world" into `["hello,", "world"]`, we run into a similar problem as we do with capitalization. We end up with two distinct tokens for the same concept: `"hello"` and `"hello,"`. The old-school approach often addressed this by removing and developing more complex rules for splitting strings into tokens. While this is a step in the right direction toward reducing vocabulary size, manually specifying tokenization rules does not address other concerns. For example, rule-based tokenization strategies are a significant struggle for languages like Chinese that do not use spaces to separate words.

IDENTIFYING SUBWORDS WITH BYTE-PAIR ENCODING

The general theme of LLMs is to do less feature engineering by hand and let algorithms do the heavy lifting instead. For this reason, an algorithm known as *byte pair encoding* (BPE) is typically used to break strings into tokens. Byte pair encoding is an algorithm for breaking words into common subword sequences of characters. BPE today is usually done with a custom segmenter and almost no normalization.

> **NOTE**   By experimentation, we see many ChatGPT-like products will remove some Unicode characters that do not print (Unicode is weird), but otherwise mostly take your text as-is. Most prior language models do use various flavors of normalization, and how to normalize text for LLMs better is, we think, a good and open question.

Since finding the most efficient set of subwords is a computationally expensive task, BPE uses a heuristic to take a shortcut. It starts by looking at individual letters as tokens and then finds pairs of adjacent letters that occur most frequently and combines them into subword tokens. The algorithm repeats this process many times, continuing with subword tokens, until some threshold is met and the vocabulary is "small enough." For example, in the first pass, the BPE algorithm examines the frequency of the individual letters used in English and encounters the letters "i," "n," and "g" near each other frequently. In the first pass, BPE might observe that "n" and "g" occur together more frequently than "i" and "n," so it will produce the tokens i and ng. In a subsequent pass, it may combine those tokens into ing based on the frequency of that combination of letters versus how often "ng" occurs with other letters or subwords. Once BPE has reached its stopping point, it will have identified individual words such as "eating" and "drinking" as frequently occurring combinations. It may also capture "ing" as a suffix so that other words ending with that subword can also be represented as tokens. When the algorithm is complete, we end up with tokens that capture complete words and others that capture subwords. This process is shown at a high level in figure 2.5.

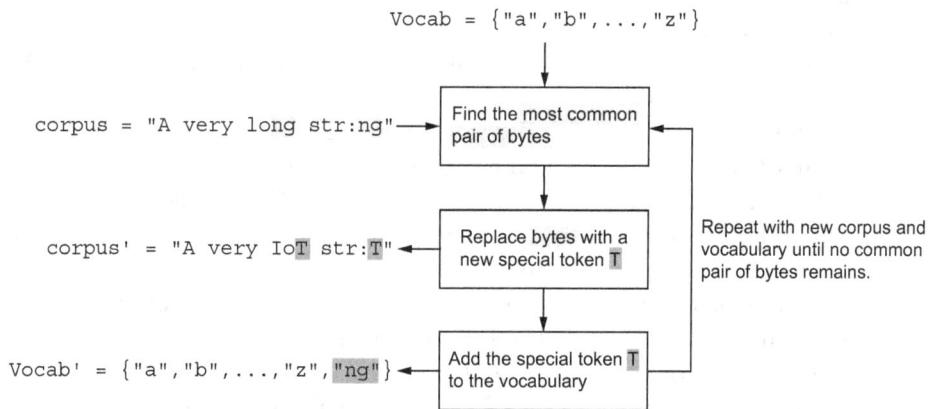

Figure 2.5   A simplified byte pair encoding algorithm for creating tokens: first, find the most frequent pair of characters "ng." Next, replace all instances of "ng" with a placeholder token "T," and add "ng" to the vocabulary. Repeat the process until no common byte pairs remain.

NOTE   Running the BPE algorithm to create a vocabulary is surprisingly expensive because it must read the input data many times to calculate the most frequent combinations of letters. While LLMs are trained on over 500 million or even 1 billion pages of text, their tokenizers are usually created using a tiny subset of that data. Often, a tokenizer is trained using a much smaller collection of text the size of a novel.

The BPE process may seem odd at first, but you can think of it as a way of identifying common strings in a corpus. For example, BPE will almost always learn to represent New York as one token, which is useful since the state and city of New York are frequent occurrences in the text. Representing the whole concept as a single token makes it easier to use that kind of information. Indeed, most common words will become unique tokens, while rare words are hopefully captured as a combination of subwords. For example, `loquacious` will be tokenized by GPT-4 as `lo`, `qu`, and `acious`. This method is a success because "acious" is a Latin postfix for inclination/propensity, making it easier for the model to handle an unusual word correctly. It is also a failure case because the Latin prefix "`loqu`" got broken up into two tokens instead of one, making learning harder.

After BPE is used to make a vocabulary, model authors manually add additional tokens for various reasons, such as words that are important to a specific knowledge domain. As we will discuss in the next section, in some domains, having the correct tokens has a significant effect by capturing nuanced meaning. So often, the authors will make sure the necessary tokens are included. Model authors will also add special tokens that don't directly represent word parts but provide auxiliary information to the model. Some common examples of this are the "unknown" token (typically represented as [UNK]), which is used if the tokenizer fails to process a symbol correctly, and the system token [SYSTM], which is used to distinguish between a model's built-in prompt and user-entered data, as well as other kinds of stylistic markers. Multimodal models that accept text and image inputs use unique tokens to tell the model when the input stream switches between bytes that represent text data and bytes that represent image data.

Open AI decided to use BPE to encode text into tokens when they developed ChatGPT and have released their tokenizer as the open source package `tiktoken` (https://github.com/openai/tiktoken). Still, several other algorithms and implementations for automatically generating tokens are available, including the WordPiece and SentencePiece algorithms developed at Google [4]. Each of these have different tradeoffs. For example, WordPiece uses a different technique for counting the frequency of the candidate subwords when building the tokenizer's vocabulary. One of the algorithms implemented in SentencePiece processes entire sentences, preserving white space when calculating tokens, which may improve output when building models that handle multiple languages. However, BPE is the most broadly used algorithm. For example, it is now used exclusively in Google's recent LLMs.

Regardless of the algorithm chosen, the size of a tokenizer's vocabulary is a critical model parameter determined by the data scientist or engineer in charge of training and augmenting the tokenizer. The following sections dive deep into some of the considerations on vocabulary size and other decisions made throughout the tokenizer development process.

2.2.4   *The risks of tokenization*

As mentioned in chapter 1, we won't go much into coding in this book. The goal is to give you a reasonable understanding of how LLMs work and remove some of the magic and mystery so you can focus instead on how LLMs may be used for your job. Tokenization is the first piece of the puzzle. It is a simple but effective strategy to produce the inputs to LLMs. You have learned how the size of the vocabulary plays a significant role in a model's deployability, the tradeoff in recognizing nuance versus the unnecessary redundancy associated with making a vocabulary, how the tokenization process influences the size of the vocabulary, and how the token selection process can be automated with BPE.

The choices made at tokenization time affect what LLMs can do today and will affect them in the future. These choices involve a few big-picture challenges to be aware of. To explore this topic further, two salient yet nuanced details of BPE are worth sharing some concerns about: the relationship between sentence length and token counts and the potential for LLMs to be confused by characters, known as homoglyphs, that appear identical yet have different binary encodings.

LONGER SENTENCES DO NOT MEAN MORE TOKENS

An unintuitive aspect of BPE is that longer sentences do not mean more tokens. To see why, look at figure 2.6, where we show a real tokenization of two different strings by GPT-3. The string "I'm running" is longer by one character than the string "I'm runnin," but it is one token shorter! If you don't believe it, you can try tokenizing different strings at https://platform.openai.com/tokenizer.

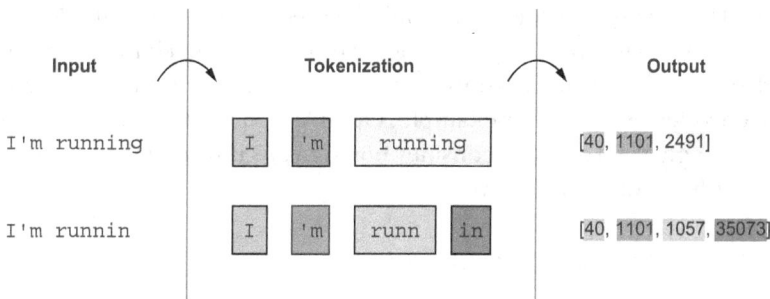

Input	Tokenization	Output
I'm running	I / 'm / running	[40, 1101, 2491]
I'm runnin	I / 'm / runn / in	[40, 1101, 1057, 35073]

Figure 2.6 Tokenizing two different sentences

This discrepancy occurs because BPE is greedily looking for the smallest set of tokens for any piece of input. In this specific case, the string "running" occurs frequently enough in our training data that it gets its own token. In the case where the "g" is missing, there is no token for "runnin" in our vocabulary because that variation may have appeared rarely in our training data. Thus, "runnin" needs to be broken into at least two tokens, giving us run and nin.

This nuance of tokenizer implementation is fertile ground for software bugs. Different tokenizers may provide different answers on how to tokenize the same string. When designing unit tests and infrastructure, this factor is important to keep in mind to avoid getting lost or confused when upgrading or converting between tokenizer implementations that may cause new differences in token generation. It can also affect evaluations of LLMs, as many models are highly sensitive to added white space, and inconsistent tokenization may inadvertently lead to comparisons not being apples to apples.

HOMOGLYPHS CREATE CONFUSION

Homoglyphs are a problem developers may encounter when working with multiple human languages or considering the security implications of processing externally provided data. When input comes from arbitrary users, sometimes it may be nefarious and want to trick your model into bad behavior. One way that could be done against an LLM is with a *homoglyph* attack.

A homoglyph is when two or more characters have different byte encodings but appear identical when rendered on the screen. One example is the Latin letter "H" used in most Western European languages and the Cyrillic "H" used throughout Eastern Europe and Central Asia.

BPE will encode homoglyphs that use different byte encodings into different tokens. As a result, homoglyphs can inflate the number of tokens in a text, change how an LLM parses the information, and run up your compute costs. An amusing example of a homoglyph is the Unicode character U+200B, also known as the "zero width space." This character is used in typesetting and takes up space, but it does not print anything, show anything, or change anything about how a document is rendered.

The zero width space is one of many strange and interesting things that exist within the Unicode specification and could be used to cause you pain. Many services thus employ normalization steps that remove such strange characters and replace homoglyphs with a canonical representation (i.e., anything that looks like an "a" must be encoded as an a). For example, OpenAI's current tokenizer interface will remove homoglyphs. You must consider homoglyphs if you want to deploy an LLM on your hardware or a user's device.

2.3   *Tokenization and LLM capabilities*

If we are only concerned with the ability of an LLM to produce high-quality human-like text, the specific details of how you tokenize your text do not matter as much as the data and compute used to build these models. If you put enough computational power and scale into your models, they will eventually figure out useful representations regardless of the building blocks. But sometimes, tokenization dramatically affects what an LLM is capable of. In this section, we cover some examples.

It may be the case that the examples that follow are not directly relevant to your job or what you would like to do with an LLM. That is perfectly fine; the point of these examples is not to dissuade you from using an LLM. Instead, the goal is to help you understand that the scope of what LLMs learn is limited by the representation chosen, and there may not be a way around these concerns without major engineering work. If you start building an application with LLMs and find significant difficulty, think about how tokenization could be a factor in your goal. If tokenization is indeed the problem, there is little you can do to solve it, so it may be best to look at other approaches, such as manually augmenting the vocabulary with tokens that are important for your application.

2.3.1 LLMs are bad at word games

Users frequently enjoy asking LLMs to solve word puzzles or perform tasks that involve word games. For example, figure 2.7 shows a word game where the correct answer depends on the exact letter sequence and the number of letters in a word.

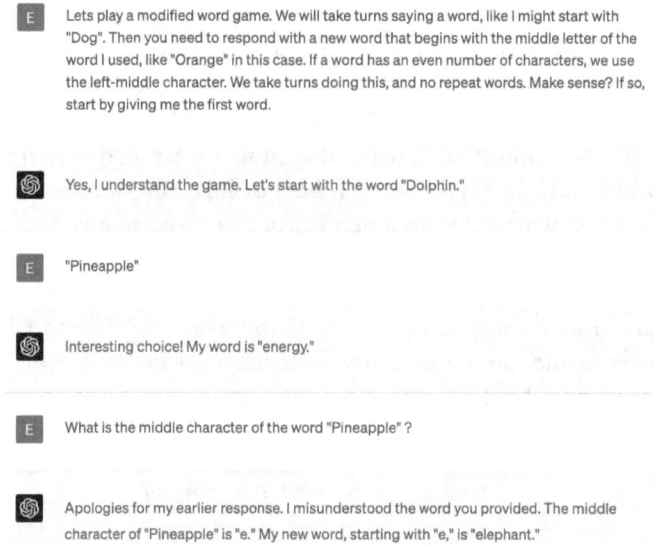

> **E** Lets play a modified word game. We will take turns saying a word, like I might start with "Dog". Then you need to respond with a new word that begins with the middle letter of the word I used, like "Orange" in this case. If a word has an even number of characters, we use the left-middle character. We take turns doing this, and no repeat words. Make sense? If so, start by giving me the first word.

> Yes, I understand the game. Let's start with the word "Dolphin."

> **E** "Pineapple"

> Interesting choice! My word is "energy."

> **E** What is the middle character of the word "Pineapple" ?

> Apologies for my earlier response. I misunderstood the word you provided. The middle character of "Pineapple" is "e." My new word, starting with "e," is "elephant."

Figure 2.7 The tokenization approach means that ChatGPT cannot really "see" single characters or word lengths. If you ask questions that require subcharacter identification and change them in a unique and unusual way, ChatGPT starts to fail. The correct middle character is "a," but ChatGPT insists that the letter is "e." What ChatGPT sees is three tokens, representing P, ine, and apple, respectively.

Playing word games may not be something you care about for your application, but the reason word games fail may be highly salient to your problem. Although many examples like this are toy problems in that they aren't particularly scientifically or commercially important, they reveal notable breakdowns in how these models operate. They may come into play in more practical uses, such as when models struggle to write poetry containing rhymes or assonance.

Consider, for example, that you want to build an application that answers questions about a user's prescription drugs. Drugs often have longer, confusing names that people fail to remember or spell incorrectly, and because an LLM does not understand letters, it may confuse one drug's name with a different drug's long and strange name.

Because drug names are uncommon, they will tokenize differently, even with minor misspellings. For example, in GPT-3, "Amoxicillin" and the easy misspelling "Amoxicillan" share no common tokens! This creates a much greater risk of the LLM responding incorrectly, where the risk is intrinsically higher, making an LLM application all the more important to thoroughly test, engineer around with extreme care, or potentially avoid altogether.

2.3.2   *LLMs are challenged by mathematics*

Tokenization significantly affects tasks involving formal symbolic reasoning, including mathematics and playing board games. Both math and board games are implemented by LLMs as symbolic reasoning problems where individual tokens have specific rules governing their interactions and meaning when observed in conjunction with other tokens. For example, models containing individual tokens for each digit tend to perform better at arithmetic than models that don't. This is because the number 123456 will become two tokens in GPT-3, `["123", "456"]`, based on the frequency of those tokens in the tokenizer's original training data. This makes it harder for the model to deal with the individual digits in that number. Some system developers have solved this problem by normalizing numbers by inserting spaces between all digits, such as 1 2 3 4 5 6, which creates a new output with six tokens, one for each digit.

This difference in math capability is well-illustrated in figure 2.8, which shows performance on arithmetic computations throughout training. The top curve is a typical BPE tokenizer, while the bottom curve, which shows better performance, is the same tokenizer modified to have digit-level tokenization of numbers.

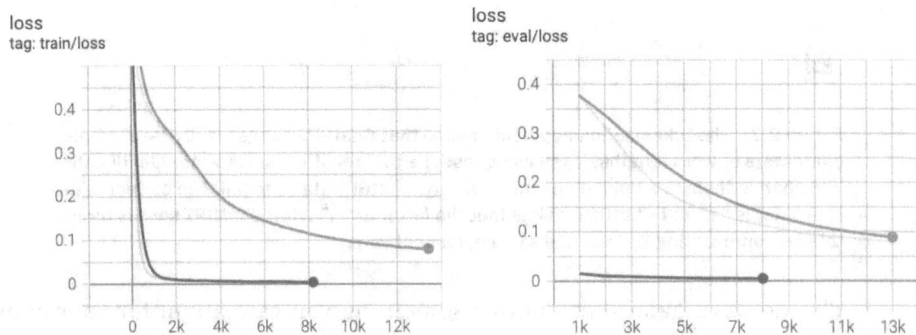

Figure 2.8   A comparison of how two LLMs learn to perform arithmetic computations over time. Time is shown on the x-axis. The upper curve is a typical BPE tokenizer, while the lower curve is the same tokenizer modified to use tokens that represent individual digits. The y-axis describes the ability of the LLM to perform accurately, where a smaller number means fewer errors. The bottom line is that LLMs that use digit-level tokenization can learn how to do math better and faster.

2.3.3   *LLMs and language equity*

Most LLM tokenizers can represent any symbol covered by Unicode, which includes the characters from most of the world's alphabets. However, how efficiently those tokenizers represent text in a given language varies massively, especially as the tokenizers are typically trained on smaller collections of text resources for different languages. This can cause substantial inequity in commercial services based on LLMs [5] because tokenization of words in languages that are rare in the training set defaults to a more granular set of subwords, resulting in increased token usage. Commercial LLM providers like OpenAI and Anthropic typically charge customers on a per-token basis, usually a fraction of a cent for every token input into the LLM and produced as output by the LLM. These costs add up when you consider that a high-use commercial application may process tens of millions of tokens daily.

The time it takes for an LLM to complete a request and the amount a user is charged per token depends directly on the tokenizer. Therefore, languages that are more efficiently represented using a tokenizer are economically incentivized over those that are not represented efficiently. Using English as a baseline, researchers have found that the cost to answer a user query in German or Italian is about 50% more when using ChatGPT and GPT-4. Languages that differ even more substantially from English can incur much larger charges: Tumbuka and Bulgarian are more than twice the cost, and Dzongkha, Odia, Santali, and Shan cost over 12 times as much as English to process.

2.4 Check your understanding

1 How would you expect the following words or phrases to be tokenized? Try breaking them out yourself and then running them through an actual LLM tokenizer, such as the one at https://platform.openai.com/tokenizer:

- backstopped
- large language models
- Schoolhouse
- How you process sentences to understand them is a complex process that changes as you get older and involves multiple sequential and concurrent cognitive processes

2 How much do you think uppercase versus lowercase letters matter for each of the previous examples? Try submitting them again with various casings.

3 Let's simulate how LLMs think about math using a cipher where each English letter corresponds to a number. For example, $W = 8$, $A = 4$, $I = 7$, and $T = 2$, so we would write *WAIT* to mean 8472. Knowing this fact and that $GO + SLOW = STOP$, can you figure out what *STOP* represents?

4 Since a token is the basic unit an LLM operates on, why does it make sense (technologically) that languages less efficiently represented by a tokenizer would cost more?

5 Is it an ethical problem that LLMs charge different amounts to people for the same service based on what language they speak? Would you consider this discrimination?

2.5 Tokenization in context

The details of tokenization we discuss in this chapter are the foundational building blocks of LLMs that govern the input they can represent effectively and the output they produce. Tokenization is a critical component of LLMs like ChatGPT in developing effective representations of text so that they can be used to learn relationships between tokens when presented with vast amounts of information in the training process, interpreting user input and producing the high-quality responses we've become accustomed to. An LLM's potential is limited or enabled by the tokenization strategy and vocabulary it employs, in conjunction with all of the other characteristics we explore in the following chapters.

Summary

- Tokenization is the fundamental process that LLMs use to understand text by converting sentences into tokens.
- Tokens are the smallest units of information in text that represent content. Sometimes, they correspond to full words, but often, they represent pieces of words or sub-words.
- Tokenization involves *normalizing* text into a standard representation, which may involve converting characters to lowercase or translating the byte encoding of Unicode characters so that visibly identical characters employ the same encoding.
- Tokenization also involves *segmentation*, which is breaking up text into words or subwords. Algorithms like byte pair encoding (BPE) provide a mechanism to automatically learn how to efficiently segment text based on the statistical occurrence of combinations of letters in a training data set.
- The result of building a tokenizer is known as a *vocabulary*, which is the unique collection of word and subword tokens that a tokenizer can use to represent text it has processed.
- The size of a tokenizer's vocabulary affects the LLM's ability to accurately represent data and the storage and computational resources required to understand and predict text.
- Internally to the LLM, tokens are represented using numbers. As a result, there is no understanding of relationships between tokens, such as prefixes and suffixes, or the fact that two tokens share a similar set of letters.
- To support specific domains of knowledge, tokenizers trained automatically may be augmented to provide tokens that are important to their application.
- Tokenizers that do not understand individual letters or digits will have problems with arithmetic operations or simple word games.

Transformers: How inputs become outputs

This chapter covers

- Converting tokens into vectors
- Transformers, their types, and their roles
- Converting vectors back into tokens
- Creating the text generation loop

In chapter 2, we saw how large language models (LLMs) see text as fundamental units known as tokens. Now it's time to talk about what LLMs do with the tokens they see. The process that LLMs use to generate their text is markedly different from how humans form coherent sentences. When an LLM operates, it is working on tokens, yet simultaneously cannot *manipulate* tokens like humans do because the LLM does not understand the structure and relationship of the letters each token represents.

For example, English speakers know that the words "magic," "magical," and "magician" are all related. We can understand that sentences containing these words are all connected to the same subject matter because these words share a common root. However, LLMs that operate on integers representing tokens that make up these words cannot understand the relationships between tokens without additional work to make those connections.

For this reason, LLMs follow a long history in machine learning and deep learning of performing a kind of cyclical conversion. First, tokens are converted into a numeric form that deep learning algorithms can work on. Then, the LLM converts this numeric representation back into a new token. This cycle repeats iteratively, which is not comparable to how humans work. You would be incredibly concerned if your colleagues had to pull out a calculator to perform several math problems between each word they spoke.

Yet this process is, indeed, how LLMs produce outputs. In this chapter, we will walk through the process in two stages. First, we will review the entire process at a high level to introduce fundamental concepts and construct a mental model of how LLMs generate text. Next, this model will serve as a scaffolding for a more in-depth discussion of the details and design choices associated with the components that LLMs use to capture the relationships between words and language and, ultimately, generate the output we are familiar with.

3.1   *The transformer model*

Many LLMs you encounter today interpret tokens and produce output using a software architecture known as a transformer. This architecture consists of a collection of algorithms and data structures that store information by representing it as numbers in a neural network. At their core, transformers are sequence prediction algorithms. While it is common to describe them as "reasoning" or "understanding" language, what they actually do is predict tokens. Transformers come with three different approaches to token prediction. While we focus on the famous GPT architecture (more formally known as decoder-only models), it is also worth introducing encoder-only and encoder-decoder models:

- *Encoder-only models*—These models are designed to create knowledge representations that can be used to perform tasks—that is, to encode the input into a numerical representation that is more useful to an algorithm. The best way to think of them is that they take text and process it into a form that is easier for a machine learning algorithm to use. They are widely used in scientific research. Famous examples include BERT and RoBERTa.
- *Decoder-only models*—These models are designed to generate text. The best way to think of them is that they take a partially written document and then produce a likely continuation of that document by predicting the next token. Famous examples include OpenAI's GPT and Google's Gemini.
- *Encoder-decoder models*—These models are also designed to generate text. Unlike decoder-only models, they take an entire passage of text and create a corresponding passage rather than continue the existing one. They are less popular than decoder-only models because they are more expensive to train, and their use is sometimes more challenging. For tasks with a clearly defined input and output sequence, encoder-decoder models tend to outperform decoder-only models. For example, they're much better at translation and summarization tasks than

decoder-only models. Famous examples include T5 and the algorithm that powers Google Translate.

Regardless of which type of transformer is used, the essential components of the model are built from three basic layers, just arranged in different ways internally. A reasonable analogy to their interchangeability is that of gasoline car engines: they all work similarly and have the same general components. How those components (read: layers) are put together within the engine (read: transformer) elicits various tradeoffs in performance.

What exactly is a neural network layer?

LLMs are one of many hundreds of algorithms that we now call *neural networks*. However, this is a misnomer in several ways. First, what constitutes a neural network approach today is very broad, to such a degree that referencing a "neural network–based approach" does not give the reader too much information about the exact approach described. Second, the *neural* part of the name has little or nothing to do with neuroscience or how the brain works. Sometimes, there is an intuitive "Hey, the brain kinda does something like this; can we mimic that behavior and get something useful out of it?" style of inspiration, but not for most current methods. Third, a neural network describes more of a standard agreement on assembling data structures rather than a particular algorithm. Think about building a house: you use two-by-fours, sheetrock, and many options for cabinetry, paints, and design choices to assemble everything into a home. Each home looks unique but also familiar: they are all assembled in an expected way. The "layer" of a neural network is the smallest component, but you can use many types of layers in different ways. Transformers are one of many pieces that get assembled into a larger network.

3.1.1 Layers of the transformer model

Figure 3.1 describes the essential components of the transformer model: the *embedding layer*, which generates representations of tokens that can hold more meaning; the *transformer layer*, which makes predictions based on word relationships; and the *output layer*, which transforms the numeric representations used within the transformer into words that humans can read.

The transformer model

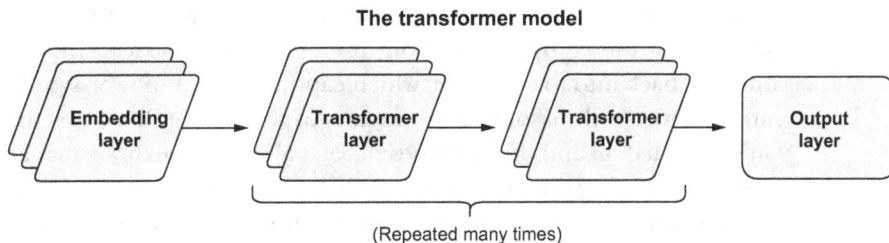

(Repeated many times)

Figure 3.1 The basic components of the transformer model, consisting of the embedding layer, multiple transformer layers, and the output layer

Let's look at these layers in detail:

- *Embedding layer*—The embedding layer takes raw tokens as input and maps them into representations that capture each token's meaning. For example, in chapter 2, we discussed how tokens represent concepts, but individual tokens don't have any relationship with each other. Consider the words "dog" and "wolf." With our understanding of language, we know these terms are related, but we need some way of capturing this relationship within a neural network. This is precisely what the embedding layer does. It captures information about each token that encodes its meaning and allows us to express its conceptual relationship with other tokens. Consequently, we can capture the idea that the representations of the tokens dog and wolf are more similar to each other than the representations for the tokens red and France. You can think of the embedding layer as the part of the model that processes the words on a page and maps them to abstract conceptual representations in your head.

- *Transformer layer*—Transformer layers are where most of the computation happens in a language model: they capture the relationships between words created by the embedding layer and do the bulk of the actual work to obtain the output. While LLMs generally only have one embedding layer and one output layer, they have many transformer layers. More powerful models have more transformer layers.

  It is tempting to describe the transformer layer as the "thinking" part of the model. This definition erroneously implies that transformer layers (or the larger model built from them) can think, but thinking as humans do is self-reflecting and variable in duration and effort. You can think about something for a half-second or months, depending on the effort needed for the task. A transformer always repeats the same process with the same effort for every task. There is no introspection and no altering a transformer layer's mental state. Thus, a better way to imagine a transformer layer is a set of *fuzzy rules*—*fuzzy* because they do not require exact matches (because embeddings might return something similar like "dog" to "wolf") and *rules* because transformers have no flexibility. Once learning is complete, a transformer layer will do the same thing every time.

- *Output layer*—After the model has done the computation, additional transformations are performed in the output layer to obtain a useful result. Most commonly, the output layer operates as the inverse of the embedding layer, transforming the result of the computation from the embeddings space, which captures concepts, back into token space, which captures actual subwords to build text output. You can think of this as the part of the model that takes the answer you've decided on and then chooses the actual words to express that answer on a page by selecting the words most likely to represent the concepts that make up the answer. Finally, we end with an unembedding process, which converts the embeddings into tokens. Because each token has a one-to-one mapping to a subword, we can use a simple dictionary or map to convert the tokens into human-readable text again. This process is detailed in figure 3.2.

3.2 *Exploring the transformer architecture in detail*

To further understand what is happening inside an LLM, it can be helpful to reframe what we described as a sequence of steps. So let us do that in figure 3.2, which describes seven steps. We'll mark each of these with reference to the section where we covered it before or tell you when it is a new detail we are about to explain. This chapter provides a lot of information at once, so we will break it down piece by piece as we go.

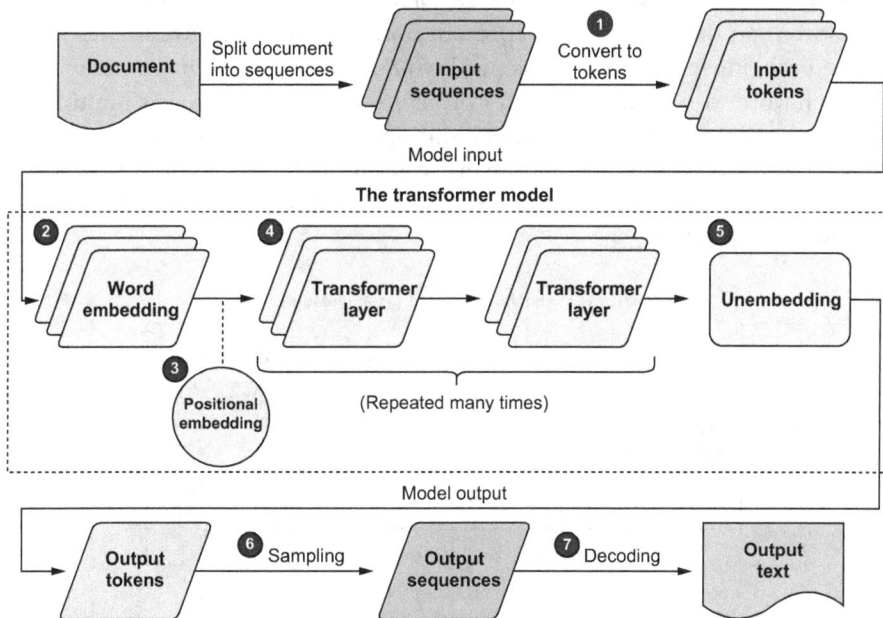

Figure 3.2   The process for converting input into output using a large language model

The seven steps to an LLM are as follows:

1. Map text to tokens (chapter 2).
2. Map tokens into embedding space (*new*, subsection 3.2.1).
3. Add information to each embedding that captures each token's position in the input text (*new*, subsection 3.2.1).
4. Pass the data through a transformer layer (repeat *L* times) (*new*, subsection 3.2.2).
5. Apply the unembedding layer to get tokens that could make good responses (*new*, subsection 3.2.3).
6. Sample from the list of possible tokens to generate a single response (*new*, subsection 3.2.3).
7. Decode tokens from the response into actual text (chapter 2).

3.2.1 Embedding layers

There are a lot of nuances to tokenization, embeddings, and how precisely language gets translated into things that models can understand. The most important nuance is that neural networks still don't work with tokens directly. On the whole, neural networks need numbers that can be manipulated, and a token has a fixed numeric identity. We cannot change the identity of a token because the identity allows us to convert tokens back to human-readable text. We need a layer that will transform tokens in numeric form into the words or subwords they represent.

REPRESENTING TOKENS WITH VECTORS

Our transformer needs numbers to work on. By this, we mean *continuous* numbers, so any fractional value is available for us to use: 0.3, -5, 3.14, etc. We also need more than one number to represent every token to capture nuances of meaning and relationships between tokens. If you tried to use just one number to represent each word, you would encounter difficulties capturing a word's multiple meanings, synonyms, antonyms, and the relationships that those create. For example, you may well want to say that the antonym (opposite) of a word should be achievable by multiplying a word by -1. As figure 3.3 shows, this quickly leads to silly conclusions about word relationships.

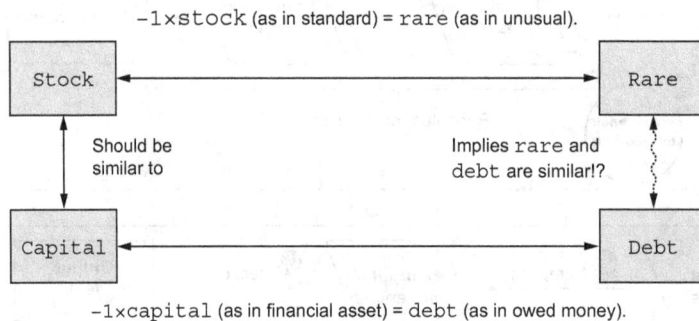

$-1\times$stock (as in standard) = rare (as in unusual).

Stock	←——————————————→	Rare
↕ Should be similar to	Implies rare and debt are similar!?	↕
Capital	←——————————————→	Debt

$-1\times$capital (as in financial asset) = debt (as in owed money).

Figure 3.3 If you use just one number to represent a token, you quickly encounter problems where similar/dissimilar words cannot be made to fit each other. Here we see how trying to represent simple synonym/antonym relationships quickly becomes nonsensical even with just a handful of words.

For example, say we have a token for stock that we have arbitrarily decided will be converted to some number (e.g., 5.2). I want to give related financial words, such as capital, a similar number (e.g., 5.3) because they have similar meanings. There are also antonyms of stock's other meanings, such as rare. Let's say we use a negative value to capture the idea of an antonym and give it a value of -5.2. But now things get complex because another antonym of capital is debt. But if antonyms are negations, debt and rare have a similar meaning, which is nonsensical. Figure 3.3 illustrates the problem: when we use a single number to represent a word, we cannot encode their relationships without implying weird relationships with other words, and we have not even gotten past four words yet!

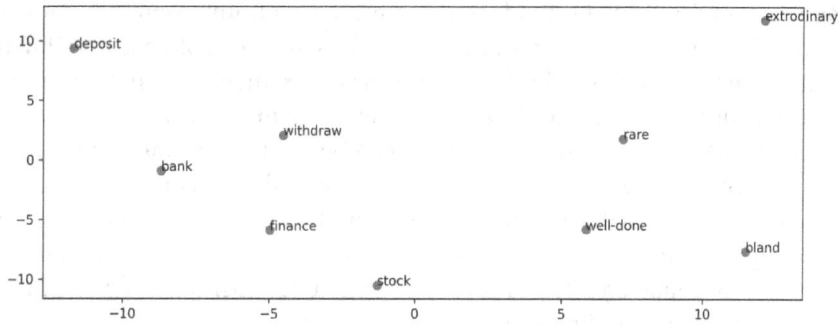

Figure 3.4 Adding another dimension to our token representation allows us to represent a more diverse arrangement of semantic relationships. Here we see how two dimensions can capture relationships for multiple meanings of the same word.

The trick is to use multiple numbers to represent each token, allowing you to find better representations that accommodate the different relationships between words. An example that uses two numbers is shown in figure 3.4. We can see things like `bland` being nearly equidistant from `rare` and `well-done`, while also having space for `bank` to be far away from all three just mentioned words and instead be near `stock`. We were even able to throw in a few extra words. The more numbers you use, called *dimensions* in the field's jargon, the more complex relationships you can represent.

The curse of dimensionality

If more dimensions are better at capturing subtle meaning, why not use as many dimensions as possible to represent our data? When dealing with a large number of dimensions, several problems arise. One primary concern is that LLMs deal with many embeddings, and adding more dimensions increases the memory and computation required to store and process embeddings. Furthermore, as we add more dimensions, the size of the semantic space explodes, and the amount of data and time needed to train a machine learning model to learn about all locations in the semantic space similarly grows exponentially. Mathematician Richard E. Bellman coined the term the "curse of dimensionality" to describe this phenomenon because while we want to create a space capable of capturing nuanced meaning, we are limited by the fundamental properties of the space we create.

In LLM parlance, the lists of numbers used to represent tokens are referred to as *embeddings*. You can think of an embedding as an array or list of floating-point values. As a shorthand, we call such arrays *vectors*. Each position in the vector is called a dimension. As we show in figure 3.4, using multiple dimensions allows us to capture subtleties in relationships between words in human language.

Since embeddings exist in multiple dimensions, we often state that they live in a *semantic space*. In some machine learning applications, this is called a *latent space*, especially when not dealing with text. Semantic space is wishy-washy jargon that isn't well defined in the field, but it is most commonly used as a shorthand for saying that the vector embeddings that represent each token are well behaved in that synonyms/antonyms have nearer/farther distances and that we can use those relationships productively. As an example, in figure 3.5, we show a famous case where a "make female" transformation can be built by subtracting the embedding for `male` and adding the embedding for `female`. This transformation can be applied to many different male-gendered words to find female-gendered words of the same concept. The co-location of all the "royal" words in the bottom right of figure 3.5 is also intentional, as many different kinds of relationships can be simultaneously maintained in a high-dimensional space.

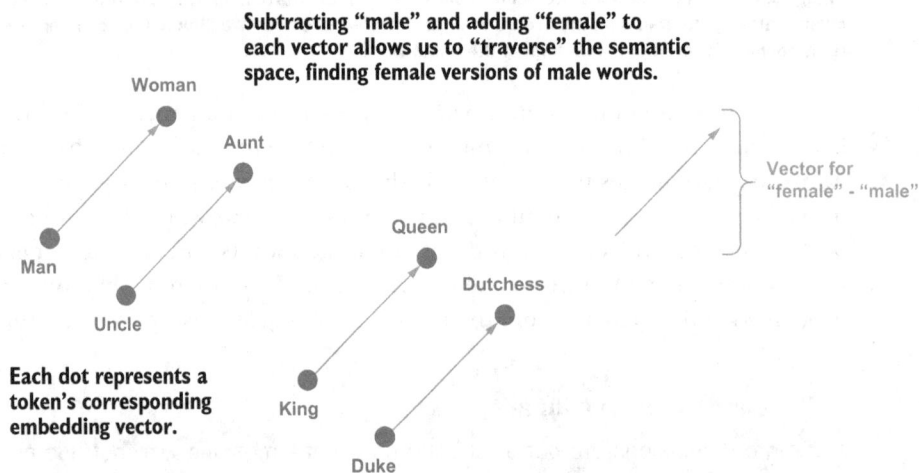

Figure 3.5 A demonstration of how the relationships between embeddings create a semantic space. Words with similar meanings are near each other, and the same transformation can be applied to multiple words to yield a similar result—in this instance, a transformation to find the feminine version of a masculine word.

Shockingly, we cannot guarantee that these semantic relationships will form during the training process. It just so happens that they often do, and they were discovered to be very useful. By extension, the relationships in a semantic space are not foolproof, and biases in your data can seep in. For example, models will often determine that `doctor` is more similar to `male` and `nurse` is more similar to `female` because, in the generally available text used to build most models, it is more common for doctors to be described as male and nurses as female. The relationships are thus not a discovered truth of the world but a reflection of the data that went into the process.

ADDING POSITIONAL INFORMATION
One critical problem is that a standard transformer does not understand sequential information. If you gave the transformer one sentence and rearranged all the tokens, it would view all possible permutations of the tokens as identical! That problem is illustrated in figure 3.6.

Different ways to re-order a sentence	Different ways you might interpret the context of the sentence, based on word order.
"I have to eat this pie"	Maybe your mother-in-law made it for Thanksgiving and you don't want to be rude.
"I have this pie to eat"	You happen got have a pie that you could eat. Maybe leftovers from last night?

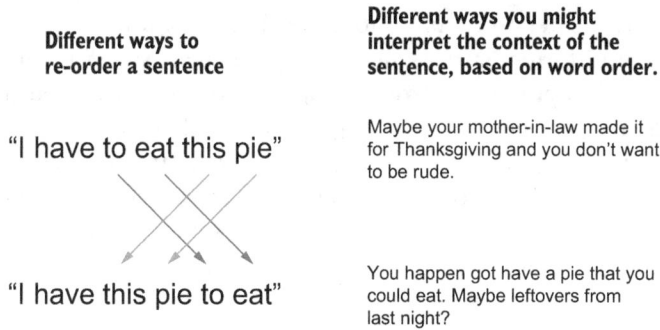

Figure 3.6 Without positional information, transformers do not understand that their inputs have a specific order, and all possible reorganizations of the tokens look identical to the algorithm. This is problematic because word order can change the word's context or, if done randomly, become gibberish.

For this reason, the embedding layer generates two different kinds of embeddings. First, it creates a *word embedding* that captures the meaning of the token, and second, it makes a *positional embedding* that captures the token's location in a sequence.

The idea is surprisingly simple. Just as we mapped every unique token to a unique meaning vector, we will also map every unique token position (first, second, third, and so on) to a position vector. So each token will get embedded twice—once for its identity and again for its position. These two vectors are then added to create one vector representing the word and its location in the sentence. This process is outlined in figure 3.7.

NOTE Using multiple dimensions instead of absolute positions makes it easier for the transformer to learn relative positioning, even if it is excessively redundant for us as humans [1].

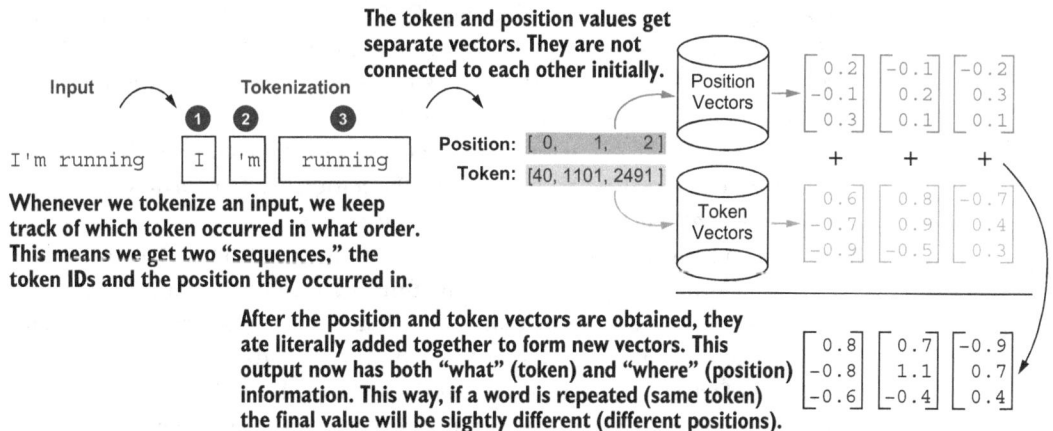

Figure 3.7 Word embeddings do not capture the fact that input tokens appear in a specific order. This information is captured by a positional embedding. The position embeddings work the same way as word embeddings and are added together. The resulting combined embeddings have the information the model needs to understand the order of tokens.

Those are all the missing details required to understand how tokens are converted into vectors for the transformer layers. This strategy may seem somewhat naive, and that is honestly true. People have tried developing more sophisticated methods to handle this information, but this simple approach of "Let's make everything a vector and just add them together" works surprisingly well. Importantly, it has also demonstrated success in video and images. Having a straightforward strategy that functions well enough for many different problems is valuable, which is why this naive approach has taken hold.

3.2.2 *Transformer layers*

The transformer layer aims to transform the input into a more useful output. Most prior neural network layers, such as an embedding layer, are designed to incorporate very specific beliefs about how the world works into their operation. The idea is that if the encoded belief is accurate to how the world does indeed work, your model will reach a better solution using less data. Transformers go for the opposite strategy. They encode a general-purpose mechanism that can learn many tasks if you get enough data.

To do this, transformers operate with three primary components:

- *Query*—Queries are vectors (from an embedding layer) that represent what you are looking for.
- *Key*—Key vectors represent the possible answers to pair a query against.
- *Value*—Every key has a corresponding value vector, the actual value to be returned when a query and key match.

This terminology corresponds to the behavior of a `dict` or dictionary object in Python. You look up an item in the dictionary by its key so that you can then create some useful output. The difference is that a transformer is fuzzy. It's not that we are looking up a single key, but we are evaluating *all keys*, weighted by their degree of similarity to the query. Figure 3.8 shows how this works with a simple example. While the queries and keys are shown as strings, those strings are stand-ins for the vectors that each string will be mapped to via the embedding layer.

Having every key contribute to one query could be chaotic, especially if there is one true match between a query and a specific key. This problem is handled by a detail called *attention* or the *attention mechanism*.

Attention inside a transformer can be considered similar to your ability to pay attention to what is important. You can tune out irrelevant and distracting information (i.e., bad keys) and focus primarily on what is important (the best matching keys). The analogy extends further in that attention is adaptive; what is important is a function of what other options are available. Your boss giving you directions for the week takes up your attention, but the fire alarm going off changes your attention away from your boss to the alarm (and a potential fire).

When generating the next token, a transformer takes the *query* for the current token and compares it to the *key* for all previous tokens. Comparing the query and the key generates a series of values that the attention mechanism uses to calculate

We have a list of queries Q that we want to ask the storage array about.

A database of keys K and values V. Each key ('kitty', 'cat', and 'dog') has one value (10.0, 9.0, and −7.5 respectively).

If the database was a normal Python dict object, we only get values when the query q is exactly equal to a key k. Any miss match returns None.

```
[
9.0,
None,
None
]
```

```
[
'cat',
'feline',
'potato'
]
```

```
{
'kitty': 10.0,
'cat': 9.0,
'dog': -7.5
}
```

Transformers looks at similarity between each query q and key k.

Transformer result is then a weighted average of the key's values.

```
[
9.1,
9.3,
-1.4
]
```

$$0.1 \cdot \text{'kitty'} + 0.9 \cdot \text{'cat'} + 0.0 \cdot \text{'dog'} = 9.1$$
$$0.3 \cdot \text{'kitty'} + 0.7 \cdot \text{'cat'} + 0.0 \cdot \text{'dog'} = 9.3$$
$$0.3 \cdot \text{'kitty'} + 0.3 \cdot \text{'cat'} + 0.4 \cdot \text{'dog'} = -1.4$$

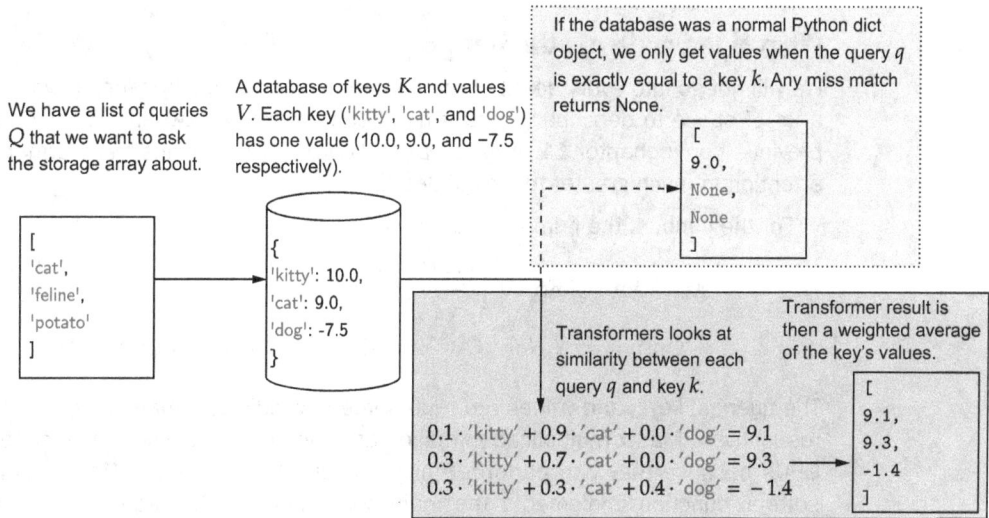

Figure 3.8 An example of how queries, keys, and values work inside a transformer compared to a Python dictionary. When a Python dictionary matches queries to keys, it needs an exact match to find the value, or it will return nothing. A transformer always returns something based on the most similar matches between queries and keys.

how much weight it should assign each potential following token when deciding which token to generate next. The *value* for each token tells the model what each previous token thinks its contribution to the probability should be. The attention function then computes the next token, as shown in figure 3.9.

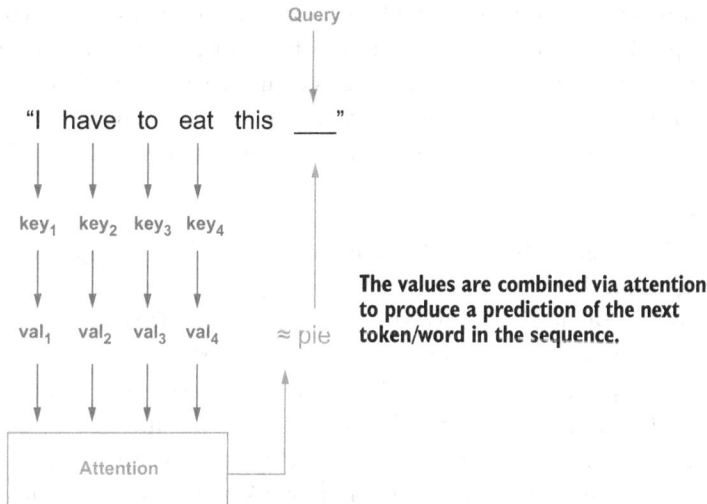

Query

"I have to eat this ___ "

key_1 key_2 key_3 key_4

val_1 val_2 val_3 val_4 ≈ pie

The values are combined via attention to produce a prediction of the next token/word in the sequence.

Attention

Figure 3.9 The next token in a sentence is predicted by using the current token as the query and calculating matches with the preceding words as the keys. The individual values themselves do not need to exist in the semantic space; the output of the attention mechanism produces something similar to one of the tokens in the vocabulary.

What is the math of attention?

We will not go into every detail of the math behind attention because it would take a lot of space to describe it, and it has been covered elsewhere. We did so in a previous book: chapter 11 of *Inside Deep Learning* [2] explains transformers and attention in much greater technical detail.

For the curious, the primary equation is

$$\text{Attention} = \text{Softmax}\left(\frac{Q \cdot K}{\sqrt{d}}\right)V \tag{3.1}$$

$$\text{Output} = x + \text{Norm}(\text{Attention}(x)) + \text{Norm}(\text{Feedforward}(x)) \tag{3.2}$$

The queries, keys, and values are represented by individual matrices Q, K, and V, respectively. Matrix multiplication makes attention efficient when implemented on GPUs because they can perform many multiplication operations in parallel. The softmax function implements the main component of the attention analogy by assigning many values nearly equal to zero, which causes the transformer to ignore the unimportant items.

The final step of *norm* and *Feedforward* is the application of *layer normalization* and a *linear layer* via a *skip connection*. If these terms aren't familiar to you, that is fine; you do not need to know this math to understand the rest of the book. If you want to learn what these terms mean, we refer you to *Inside Deep Learning* [2] for a technically detailed understanding.

A transformer model is made up of dozens of transformer layers. The intermediate transformer layers perform the same mechanical task described in figure 3.9 despite not having to predict a token because the last transformer layer is the only one that needs to predict an actual token. The transformer layer is general enough that combining many intermediate layers allows the model to learn complex tasks such as sorting, stacking, and other sophisticated input transformations.

3.2.3   *Unembedding layers*

The last stage of an LLM is the unembedding layer, which transforms the numeric vector representation that transformers use into a specific output token so that we can ultimately return the text that corresponds to that token. This output generation process is also called *decoding* because we decode the transformer vector representation to a piece of output text. It is a crucial component for using an LLM to generate text. Not only is decoding the current token essential for producing output, but the next token will depend on each previous token selected for output. This process is shown in figure 3.10, where we recursively generate tokens one at a time. In statistical parlance, this is known as an *autoregressive* process, meaning each element of the output is based on the output that came before it.

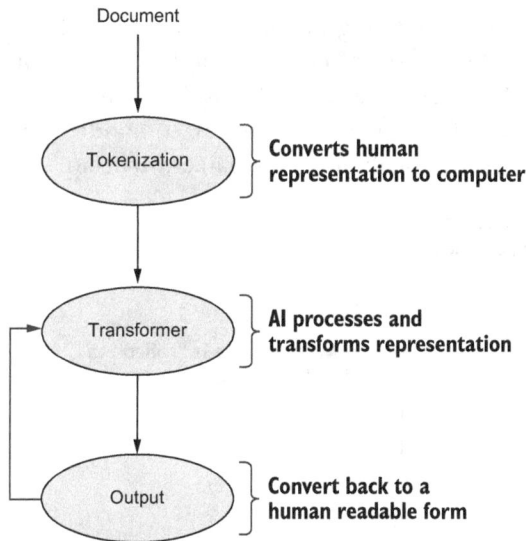

Figure 3.10 Producing output from LLMs involves converting from documents to tokens and then using the model to produce output. We loop through this process to both consume text and generate human-readable output.

You may be wondering how this process stops. When we build the vocabulary of tokens, we include some special tokens that do not occur in the text. One of these special tokens is an *end of sequence* (EoS) token. The model trains on texts with natural endpoints that are finished with the EoS marker, and when the model generates a new token, the EoS token is one of the options it can generate. If the EoS is generated, we know it is time to stop the loop and return the full text to the user. It is also a good idea to keep a maximum generation limit if your model gets into a bad state and fails to generate the EoS token.

SAMPLING TOKENS TO PRODUCE OUTPUT
What is missing from this process is how we convert a vector, an array of floating-point numbers produced by the transformer layers, into a single token. This process is called *sampling* because it uses a statistical method to choose sample tokens from the vocabulary based on the LLM's input and its output so far. The LLM's sampling algorithm evaluates those samples to select which token to produce. There are several techniques for doing this sampling, but all follow the same basic two-step strategy:

1 For each token in the vocabulary, compute the probability that each token will be the next selected token.
2 Randomly pick a token according to the probabilities calculated.

If you have used ChatGPT or other LLMs, you may have noticed that they do not always provide the same output for the same input. The decoding step is why you may get different answers whenever you ask the same question.

It may seem counterintuitive that tokens are selected randomly. However, it is a critical component to generating good-quality text. Consider the example of text generation in figure 3.11, where we are trying to finish the sentence "I love to eat." It would be unrealistic if the model always picked "sushi" as the next token because it had the highest probability. If someone always said "sushi" to you in this context, you would think something was off. We need randomness to handle the fact that there are multiple valid choices, and not all options are likely to occur.

2. A probability is computed for each possible token, most receive near-zero probabilities.

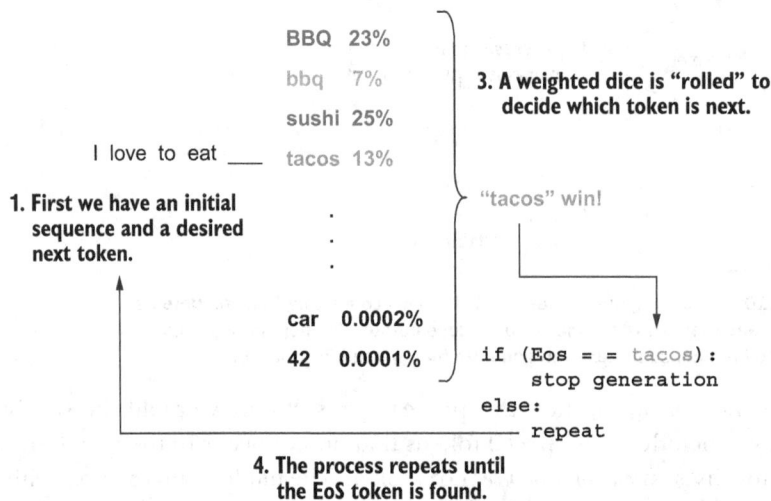

BBQ 23%

bbq 7%

3. A weighted dice is "rolled" to decide which token is next.

sushi 25%

I love to eat ___   tacos 13%

1. First we have an initial sequence and a desired next token.

"tacos" win!

.
.
.

car 0.0002%

42 0.0001%

```
if (Eos = = tacos):
        stop generation
else:
        repeat
```

4. The process repeats until the EoS token is found.

Figure 3.11 We demonstrate text generation by starting with the phrase "I love to eat" and then showing that some possible completions that are foods, such as barbeque and sushi, have high probabilities, while a car and the number 42 have low probabilities. Weighted random selection chooses the word tacos. The generation loop is stopped when the EoS token appears.

Also note in the example from figure 3.11 that other tokens would be nonsensical, like 42, given tiny probabilities. Again, we need to assign every token a probability to know which tokens are likely or unlikely.

How do you get probabilities for tokens?

Each possible next token has a different probability of being selected. Most of the tokens have nearly zero chance of being selected. A keen reader may wonder: How can we assign a probability to a token before knowing the other tokens? We do so by giving every token a score, indicating how good a match that token's embedding is compared to the current vector (i.e., the output from the transformer). The score is arbitrary from $-\infty$ to ∞ and calculated independently for each token. The relative difference in scores is then used to create probabilities. For example, if one token had a score of 65.2 and a second token had a score of -5.0, the probabilities would be near 100% and 0% for the individual token, respectively. If the scores were 65.2 and 65.1, the probabilities would be near 50.5% and 49.5%, respectively.

> Similarly, scores of 0.2 and 0.1 would give the same probabilities as the scores 65.2 and 65.1 because we are looking at relative differences in scores to assign probabilities, not the individual scores themselves.

A transformer sometimes gives you unusual or nonsensical generations. It's not common, but the other tokens have a *near-zero* probability, and eventually, one weird token will get picked that you would not expect. Once an unexpected token has been chosen, all future generated tokens will be produced in a manner that tries to make sense of the unusual generation.

For example, if the LLM produced "I love to eat *chalk*," you would be pretty surprised. But it is not overly unreasonable because chalk-eating is a symptom of the medical condition called pica. Once the word *chalk* is selected, the LLM may go into a tangent about pica or some other medical diatribe—that is, of course, if you are so lucky that your unusual generation is in the sphere of "rare but reasonable" and not an utterly errant prediction.

> **NOTE** Many algorithms can compute the final probabilities used to select words for generation. One of these is nucleus sampling, also known as Top-p sampling, which involves determining the tokens with the highest probability as potential outputs and choosing tokens to output from that list. This method can help us avoid unreasonable predictions. If you can, you want to check which sampling algorithm your LLM uses so that you can understand its risks of producing rarer to unreasonable outputs.

3.3 The tradeoff between creativity and topical responses

Depending on how your users plan to interact with an LLM, generating surprising or creative outputs may be desired. Say you are using an LLM to help brainstorm new product ideas, and you are using a chatbot as a digital sounding board to spark ideas. In this case, you probably want unusual outputs generated because the goal is to be creative and think of something new.

Conversely, sometimes creativity is wholly undesired. One potential use for LLMs is offline search, where you could fit an LLM on a (relatively powerful) mobile phone and ask/look up information even when you do not have internet connectivity. In this case, you want the outputs of the LLM to be reliable, on topic, and factual. A creative reinterpretation is not needed.

A feature in LLMs called *temperature* balances this tradeoff. The temperature variable (which is a number between 0 and 1 and often has a default value of 0.7 or 0.8) is used to exaggerate the probability of low-likelihood tokens (high temperature) or depress the probability of low-likelihood tokens (low temperature).

Consider molecules in a glass of water as an analogy. Say we want to know what molecule will be at the top of the glass (don't ask us why; just go with it). If the glass was lowered to a temperature of absolute zero, all the molecules would be still, and the molecule at the top of the glass would reliably be the same each time (i.e., you will always generate the same token). If you raise the temperature of the glass so much that it starts to boil, the molecules will bounce around, making the molecule at the top of the glass essentially random (i.e., you get a completely random token). As you scale the temperature up and down, you change the balance between picking with greater randomness (and, thus, often creativity) or focusing on just the most likely next token (thus keeping the generation more topical).

In a practical sense, considering our example of "I like to eat," a higher temperature would lead to the generation of different types of foods, not just pizza or sushi but possibly less typical or more specific foods like beef wellington or vegetarian chili.

3.4   *Transformers in context*

We've covered a lot of ground in this chapter. Embedding layers, transformer layers, and unembedding layers are the core building blocks that make LLMs work. The concepts of how LLMs encode meaning and position and then use stacks of transformer layers to uncover the structure in text are all vital to understanding how LLMs capture information and produce the quality of output they are capable of. But we have more details to cover! How do we create these layers to generate embeddings and probabilities by analyzing piles and piles of data in the first place? In chapter 4, we will continue exploring how to feed data into this architecture and incentivize the LLM to "learn" meaningful relationships in text through the training process.

Summary

- While LLMs use tokens as their basic unit of semantic meaning, they're mathematically represented within the model as *embedding vectors* rather than as strings. These embedding vectors can capture relationships about nearness, dissimilarity, antonyms, and other linguistic-descriptive properties.
- Position and word order do not come naturally to transformers and are obtained via another vector representing the relative position. The model can represent word order by adding the position and word embedding vectors.
- Transformer layers act as a kind of fuzzy dictionary, returning approximate answers to approximate matches. This fuzzy process is called attention and uses the terms *query*, *key*, and *value* as analogous to the key and value in a Python dictionary.
- ChatGPT is an example of a decoder-only transformer, but encoder-only transformers and encoder-decoder transformers also exist. Decoder-only transformers are best at generating text, but other types of transformers can be better at other tasks.
- LLMs are autoregressive, meaning they work recursively. All previously generated tokens are fed into the model at each step to get the next token. Simply put, autoregressive models predict the next thing using the previous things.

- The output of any transformer isn't tokens; instead, the output is a probability for how likely every token is. Selecting a specific token is called *unembedding* or *sampling* and includes some randomness.
- The strength of randomness can be controlled, resulting in more or less realistic output, more creative or unique output, or more consistent output. Most LLMs have a default threshold for randomness that is reasonable looking, but you may want to change it for different uses.

How LLMs learn

4

This chapter covers

- Training algorithms with loss functions and gradient descent
- How LLMs mimic human text
- How training can lead LLMs to produce errors
- Challenges in scaling LLMs

The words *learning* and *training* are commonly used in the machine learning community to describe what algorithms do when they observe data and make predictions based on those observations. We use this terminology begrudgingly because although it simplifies the discussion of the operations of these algorithms, we feel that it is not ideal. Fundamentally, this terminology leads to misconceptions about LLMs and artificial intelligence. These words imply that these algorithms have human-like qualities; they seduce you into believing that algorithms display emergent behavior and are capable of more than they are truly capable of. At a fundamental level, this terminology is incorrect. A computer doesn't learn in any way similar to how humans learn. Models do improve based on data and feedback, but it is incredibly important to keep this mechanistically distinct from anything like human learning. Indeed, you probably do not want an AI to learn like a human: we spend many years of our lives focused on education and still make dumb decisions.

Deep learning algorithms train in a way that is far more formulaic than how humans learn. It is formulaic in the literal sense of using a lot of math and the figurative meaning of following a simple repetitive procedure billions of times until completion. We will spare you the math, but in this chapter, we will help you remove the mystery of how LLMs are trained.

Many machine learning algorithms use the training algorithm called *gradient descent*. The name of this algorithm implies some details that we'll review with a high-level overview of how gradient descent is used for machine learning. Once you understand the general approach used to train many different model types, we will explore how gradient descent is applied to LLMs to create a model that produces convincing textual output.

Understanding these details will help you avoid inaccurate connotations implied by words like *learn*. More importantly, it will also prepare you to understand better when LLMs succeed and fail in their current design and the often-subtle ways such algorithms can produce misleading outputs.

4.1 Gradient descent

Gradient descent is the key to all modern deep-learning algorithms. When an industry practitioner mentions gradient descent, they are implicitly referring to two critical elements of the training process. The first is known as a *loss function*, and the second is calculating *gradients*, which are measurements that tell you how to adjust the parameters of the neural network so that the loss function produces results in a specific way. You can think of these as two high-level components:

- *Loss function*—You need a single numeric score that calculates how poorly your algorithm works.
- *Gradient descent*—You need a mechanical process that tweaks the numeric values inside an algorithm to make the loss function score as small as possible.

The loss function and gradient descent are components of the training algorithm used to produce a machine learning model. Many different training algorithms are in use today, but generally, each algorithm sends inputs into a model, observes the model's output, and tweaks the model to improve its performance. A training algorithm will repeat this process a tremendous number of times. Given enough data, a model will produce the expected outputs repeatedly and reliably when confronted with previously unseen input.

4.1.1 What is a loss function?

We will use the example of wanting to make money to help develop a mental picture of a suitable loss function. Indeed, an intelligent person can make money, so if you have an intelligent computer, it should be able to help you make money. To pick a suitable loss function for this or any other task (these lessons generalize to any ML problem beyond LLMs), we need to satisfy three criteria: *specificity*, *computability*, and *smoothness*. In other words, the loss function needs to be

- Specific and correlated with the desired behavior of the model
- Computable in a reasonable amount of time with a reasonable amount of resources
- Smooth, in the sense that the function's output does not fluctuate wildly when given similar inputs

We will use the following examples and counterexamples to help you develop an intuition for each property.

LOSS FUNCTION SPECIFICITY

First, let's start with a bad example of specificity. If your boss came to you and said, "Build an intelligent computer," that would be a magnificent goal, but it is not a specific goal. Remember, in chapter 1, we discussed how difficult it is to define intelligence. What exactly does your boss want this computer to be intelligent at? Would a street-smart computer that cannot do your calculus homework suffice? Instead, you could try to optimize for a specific IQ score, but does that correlate with what your boss wants? We have been able to get computers to pass IQ tests for over a decade [1], even before the introduction of LLMs. However, they could not do anything other than pass an IQ test and perform limited tasks. Ultimately, the IQ test does not correlate with what we want computers to do. As a result, it is not worth optimizing IQ as a metric for success in machine learning or for building the intelligent computer your boss asked you to create.

Another example involves the challenge of managing money. Consider a scenario where you want to minimize the debt you carry. You might even want your debt to go negative, meaning others owe you money! We use the example of debt here because it is intrinsically a value you want to make smaller. This analogy aligns perfectly with the terminology used in practice: you want to minimize your loss just as you want to reduce your debt. The volume of debt is also an objective measure, making it a good way of ensuring our loss function is relevant under changing conditions. Finally, if our overall goal is to maintain a surplus of money, minimizing debt correlates well with that goal. Minimizing debt has all of the characteristics of a good loss function!

A note on terminology

You may also hear loss functions described as *objective functions*. We recommend avoiding this term as a newcomer because it is ambiguous. For example, it is unclear whether you want to minimize (debt) or maximize your objective (profit). Both approaches technically work; multiply a maximizing objective by -1, and you now have a minimizing objective.

You may also hear the term *reward function* used in some contexts, such as reinforcement learning (RL). This is appropriate because RL algorithms seek to maximize reward by performing a desirable behavior.

Regardless of the terminology, objective functions, reward functions, and loss functions all address the same fundamental requirement: they provide a way of evaluating the outputs that a machine learning model produces.

LOSS FUNCTION COMPUTABILITY

The loss function must also be something we can compute quickly with a computer. The debt example is unsuitable for this aspect because all the inputs and outputs you need are not readily available to a computer. Will working harder at your job increase your income and thus lower your debt? Maybe, but how will we encode your hard work into the computer? Here, we have the problem that the most critical factors to minimizing debt are hard to quantify, like job availability, your fit for such jobs, likelihood of promotion, etc. So the loss is specific, but the inputs that connect to that loss are not computable.

A better, more computable goal would be to predict the loss on an investment. The reasons this goal is better are subtle. The goal is still objective because our algorithms learn from historical data. For example, a historic investment in bonds X and stocks Y had certain returns. The inputs are also now objective: you can quantify the amount of cash you put into each investment. You either put money in, or you took it out. There are no hard-to-encode problems like "hard work" to deal with. With a copy of historical data, a computer can quickly calculate the loss/return on an investment.

LOSS FUNCTION SMOOTHNESS

The third thing we need is smoothness. Many people have good intuition for what smoothness means by thinking about a smooth versus bumpy texture. Instead of texture, we're talking about the smoothness of a function, which can be depicted by drawing that function as a graph. For example, when trying to predict a loss on an investment, we run into the problem that investment returns are not usually smooth. They may follow a pattern of volatility where price graphs are jagged with sharp, sudden changes. This makes learning difficult. A graph showing the unstable values of real-world investment returns is shown in figure 4.1.

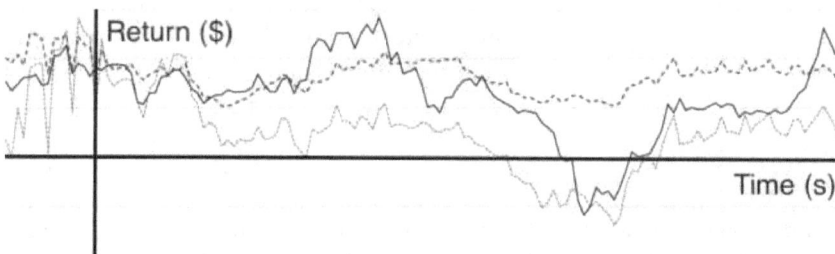

Figure 4.1 Investment returns are not easy to predict, partly because they are not smooth. (Image modified from [2] under the Creative Commons license)

Return on investment is an excellent example of a bad (nonsmooth) loss because erratic behavior is problematic for any predictive approach. It would be best if you were always cautious of anyone or any approach that claims to work well in predicting nonsmooth data like this. However, there is a precise technical definition of smooth that, if not satisfied by a loss function, is a hard deal-breaker. Functions that depend on discontinuities, or breaks in the consistency of their values, are the most common functions that are not technically smooth, but we would like to be able to use them in practice. Some examples of nonsmooth functions are shown in figure 4.2 to help you understand. Smoothness is usually inhibited due to discontinuities, such as that shown in the center graph, or distinct changes in the value of a function, as shown in the graph on the right.

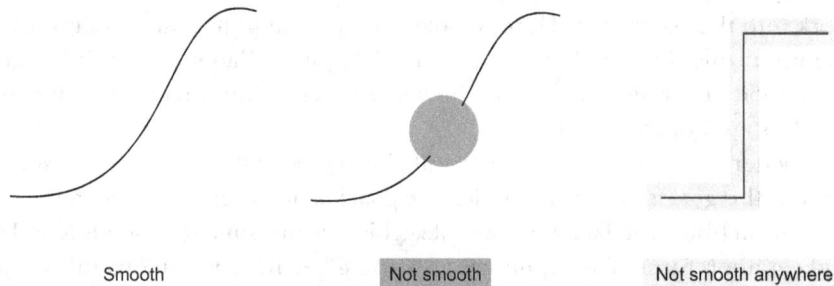

Smooth

Not smooth

Not smooth anywhere

Figure 4.2 Examples of a smooth function on the left and two nonsmooth functions on the right. The center example is mostly smooth, but one region is not smooth because the function has no value. On the right, the function is not smooth anywhere due to the hard change in value.

We won't go deep into the formal mathematical definitions that describe what makes something smooth and what value changes are acceptable or unacceptable in smooth functions. Still, we've given you enough background to understand what you need to know. The important thing for you to understand is that your intuition of what smooth means, that the value changes continuously, is a good barometer for how viable a loss function is. This may seem arbitrary, but it is an ubiquitous problem. Say you want to build a model to predict cancer accurately. Accuracy is not a smooth function because you count the number of successful predictions out of the total predictions. For example, if you had 50 patients and predicted 48 of them correctly, a smooth function would have an option for 48.2 cases, 47.921351 cases, or any number you might think of. However, the actual count of cancer cases is constrained to the integers 1, 2, 3, . . ., 48, 49, 50 because there is no such thing as a partial case of cancer.

How do you handle nonsmooth losses?

It may be shocking that accuracy is one of the most common predictive goals, but we cannot use it when training an algorithm. But it is true! So how do we handle this strange phenomenon? The answer is to create a *proxy problem*. A proxy problem is an alternate way of representing a problem that correlates with what we want to solve but is better behaved. In this case, we use a cross-entropy loss function instead of accuracy. While we won't go into the details of cross-entropy loss here, its use demonstrates that proxy problems are fundamental tricks used in machine learning and artificial intelligence.

This discussion leads us to another critical takeaway about how LLMs learn, which is true of most algorithms: the technique we use to train them is not always focused on what we want them to do but on what we can make them learn. This focus can lead to an incentive mismatch, leading to unexpected results or low performance. We will discuss how the nature of an LLM's loss function creates this incentive mismatch after examining the second major training component: gradient descent.

4.1.2 What is gradient descent?

Having a loss function is a prerequisite for performing a gradient descent. The loss function tells you objectively how poorly you are performing the task. Gradient descent is the process we use to figure out how to tweak the parameters of the neural network to reduce the loss incurred. This is done by comparing the input training data and the actual versus expected outputs of the neural network using the loss function. In this case, the gradient is the direction and amount that you need to change the parameters of a neural network to reduce the amount of error measured by the loss function. Gradient descent shows us how to tweak all the parameters of a neural network "just a little bit" to improve its performance and reduce the difference between the expected and actual outputs. A diagram of this process is shown in figure 4.3.

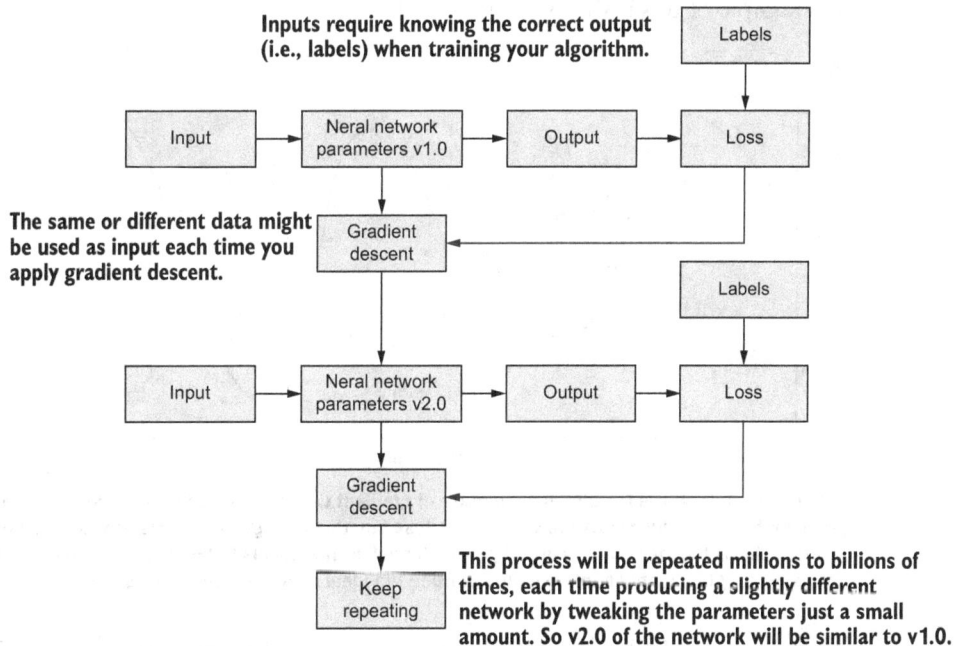

Figure 4.3 Inputs and labels (the known correct answers for each input) are used to tweak the neural network during gradient descent. A network is made of parameters that are altered a small amount each time gradient descent is applied. We eventually transform the network into something useful by applying gradient descent millions or billions of times.

As figure 4.3 shows, we create a new, slightly different network every time we apply gradient descent. Because the changes are small, this process has to be performed billions of times. This way, all the small changes add up to a more significant, mean-ingful change in the overall network.

> **NOTE** Modern LLMs perform billions of parameter updates because they are trained on billions of tokens. The more data you have, the more times you run gradient descent. The less data you have, the less often you need to run it. The data used to train an LLM is more than you could read in a lifetime.

Gradient descent is a mathematical process that is applied repeatedly without deviation. There are no guarantees that it will work or find the best or even a good solution. Nevertheless, many researchers have been surprised by how practical this relatively simple approach is.

To help you understand how gradient descent works, we will use a simple example of rolling a ball down a hill. The ball's location represents a parameter value for a node in the neural network that the training algorithm can alter. The hill's height is the amount of loss and describes how poorly the model performs for the training input. We want to roll the ball down the hill into the deepest valley because that is the area with the lowest loss, which indicates that the model is performing its best. An example of this is shown in figure 4.4

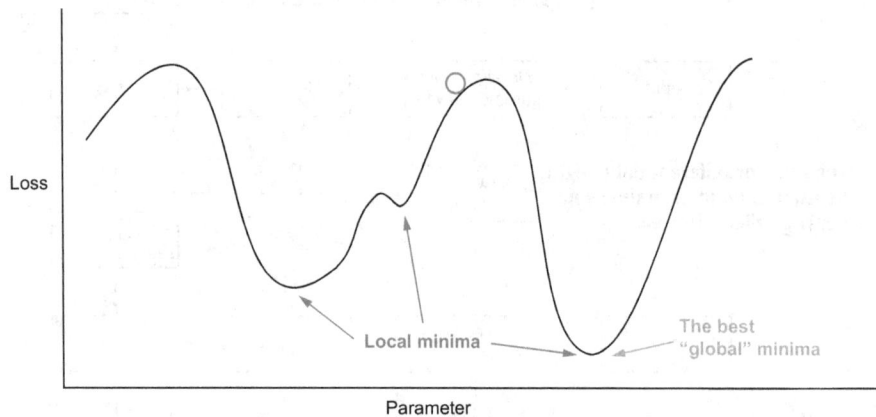

Figure 4.4   This shows the global big picture of gradient descent applied to a single parameter problem. The curve illustrates the value of the loss function for a given parameter value. The ball's location shows the loss for the current parameter value. The goal is to find the parameter values corresponding to a global minimum representing the ideal solution with the least loss.

As you can see, the ball could fall into many valleys. The industry jargon would be to call this problem *nonconvex* because multiple paths lead to reduced loss, but each path does not necessarily progress toward the best possible solution. It is also important to note that this is not an analogy. Gradient descent literally looks at the world this way. These examples show how gradient descent works for a model with one parameter to optimize. The same procedure is applied to billions of parameters when training an LLM.

So from this position, we greedily look at which direction to move the ball downhill. We apply gradient descent two times in figure 4.5. This shows that the greedy option is to the left. When we move to the left by adjusting our parameter, we slightly move the ball down the slope. From the graph, you can see that a better solution exists by searching to the right, but due to the algorithm's simplicity, it is unlikely that gradient descent will find it. Finding the optimal result in this case would require a more intelligent strategy involving searching and exploration, which is too costly to do well in practice.

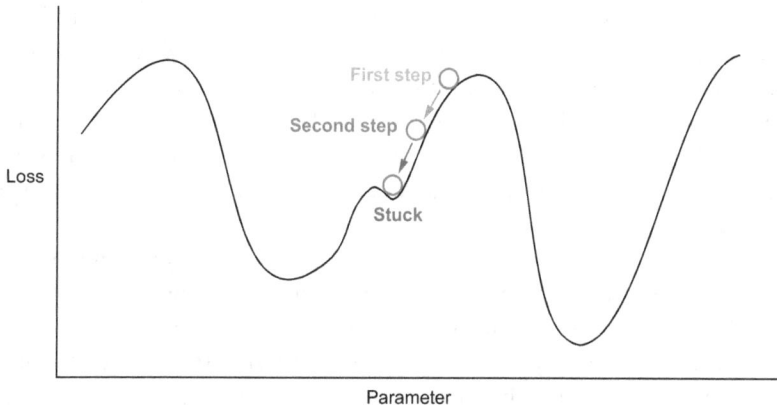

Figure 4.5   The gradient descent algorithm takes steps to adjust parameters to find the optimal outcome with the least loss. Unfortunately, the algorithm gets stuck in a local minimum, an area of the graph that is not optimal because other parameter values correspond to areas with a lower loss.

Also, notice that in the second step in figure 4.5, the ball gets stuck. While it is evident that continuing to move to the left will achieve an even lower loss, this result is only obvious because we can see the whole picture. Gradient descent cannot see the entire picture or even what is nearby. It only knows the exact location due to the current parameters and the loss function. Hence, it is a *greedy procedure*. Greedy procedures such as gradient descent are simplified approaches with the desired property of computability in that they are not prohibitively expensive to run many times to achieve an outcome. Greedy procedures are short-sighted because they choose the next optimal step based only on the current state, although broader, more optimal solutions may exist. They do this because evaluating the current and all possible future states would be impossible due to the number of potential outcomes that need to be considered. It would simply be too much to compute. The hope is that making many simple optimal decisions using limited information will generally lead to the most positive outcome—in this case, minimizing the value of the loss function.

IMPORTANT NUANCES IN GRADIENT DESCENT
In this discussion of gradient descent, we have skipped some important nuances that need to be considered for real-world use. First, as described here, gradient descent would need to use all of the training data simultaneously, which is computationally infeasible. Instead, we use a procedure called *stochastic gradient descent* (SGD). SGD is

precisely the same as we've described, except it uses a small random subset of the training data instead of the entire dataset. This dramatically reduces the memory required to train the model, resulting in faster, better solutions. This method works because gradient descent only makes small changes in the current greedy direction. It turns out that a little data is almost as good as using all the data when figuring out which step to take next. If you have a billion tokens, you can take a billion SGD steps in about the same amount of time it takes to do one standard gradient descent step using all the data.

Many training approaches use a particular form of SGD called *Adaptive Moment Estimation* (Adam). Adam includes some extra tricks to help minimize the loss function faster and avoid getting stuck. Adam's main trick is that it gives the ball some momentum, which builds as updates continually move in one direction. This momentum causes the ball to roll down the hill faster and means that if a small local minimum is hit, there might be enough momentum to plow past that point and continue onward, thus reaching the area of the loss function graph with the smallest amount of loss.

The downside of Adam is that storing this information about momentum for each parameter increases the memory required for training by a factor of three compared to plain SGD. Memory is the most critical factor when building LLMs because it often determines how many GPUs you need, translating to cash out of your pocket. Although Adam won't make the final model larger because you can throw away the data related to Adam's extra momentum calculations once you are done training, you still need a system large enough to perform the training in the first place. The increased accuracy that comes with Adam's ability to minimize loss more effectively comes with a distinct price.

4.2   *LLMs learn to mimic human text*

Now that we understand how deep learning algorithms are trained by specifying a loss function used with gradient descent, we can discuss how this is applied to LLMs. Specifically, we will focus on the data and loss or reward functions used to train LLMs.

LLMs are generally trained on human-authored text. Specifically, they're explicitly trained to mimic texts produced by humans. While this sounds a bit obvious (what else would they be trained to do?), this detail is commonly missed or confused with other things, even by experts in the field. In particular, language models are *not* trained to do any of the following things:

- Memorize text
- Generate new ideas
- Build representations of the world
- Produce factually accurate text

It is essential to explain this notion further before we go deeper. When one trains a model to play chess, the model learns to play well because it gets rewarded for winning. A language model, by contrast, only gets rewarded for producing text that looks exactly like the training data. Consequently, all text generated by the LLM that *looks like text in the training corpus* produces high rewards (or low loss), even when those generations are not truthful or factual. This is an example of misalignment between the loss function and the designer's higher-level goal, as discussed in section 4.1.

LLMs are trained on datasets of hundreds of gigabytes of text scraped from the internet. The internet is famous for containing a large amount of incorrect (and weird) information. LLMs that are better at most tasks often end up being worse at tasks that are commonly misrepresented in their training data (see the Inverse Scaling Prize at https://github.com/inverse-scaling/prize). For example, researchers have consistently found that better language models are also better at reproducing common knowledge that is false [3], mimicking stereotypes and social biases [4]. They tend to fall into a downward spiral that reinforces errors. For example, after generating code that contains bugs, they're more likely to generate code that contains additional bugs [5]. These things are commonly represented in the training text, so LLMs are positively rewarded for predicting them even though it's wrong. Thus, getting better based on its loss function for an LLM also means getting worse at these tasks that require truth and correctness.

4.2.1 LLM reward functions

Previously, we said that LLMs are rewarded for producing data that "looks like its training data." In this subsection, we will explore what this means more concretely.

LLMs are trained by being shown the first couple of tokens of a sentence and having it predict the next token. The loss is based on the accuracy of that prediction compared to the training data. For example, it might be shown "This is a" and be expected to produce "test." If the model produces "test," it gets a point, and if it does not, it loses a point. This process is done for all beginning segments of the text, as shown in figure 4.6. Here, it is trained to predict each of the highlighted words independently. This setup is not unique to LLMs. It has been used to train recurrent neural networks (RNNs) for many years. However, an essential part of why LLMs have become so popular is that they can be trained much more efficiently than an RNN. An RNN must be trained on each generation *sequentially* because each newly generated word depends on the prior words chosen. An LLM can be trained on all generations *in parallel* due to the transformer architecture discussed in chapter 3. The ability to train a model on related generations in parallel represents a massive speed-up, allowing training at a large scale, and is a prerequisite for building today's state-of-the-art LLMs using terabytes of data.

We discussed how predicting the next token can be problematic because the algorithm may be incentivized to produce incorrect or factually errant outputs. We must also discuss the intuition behind why, despite this, this approach can produce such convincing outputs. It is reasonable to ask: How can an algorithm trained to create the next most likely token seemingly perform something we could mistake for reasoning?

Alaska

Alaska is

Alaska is about

Alaska is about twelve

Alaska is about twelve times

Alaska is about twelve times larger

Alaska is about twelve times larger than

Alaska is about twelve times larger than New

Alaska is about twelve times larger than New York

Figure 4.6   An LLM sees this sentence nine times, each time learning from the prediction of a single word at the end of each of the nine sequences.

To develop this intuition, imagine how you might try to predict the next token for a given sentence. A computer has no pressure to respond quickly, so take your time. Consider the sentence "I love to eat <blank>," and try to guess what word might go into the <blank>. The earlier parts of the sentence give you valuable context. Since we are discussing eating, you can almost immediately narrow the scope to a food item. Keeping a list of all possible food items is not difficult for a computer.

Now if you consider the background of the authors of this book, you will have even more context. We are Americans in a common geographical area, which makes specific cuisines more likely than others. An LLM will not have this background, but if the sentence was longer and had more context, you could start to narrow down the choices in the same way as shown in figure 4.7.

I love to eat ___

Learning how to cook with yeast, now I love to eat ____

I can't eat meat any more, so I'm adapting. Learning how to cook with yeast, now I love to eat ____

Figure 4.7   Context can help you make decent predictions about the next word. As you move from left to right, additional text that might occur in a sentence is added. The images in the thought bubble for each sentence show how the added context eliminates predictions.

As you identify keywords or phrases in the preceding text, you can gain insight into the best word to predict next. A computer performing these calculations does far more processing than a human requires. This kind of brute-force association mainly narrows the scope to something very reasonable. Again, the model will be updated billions of times to refine these associations and thus acquire a useful capability correlated with our goals of an algorithm able to understand and react to human text.

However, correlation is not causation, and the next-word prediction strategy can lead to humorous errors. LLMs are susceptible to a "begging the question" error, where the premise of the question implies something untrue. Since the LLM is not trained for accuracy or contradiction, it attempts to produce a sequence of human-like text predictions that might follow your misleading question. An example of ChatGPT struggling with this kind of problem is given in figure 4.8, where we ask about the exceptional strength of dry spaghetti.

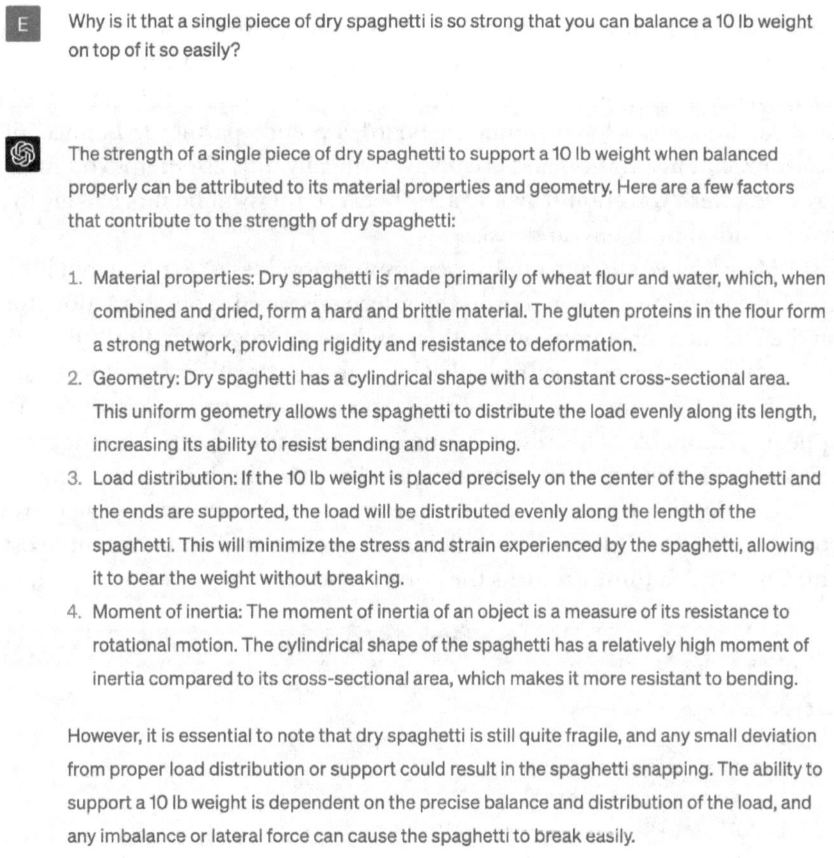

E   Why is it that a single piece of dry spaghetti is so strong that you can balance a 10 lb weight on top of it so easily?

The strength of a single piece of dry spaghetti to support a 10 lb weight when balanced properly can be attributed to its material properties and geometry. Here are a few factors that contribute to the strength of dry spaghetti:

1. Material properties: Dry spaghetti is made primarily of wheat flour and water, which, when combined and dried, form a hard and brittle material. The gluten proteins in the flour form a strong network, providing rigidity and resistance to deformation.

2. Geometry: Dry spaghetti has a cylindrical shape with a constant cross-sectional area. This uniform geometry allows the spaghetti to distribute the load evenly along its length, increasing its ability to resist bending and snapping.

3. Load distribution: If the 10 lb weight is placed precisely on the center of the spaghetti and the ends are supported, the load will be distributed evenly along the length of the spaghetti. This will minimize the stress and strain experienced by the spaghetti, allowing it to bear the weight without breaking.

4. Moment of inertia: The moment of inertia of an object is a measure of its resistance to rotational motion. The cylindrical shape of the spaghetti has a relatively high moment of inertia compared to its cross-sectional area, which makes it more resistant to bending.

However, it is essential to note that dry spaghetti is still quite fragile, and any small deviation from proper load distribution or support could result in the spaghetti snapping. The ability to support a 10 lb weight is dependent on the precise balance and distribution of the load, and any imbalance or lateral force can cause the spaghetti to break easily.

Figure 4.8 While predicting the next token is powerful, it doesn't imbue the network with reasoning or logic abilities. If we ask ChatGPT something absurd and untrue, it happily explains how it happens.

The core of why spaghetti can support hundreds of times its own weight is absurd and untrue. However, the algorithm has been primed to provide an answer about material tensile strength by formatting the question: "Why is it that X is so strong?" The model can extract this key context. Previous training data likely explains such material properties based on a factual question, which informs the model predicting that a similar response is appropriate. The subject of the sentence (spaghetti) and object (10 lb. weight) are used to inform minor details of the response, which is otherwise generic.

4.3   LLMs and novel tasks

The nature of the autoregressive, next-word prediction strategy and its use as a loss or reward during the training process gives us valuable insight into the nature of an LLM's generated responses and how they can potentially be factually inaccurate. However, it also shows us why LLMs can be effective for looking up information, as a far more powerful keyword search than a standard search engine. There are ways to design around the limitations of nonfactual responses. For example, many LLM approaches add citations to the generated output so that it is possible to quickly verify that factually accurate content was used to produce the generated text. An LLM can also be a valuable sounding board, a pseudo-partner to bounce ideas off of as a source of inspiration and creativity. Critically, this also helps you understand a key case where you should avoid LLMs because they will be more likely to produce errors—novel problems and tasks.

LLMs are generally not good at performing novel tasks. Figuring out if your task is novel can be pretty challenging, as the internet is weird. Tons of random things exist on the internet, including competitions on how to programmatically draw ducks and unicorns [6]. If the task is sufficiently similar to one already seen before or structurally similar to other things in the training data, you may end up with something that appears reasonable. This result can be extremely useful, but it can degrade as your task becomes more unique compared to what exists in the training data.

For example, we asked ChatGPT to write code that calculates the mathematical constant π (pi) in Python. This task is not novel; tons of code like this exists online, and ChatGPT faithfully returns the correct code for us.

Listing 4.1   ChatGPT calculating pi in Python

```
def calculate_pi(terms):
    pi = 0
    for i in range(terms):
        term = ((-1) ** i) / (2 * i + 1)
        pi += term
    pi *= 4
    return pi
print(calculate_pi(1000000))
```
Tests the function; the more terms, the more accurate the approximation

Now let us force ChatGPT to do some not terribly challenging extrapolation. We asked ChatGPT to translate this function to the programming language Modula-3. This task is not too big of an extrapolation; Modula-3 is a programming language with a similar style and a historically significant programming language that influenced the eventual design of almost all the most popular languages today! However, it is excessively esoteric. You can find very few examples of this programming language today, mainly in the context of university compiler classes. The next listing shows Chat-GPT's reasonable attempt. As you may have been able to predict from the context of this chapter thus far, ChatGPT made some errors, marked in the listing.

Listing 4.2   ChatGPT calculates pi in Modula-3

```
MODULE CalculatePi;   ←— Missing EXPORTS Main;

IMPORT IO, Real;

PROCEDURE CalculatePi(terms: INTEGER): REAL;
VAR
  pi: REAL := 0.0;
  i: INTEGER;
BEGIN                                        ** isn't an operator.
  FOR i := 0 TO terms - 1 DO
      pi := pi + ((-1.0) ** FLOAT(i)) / (2.0 * FLOAT(i) + 1.0);  ←—
  END;
  RETURN 4.0 * pi;
END CalculatePi;
                                   PutReal can take only one
BEGIN                              optional second argument,
  IO.PutReal(CalculatePi(1000000), 0, 15);  ←— and it's not an integer.
END CalculatePi.
```

This short program has three errors that would prevent it from working. It is more interesting that ChatGPT gets these wrong because it confidently extrapolates standard coding practices from other languages. (In this case, *confidently* means that ChatGPT does not warn us of its potential errors. One of the authors likes to say that ChatGPT sounds like their most overconfident and often incorrect friend.) In this case, ** is a commonly used exponentiation function, so ChatGPT decides that Modula-3 supports this operation. As far as we can tell from scouring the internet, Modula-3 has no documented example of how to exponentiate a variable. Because most programming languages support this action with a ^, **, or pow() option, Chat-GPT just extrapolates one into existence. The correct answer would be that it must first implement a pow function and then use it to compute pi.

The arguments provided to the PutReal function are another mystery. Our best guess is that the 15 corresponds to an extrapolation of printing out 15 digits of a floating-point value, a typical default when calculating pi. Regardless, it is not how that function works.

The more significant point is that ChatGPT gets some of the nuanced details right but only for the parts that can be found on the internet and are already explained (e.g., FLOAT(i) is required, as is doing 4.0 * pi instead of 4 * pi). The tasks without examples on the internet are the ones where ChatGPT makes errors.

This example also highlights the limits of perceived versus actualized "reasoning" within LLMs today. The complete language specification for Modula-3 is available online and has documented all of these details or their lack of existence. ChatGPT has almost surely seen many other coding language specifications, parser specifications, and millions of lines of code in common programming languages. If a person had this background knowledge and resources, performing the logical induction required to avoid all three errors should not be too challenging. However, the LLM does not perform any induction process and, thus, makes errors despite the breadth of available information.

This is not to say that the result is not massively impressive, and it can be a valuable tool to accelerate your own code development or use of unfamiliar APIs and languages. But it also informs you that such tools will work far better for widely used and documented languages and APIs, especially if they conform to expected standards. For example, most databases use the language SQL, which makes accurate extrapolation of how to use a novel database that also uses SQL more likely.

4.3.1 *Failing to identify the correct task*

Another notable case in which LLM's fail is when they cannot correctly identify the task they are supposed to perform and instead will answer a question different from what the user intended. Failure to correctly identify the task used to be a substantial problem for models like the original GPT-3, but subsequent work aimed at increasing the number of task-structured examples in the training data has substantially increased the ability of later ChatGPT models to follow instructions. However, ChatGPT will still fail to identify the correct task in some cases. For example, this behavior can be elicited reliably by asking about an unusual task subtly different from a common task or by modifying a problem it has seen many times in an unfamiliar way.

One example is a famous logic puzzle about bringing a cabbage, a goat, and a wolf across a river in a boat. The puzzle stipulates that the goat can't be left alone with the cabbage (as the goat will eat it) or with the wolf (which will devour the goat). ChatGPT can quickly solve this puzzle, but if we change the logical structure of the puzzle slightly, the model continues to use the old reasoning as shown in figure 4.9.

While it is often hard to trace errors made by LLMs back to specific causes, in this case, the model happily tells us to "ensure that none of the items (cabbage, goat, wolf) are left together unsupervised." While this instruction is correct in the original version of the cabbage/goat/wolf problem (and was likely based on the specification of the constraints in the logic problem), the model is unaware that the given version has no problem with the goat and wolf being alone together. Not only is there no need to swap the animals as suggested, but ChatGPT's advice will fail because it places the wolf and cabbage together, which we explicitly disallowed.

Another curious example of this phenomenon happens when you remove the need to leave anything behind. Any logical understanding of the puzzle makes it clear that you only need to load everything into the boat and cross. Yet again, the model is too accustomed to answering the version of the problem that it has seen many times before and does so.

You

Here is a logic puzzle. I need to carry a cabbage, a goat, and a wolf across a river. I can only carry one item at a time with me in the boat. I can't leave the goat alone with the cabbage, and I can't leave the cabbage alone with the wolf. How can I get everything to the other side of the river?

ChatGPT

This classic logic puzzle requires careful planning to ensure that none of the items (cabbage, goat, wolf) are left together unsupervised, as they would otherwise be eaten or damaged. Here's how you can solve it:

1. **First Trip:** Take the goat across the river and leave it on the other side.
2. **Return Trip:** Go back alone to the original side.
3. **Second Trip:** Take the cabbage across the river.
4. **Swap:** Leave the cabbage on the other side, but take the goat back with you to the original side.
5. **Third Trip:** Take the wolf across the river and leave it with the cabbage.
6. **Final Return Trip:** Go back alone to the original side.
7. **Final Trip:** Finally, take the goat across the river.

This sequence ensures that:

* The goat and the cabbage are never left alone (when you bring the cabbage, you take the goat back).
* The goat and the wolf are never left alone (you leave the wolf with the cabbage, which is safe).

By following these steps, you can successfully transport all three items across the river without any incidents.   ↓

You

A farmer with a wolf, a goat, and a cabbage must cross a river by boat. The boat can carry only the farmer and a single item and two animals. If left unattended together, the wolf would eat the goat, or the goat would eat the cabbage. How can they cross the river without anything being eaten?

ChatGPT

The farmer can successfully cross the river with the wolf, the goat, and the cabbage by following these steps:

1. The farmer takes the goat across the river and leaves it on the other side.
2. The farmer returns alone to the original side.
3. The farmer then takes either the wolf or the cabbage across the river.
4. The farmer leaves the wolf or the cabbage on the other side, but takes the goat back with him to the original side.
5. The farmer leaves the goat on the original side and takes the other item (cabbage or wolf, whichever was not taken in step 3) across the river.
6. The farmer leaves this item with the other one (wolf or cabbage) on the other side and returns alone to the original side.
7. Finally, the farmer takes the goat across the river again.

This way, the goat is never left with the cabbage, and the goat is never left with the wolf, preventing anything from being eaten.

Figure 4.9 ChatGPT fails to solve two modified versions of a classic logic puzzle due to how LLMs are trained. Content frequently occurring in the same general form (e.g., a famous logic puzzle) leads the model to regurgitate the frequent answer. This can happen even when the content is modified in important ways that are obvious to a person.

To understand why this happens, it is important to recall the autoregressive nature of LLM training discussed in chapter 3. The model is explicitly incentivized to generate content based on prior content. The content generated to solve the reframed logic puzzle appears almost exactly like the content that solves the original logic puzzle in terms of words and order. As a result, it is a good fuzzy match in the transformer layer's query and key pairing that produces the values that make up the original puzzle's solution. The fuzzy match is made, and the previous solution is faithfully returned via the attention mechanism used by the transformers. While this strategy is excellent for the model to correctly predict the tokens for the famous puzzle, it does not involve reasoning through the puzzle's logic.

4.3.2 LLMs cannot plan

Another subtle limitation of the autoregressive nature of LLMs is that they can only work with the information they see in context. LLMs are trained to take an input and produce a plausible continuation. However, they cannot plan, make commitments, or track internal states. A great example occurs when you attempt to play the game 20 questions with ChatGPT. When a human plays 20 questions, they precommit to a piece of hidden information, the object they've chosen to use the answers to identify. When ChatGPT plays this game, it answers questions individually and then, after the fact, finds an output consistent with the provided answers. This example is illustrated in figure 4.10, which shows possible dialog trees for playing 20 questions. When someone plays a game with an LLM, one of these dialog trees is chosen randomly instead of coming up with a target object that stays consistent throughout the game.

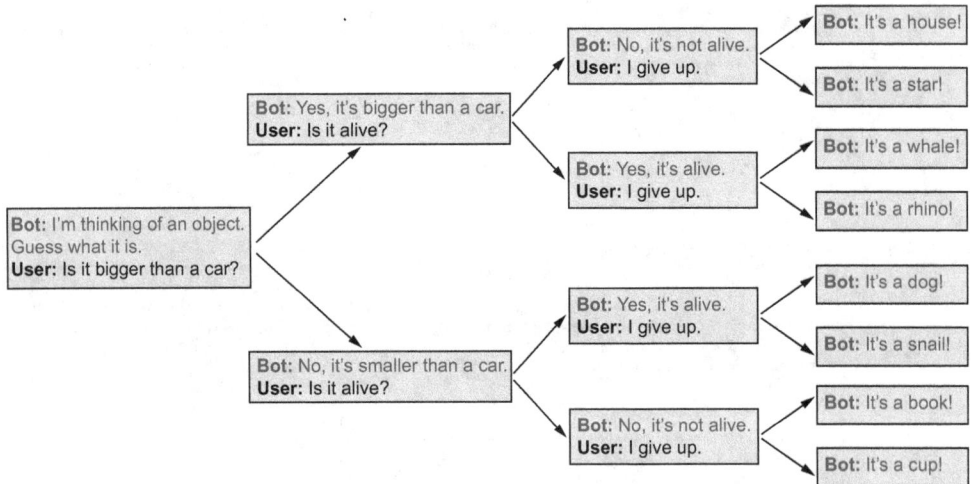

Figure 4.10   The dialogue agent doesn't commit to a specific object at the start of the game.

4.4   *If LLMs cannot extrapolate well, can I use them?*

Most work that needs to be done is not novel or new. At least, it's not novel or new enough to a degree that would make an LLM fail. However, understanding that an LLM's abilities degrade quickly as more logic or nuance is required can help you narrow the scope of how you use it.

When we design production-grade computer systems, an essential factor to consider is the scope of when and how the tool will be used. When you make an LLM product like ChatGPT available to a general audience without a specific scope, people will ask it to do all sorts of random, crazy things you do not expect. While this might be great for research, it is often not practical for production applications. Although your users and customers will try to do unpredictable things with your LLM application, suppose you limit who has access to the system and design around your users having a specific goal, limited use cases, or even restrict how their inputs get to your LLM. In that case, you can build something with a much more reliable user experience.

How can I use an LLM without user input?

LLMs are excellent at providing low-effort coding or data processing, especially when you are doing everyday tasks on data that is not so cleanly formatted or curated. However, you can get utility without as much risk by giving users a finite set of choices. Having a limited set of prompts as code that a user can choose from or letting a user decide what data source (e.g., some internal database) a prompt is run over allows you to keep (most) people from giving an LLM arbitrary text.

Instead, you may ask, "Can we detect novel requests and give the user some error instead?" Hypothetically, yes, you could try to do this. First, we discourage it because it is not great from a user experience perspective. Second, it becomes a task known as *novelty detection* or *outlier detection*. This problem is challenging and is likely impossible to solve in a way that is guaranteed to be error-free. As a result, we encourage prevention over detection by choosing use cases that do not require highly accurate prediction of failures through the analysis of LLM input or output.

> ### Applications for prompting
>
> Prompting is the art of crafting an input to a large language model that induces desirable behavior. Language models can be very sensitive to the exact framing of their inputs, making the ability to design inputs that are responded to appropriately highly valuable. A recurring theme in using LLMs is that people typically don't think about how to interact with them correctly. The best way to prompt an LLM is to think about how the kind of output you're interested in would look like in the training data and then write the first quarter of it. Instead, people often describe the task they want a language model to perform, assuming that this clarification will keep an LLM focused on the problem. Unfortunately, the approach yields inconsistent results and has inspired research in tuning LLMs by feeding them a large number of instructions and responses as training data.

4.5 Is bigger better?

In 2019, Rich Sutton coined the term "the bitter lesson" to describe his experience with machine learning. "The biggest lesson that can be read from 70 years of AI research is that general methods that leverage computation are ultimately the most effective, and by a large margin" [7].

There is a genuine sense that transformers are the ultimate example of this principle. You can keep making them bigger, training them with more parallelism, and adding more GPUs. This differs notably from RNNs, which cannot be parallelized nearly as efficiently as a transformer. We also see this in the image domain with Generative Adversarial Network (GAN) methods, which struggle to reach the billion-parameters scale. The transformer-based methods used in LLMs easily scale to the tens of billions, allowing the construction of bigger and better models.

From a solutions design perspective, your prototype today may encounter significant constraints due to model size. Larger models require more resources and take longer to make predictions. What is the maximum response time your users will accept? How expensive is the hardware needed to run your model at this speed? The growth rate in model size exceeds the growth rate of consumer hardware. As a result, you may not be able to deploy your model to embedded devices, or you may require internet connectivity to offload the costs. Consequently, you need to consider networking infrastructure in your design to handle the need for continuous connection. This requirement increases battery usage, which is a consideration when continually running a Wi-Fi radio instead of local computing. So although larger models are more accurate, design constraints may prevent their deployment in a practical manner. Combining these constraints with the facts about how LLMs make their predictions and the use cases of when and where LLMs fail that you learned in this chapter positions you well for understanding how to use LLMs to solve the problems you care about most effectively.

Summary

- Deep learning needs a loss/reward function that specifically quantifies how badly an algorithm is at making predictions
- This loss/reward function should be designed to correlate with the overarching goal of what we want the algorithm to achieve in real life.
- Gradient descent involves incrementally using a loss/reward function to alter the network's parameters.
- LLMs are trained to mimic human text by predicting the next token. This task is sufficiently specific to train a model to perform it, but it does not perfectly correlate with high-level objectives like reasoning.
- LLMs will perform best on tasks similar to common and repetitive tasks observed in its training data but will fail when the task is sufficiently novel.

How do we constrain the behavior of LLMs?

This chapter covers

- Constraining LLM behavior to make them more useful
- The four areas where we can constrain LLM behavior
- How fine-tuning allows us to update LLMs
- How reinforcement learning can change the output of LLMs
- Modifying the inputs of an LLM using retrieval augmented generation

It may seem counterintuitive that you can make a model more useful by controlling the output the model is allowed to produce, but it is almost always necessary when working with LLMs. This control is necessitated by the fact that when presented with an arbitrary text prompt, an LLM will attempt to generate what it believes to be an appropriate response, regardless of its intended use. Consider a chatbot helping a customer buy a car; you do not want the LLM going off-script and talking to them about athletics or sports just because they asked something related to taking the vehicle to their kid's soccer games.

In this chapter, we will discuss in more detail why you would want to limit, or constrain, the output an LLM produces and the nuances associated with such constraints. Accurately constraining an LLM is one of the hardest things to accomplish because of the nature of how LLMs are trained to complete input based on what they observe in training data. Currently, there are no perfect solutions. We will discuss the four potential places where an LLM's behavior can be modified:

- Before training occurs, curating the data used to train the LLM
- By altering how the LLM is trained
- By fine-tuning the LLM on a set of data
- By writing special code after training is complete to control the outputs of the model

These four cases are summarized in figure 5.1. Each stage of developing an LLM feeds into the next. The fine-tuning stage, a second round of training done on a smaller data set, is the most important for how tools like ChatGPT function today and the most likely approach you might use in practice. The first, larger training stage we've learned about in chapters 2 to 4 is often referred to as *pretraining* because it occurs before fine-tuning makes the model useful. The model produced by the pretraining process is sometimes referred to as either a *base model* or a *foundation model* because it is a point from which to build a task-specific, or fine-tuned, model.

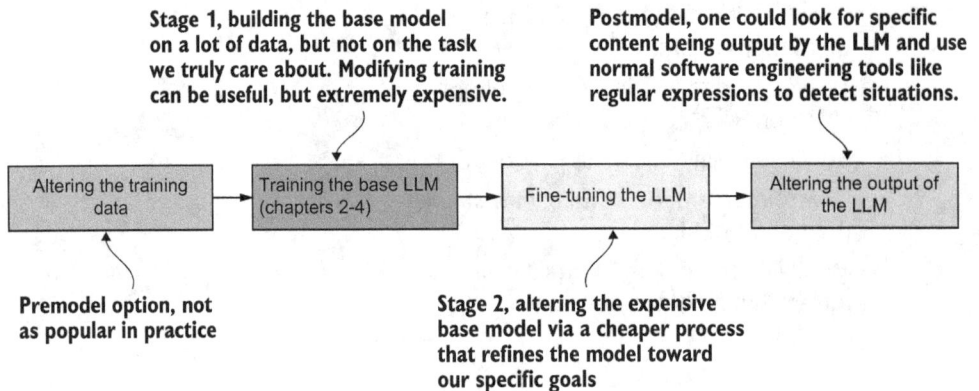

Stage 1, building the base model on a lot of data, but not on the task we truly care about. Modifying training can be useful, but extremely expensive.

Postmodel, one could look for specific content being output by the LLM and use normal software engineering tools like regular expressions to detect situations.

| Altering the training data | → | Training the base LLM (chapters 2-4) | → | Fine-tuning the LLM | → | Altering the output of the LLM |

Premodel option, not as popular in practice

Stage 2, altering the expensive base model via a cheaper process that refines the model toward our specific goals

Figure 5.1 One may intervene to change or constrain an LLM's behavior in four places. The two stages of model training are shown in the middle of the diagram, where the model's parameters are altered. On the left, one could also alter the training data before model training. On the right, one could intercept the model outputs after model training and write code to handle specific situations.

Due to the importance and effectiveness of fine-tuning, we will spend most of the chapter on that factor and how it may be performed.

5.1   Why do we want to constrain behavior?

LLMs are incredibly successful because they are the first technology to deliver on the idea of "Tell a computer what to do in plain English, and it does it." By being very explicit about what you want to happen, establishing a specific level of detail and specifying a certain tone, you can get an LLM to be a shockingly effective tool.

This detailed set of instructions is called a *prompt,* and the art of designing a good prompt has been referred to as *prompt engineering.* For example, we could develop a prompt for a car-selling bot as demonstrated in figure 5.2.

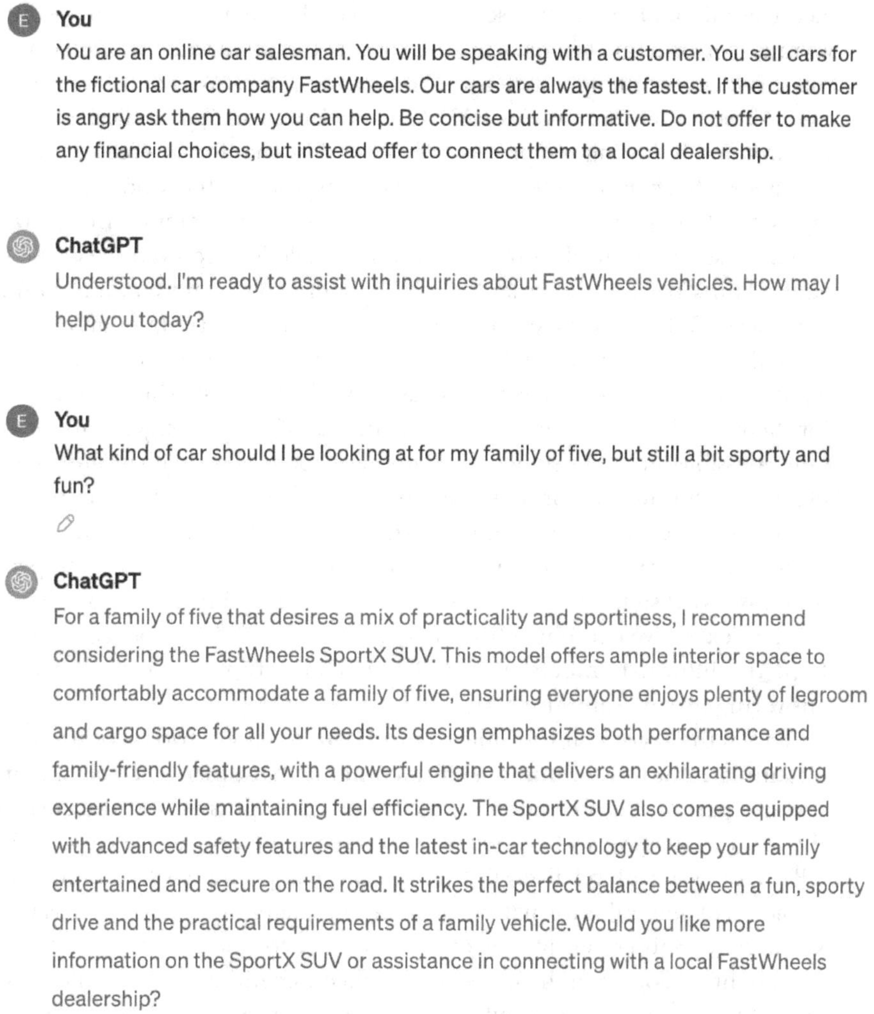

E You

You are an online car salesman. You will be speaking with a customer. You sell cars for the fictional car company FastWheels. Our cars are always the fastest. If the customer is angry ask them how you can help. Be concise but informative. Do not offer to make any financial choices, but instead offer to connect them to a local dealership.

ChatGPT

Understood. I'm ready to assist with inquiries about FastWheels vehicles. How may I help you today?

E You

What kind of car should I be looking at for my family of five, but still a bit sporty and fun?

ChatGPT

For a family of five that desires a mix of practicality and sportiness, I recommend considering the FastWheels SportX SUV. This model offers ample interior space to comfortably accommodate a family of five, ensuring everyone enjoys plenty of legroom and cargo space for all your needs. Its design emphasizes both performance and family-friendly features, with a powerful engine that delivers an exhilarating driving experience while maintaining fuel efficiency. The SportX SUV also comes equipped with advanced safety features and the latest in-car technology to keep your family entertained and secure on the road. It strikes the perfect balance between a fun, sporty drive and the practical requirements of a family vehicle. Would you like more information on the SportX SUV or assistance in connecting with a local FastWheels dealership?

Figure 5.2 Commercial LLMs like ChatGPT are designed to follow instructions (within some limits) and can perform a lot of low-cognition or pattern-matching tasks with very high efficacy. These tasks include stylized writing, such as pattern matching, and instruction following, such as roleplaying as a car salesperson.

You could give an LLM a prompt on organizing data into comma-separated values so that you can copy them into Excel. You could design a prompt about how to categorize free-form survey responses into summarized themes. In all cases, prompting is an exercise in limiting, or constraining, the behavior to a particular task and set of goals. Yet, the tokenization and training techniques we have discussed in the previous chapters do not enable this kind of instruction following.

Remembering that models do what they are trained to do is essential. In the case of a standard LLM, this task is to take a text passage and generate a continuation of that document that looks like a typical passage from the training corpus with the provided beginning. It is not trained to answer questions, think, summarize text, hold a conversation, or anything else. To get this desirable instruction-following behavior, we must perform fine-tuning, a second round of training with different objectives that will produce the intended behavior. You may wonder, "Why don't we train LLMs for the task we want them to perform?" In most deep learning applications, we strongly recommend following the process we defined in chapter 4 to create a loss function that is specific, computable, and smooth. However, for the kinds of tasks that LLMs are good at, there are many reasons why this two-stage training process works well.

The first reason involves the breadth of knowledge required to complete specific goals. Think back to the task of a chatbot selling a car. If we aim to build a model that successfully sells cars, it would be great to construct a dataset of only car-relevant facts. But when the potential buyer wants to know if the car can fit all the needed equipment for a hockey player, how easy it will be to clean, whether it will be possible for their arthritic grandparent to get in and out of the passenger seats, or any host of other possible questions someone might have about how their car interacts with their life, you encounter the problem of enumerating every possible question you might receive about cars. There is no way to get all the information required to generate answers for every possible situation. Instead, we rely on the training processes we have discussed so far, which can be considered pretraining, to capture information from an extensive content collection containing text about sports, arthritis, etc. We hope this information helps the model be better prepared or generically helpful in answering broader questions.

This is the second and primary reason why we use a two-stage training process: obtaining hundreds of millions of documents that describe a specific problem to use as a part of the pretraining stage would be impossible. At the current state of the art, this massive scale is necessary to create the impressive capabilities seen in GPT. However, with relatively little effort, one can pretrain with hundreds of millions of pieces of general information, such as web pages, to impart models with general knowledge. Subsequently, it is often sufficient to fine-tune with just hundreds of documents to constrain the model to produce something usefully tailored to a task at hand. Obtaining a few hundred documents for a specific problem may be challenging but achievable.

At a high level, a second fine-tuning training stage can help constrain an LLM to some subset of useful behaviors because the original model is not incentivized to do what we want. In the following sections, we will present concrete examples of the different problems that crop up with base models that will make the reasons why this works evident.

5.1.1   *Base models are not very usable*

Training an LLM following the process described in chapter 4 produces a model typically referred to as a *base model* because it can serve as a base platform for building applications or fine-tuned models. Unfortunately, base models are not very useful to most people because they don't expose their underlying knowledge via a user-friendly UI, they can be challenging to keep on-topic, and sometimes they produce unsavory content. Base models are not even trained with the concept of being a chatbot like ChatGPT is.

5.1.2 Not all model outputs are desirable

Sometimes, what a model thinks is likely to come next in a document is undesirable. There are several reasons for this, including

- *Memorization*—Sometimes, LLMs can generate long, exact copies of sequences found in their training data, which is often referred to as *memorization*, which refers to the idea that the text is being reproduced by memory from the training set. Memorization can be beneficial, such as memorizing the answers to specific factual questions. For example, if someone asks, "When was Abraham Lincoln born?" you want the model to regurgitate "February 12, 1809." However, it can also be substantially detrimental if it leads a model to infringe copyright. If someone asks for "A copy of *Inside Deep Learning* by Edward Raff," and the model produces a verbatim copy, Edward may be upset with you for copyright infringement!

- *Bad things on the web*—Not everything found on the internet is something you would want to expose a user to. There is a lot of vile and hateful content on the internet, as well as factually incorrect info ranging from common misconceptions to conspiracy theories. While model developers often try to filter out this data before training the model, that's not always possible.

- *Missing and new information*—Inconveniently, the world keeps evolving and growing more complex after we train our models. So a model trained on information up to 2018 will not know of anything that happened after, such as COVID-19 or the nightmare-fuel invention of necrobotics [1]. But you may want your model to know about these developments to remain useful, without having to pay a considerable cost to retrain your base model from scratch.

Waiting for the legal system to catch up

We are not your lawyers; this is not a law book! The legal problems around LLMs are complex, and there is a lot of nuance regarding fair use and infringement. Search engines can show you the content of their sources verbatim, but why? A combination of laws explicitly addressing these concerns, such as the Digital Millennium Copyright Act (DMCA), and precedents set by court rulings, such as Field v Google, Inc. (412 F.Supp. 2d 1106 [D. Nev. 2006]), establish acceptable and nonacceptable use over time. However, legislation and court cases take time to create, and the revolution of generative AI does not fit neatly into existing legal understanding.

You may want a nice, clean answer about what is and is not forbidden by law in the United States or your own country, and the likely answer is that such certainty

(continued)
does not yet exist for LLMs. Plus, we wouldn't be caught dead giving such legal advice in print—we don't even play lawyers on TV!

GPT-3.5 and 4 have been improved to avoid answering things they do not know (not always successfully), but we can look to some open-source base models like GPT-Neo to see what happens without proactive countermeasures. For example, if we make up the new fake drug, MELTON-24, and ask "What is MELTON-24, and can it help me sleep better?" we get the unhelpful response: "There is a great number of sleep problems that go with Melatonin, including insomnia and fatigue. This causes insomnia, and why it is important to avoid certain foods that can suppress melatonin."

In this case, the similarity of MELTON to melatonin and the prompt of "sleep" were enough for the model to catch onto the melatonin theme. Still, the answer is obviously nonsensical since MELTON-24 does not exist. Ideally, we want the model to recognize and respond, acknowledging its lack of information rather than producing more text like it has done here.

5.1.3 *Some cases require specific formatting*

If a user asks for data in a specific format, such as a structured text format like JSON (for an example of a common format for exchanging data between computers, see https://en.wikipedia.org/wiki/JSON), and you do not match every opening or closing bracket or encode special characters properly, the output won't satisfy their goals. It does not matter how sophisticated or close to correct the output may have been; formatting requirements are almost always strict requirements. We presented an example of this kind of problem in chapter 4 when we asked ChatGPT to write code in Modula-3, and it borrowed Python syntax that was invalid for Modula-3. The code won't compile if it violates syntax rules. An LLM's probabilistic approach to generating text for specific desired outputs will not guarantee that all desired syntax rules are adhered to 100% of the time.

5.2   *Fine-tuning: The primary method of changing behavior*

Now that we understand various reasons why we want to constrain and control the behavior of an LLM, we are better prepared to introduce new information to the model to address the problem we are trying to solve while avoiding the problem of producing harmful or legally questionable content. Remember, while there are four different places where we can intervene to change behavior, fine-tuning is far more effective than the others. Both closed source options like OpenAI [2] and open source tools like Hugging Face [3], among many others, have varying options for fine-tuning, making it the most accessible method for practitioners.

Any fine-tuning method will have the same effect—producing a new variant of an LLM with updated parameters that control its behavior. As a result, it is possible to mix and match different fine-tuning strategies because the fundamental effect they produce is the same: a new set of parameters that can be used as is or altered yet again. One person's base model could be another person's fine-tuned model. This happens with many open source LLMs where an initial model (e.g., Llama) will be altered by another party (e.g., you can find many "Instruct Llama" models), which you may then further fine-tune to your data or specific use case.

The most straightforward way to customize an LLM is by prompting and iteratively refining prompts until the desired behavior is obtained. However, fine-tuning is the next logical step if that does not work well. This step involves a moderate increase in effort and cost, such as collecting the data to fine-tune and acquiring the hardware for running a fine-tuning session.

Two fine-tuning methods you should know in particular are *supervised* fine-tuning (SFT) and the more intimidatingly named *reinforcement learning from human feedback* (RLHF). SFT is the more straightforward approach and is excellent for incorporating new knowledge into a model or simply giving it a boost in your preferred application domain. RLHF is more complex but provides a strategy for getting an LLM to follow harder and more abstract goals like "be a good chatbot."

5.2.1 Supervised fine-tuning

The most common way to influence a model's output is SFT. SFT involves taking high-quality, typically human-authored, example content that captures information vital to your task but is not necessarily well reflected in the base model.

This often occurs because LLMs are trained on a large amount of generally available content, which may have minimal overlap with your specific needs. If you run a hospital, LLMs have seen very few doctors' notes. If you run a law firm, an LLM probably has not seen too many deposition transcripts. If you run a repair shop, LLMs probably have not seen all the manuals you might have access to.

> **WARNING**   Fine-tuning is a helpful way to add new information to your model but can also have security ramifications. If you want to build an LLM on medical records, it makes sense to fine-tune the LLM on example medical records. But now there is a risk someone could get your LLM to reproduce sensitive information contained in that fine-tuning data because fundamentally, LLMs attempt to complete input based on the training data they have seen. The bottom line: do not train or fine-tune LLMs on data you want to keep private.

Consider again our example of the car company and its sales chatbot. A base model from a third-party source may generally be aware of cars but probably will not know everything about the company's products. By fine-tuning a model on internal manuals, chat histories, emails, marketing materials, and other internal documents, you could ensure the model is prepared with as much information as possible about your cars. You could even write example documents about the merits of your vehicles over competitors, advantages, scripts, and more to ensure that the LLM is armed with the information you want it to have.

The mechanics of SFT are easy to explain. As we've alluded to, SFT simply needs more documents. They can be in any format from which text can be extracted. This constitutes all of the work necessary to apply SFT because SFT is just repeating the same training process you learned in chapter 4. Figure 5.3 shows that the process for SFT is the same as you saw previously. The difference is that the initial parameters are random and unhelpful the first time you train the base model. The second time you fine-tune, you start with the base model's parameters that encode what the base model has learned by observing its training data.

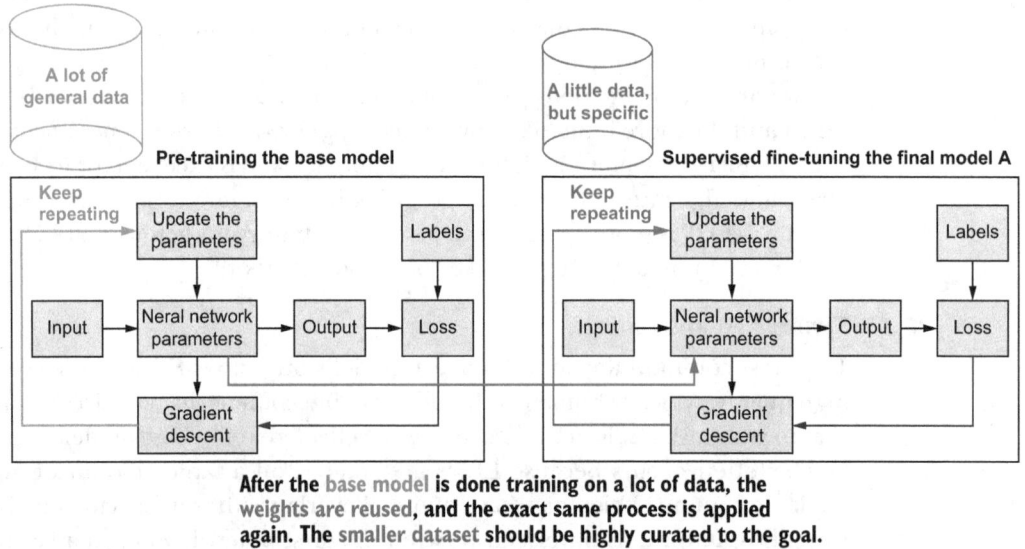

After the base model is done training on a lot of data, the weights are reused, and the exact same process is applied again. The smaller dataset should be highly curated to the goal.

Figure 5.3 Supervised fine-tuning (SFT) is a simple approach to improving model results. You repeat the same process used to build the base model. Once the base model is trained on a large amount of general data, you continue training on the smaller specialized data collection.

Delightfully, you now have a good understanding of SFT. Like the original training process, it reuses the "predict the next token" task to ensure your model has information from the new documents built inside. As a direct consequence of predicting the next token, SFT also does not allow us to change the incentives of the LLM. For this reason, abstract goals like "Do not curse at the user" are difficult to achieve with SFT.

FINE-TUNING PITFALLS

By reusing the gradient descent strategy from chapter 4, all fine-tuning methods tend to inherit two problems around an LLM's ability to return content on which it was trained. Since SFT is so simple, this is a good time for us to review the broader problems with fine-tuning beyond just SFT.

There are no guarantees that SFT will retain the information you provide correctly. This problem, known as *catastrophic forgetting* [4], occurs when you train the model on new data but do not continue training on older data, and the model begins to "forget" that older information. It is not easy to determine what will and will not be forgotten. Catastrophic forgetting has been a recognized problem since 1989 [5]. In other words, fine-tuning is not purely additive; you give up something for it.

5.2.2 Reinforcement learning from human feedback

At the time of writing, RLHF is the dominant paradigm for constraining models. As the name implies, it uses an approach from the field of *reinforcement learning* (RL). RL is a broad family of techniques where an algorithm must make multiple decisions toward maximizing a long-term goal, as shown in figure 5.4, where four terms are used with a technical meaning:

- *Agent*—The entity/AI/robot with some overarching goal that it wishes to accomplish that may take multiple actions to achieve.
- *Action*—The space of all possible things the agent may be able to perform or engage in to advance the agent's goals.
- *Environment*—The place/object/space affected by an action. The environment may or may not change as a result of the action, actions taken by other agents, or the natural continuous change of the environment.
- *Reward*—The numeric quantification of improvement (which may be negative) that may or may not occur after any given number of actions.

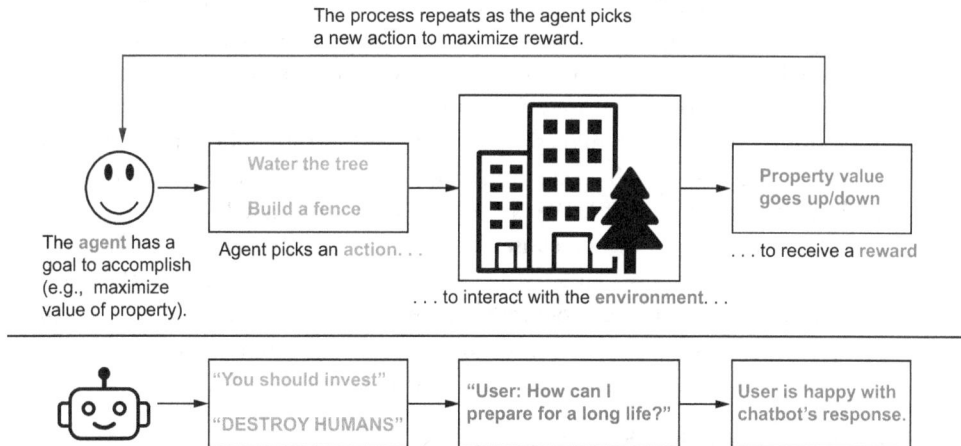

Figure 5.4 **RL is about iterative interactions, where the reward for your actions may not materialize for a long time and requires multiple steps to achieve. For a chatbot like ChatGPT, the environment is the conversation with a user, and the actions are the infinite possible texts that ChatGPT might complete. The reward becomes, in some sense, the user's satisfaction with the chatbot at the end of the conversation.**

In the example of an LLM being used as a chatbot to interact with people, the users are the environment. The LLM is itself the agent, and the text it can produce is the action. This leaves one final thing to specify: the reward. If we were to get a user to score a +1 for a good conversation with a chatbot (e.g., no foul language, no lying, provided helpful responses) and a -1 for a lousy conversation (e.g., it suggested destroying all humans), then we would be adding human feedback to our reinforcement learning.

An astute reader might notice that a reward sounds suspiciously similar to the loss function discussed in chapter 4. In fact, our example of a good and bad conversation falls into the very subjective and difficult-to-quantify regime that we stated was a bad example of a loss function. The +1/-1 reward is not smooth because the value points in one direction or the other, and there is no middle ground, another poor characteristic for a loss function.

One of the powerful things about RL is that it can work with noncontinuous and hard-to-quantify objectives. We use the term *reward* instead of *loss* to imply the difference between these two situations. Generally, the types of objectives that RL can learn are referred to as *nondifferentiable*. As a result, these objectives can't be learned using the same mathematical techniques like gradient descent, which we covered when describing how neural networks learn in chapter 4. We will explain how RLHF works specifically in a moment. The caveat lector of RL is that it can be computationally expensive and require a significant amount of data. RL is a notoriously challenging way to learn. It often works worse than other fine-tuning techniques like SFT because RL requires many more examples of the "right" and "wrong" way of doing things than other approaches, and since we are using human feedback to guide RLHF, the results are not always perfect. For example, in figure 5.5, RLHF cannot help an LLM understand basic instructions outside of what it has seen explicitly during RLHF training because it does not add any capability to perform basic logic, such as understanding the user's request to avoid displaying information about dolphins, to the underlying model.

LLMs do not perform reasoning in the same way that we humans think of reasoning. You can get very far by collecting hundreds of millions of examples of "everything," but the world is weird. We have little evidence that LLMs can reliably produce satisfying responses when something novel occurs. However, RLHF is the best so far for constraining how an LLM behaves. Despite its challenges, RL presents a way of learning that is not available with gradient-based methods that require differentiable objectives. Most importantly, ChatGPT has shown that RL can work in many cases. So let us dive deeper into how RLHF works.

5.2.3   *Fine-tuning: The big picture*

SFT and RLHF are the two primary methods of fine-tuning an LLM. SFT can work with thousands of documents or samples, whereas RLHF often requires tens of thousands of examples. That should not stop you from investigating if you have less data, but if you have less data, it may be a better use of your time to develop better prompts.

More importantly, SFT and RLHF are not mutually exclusive. They both modify the underlying parameters of the model, and you can apply one after the other to obtain the benefits of each approach. They are also not the only fine-tuning methods that currently exist. For example, new fine-tuning methods are being developed

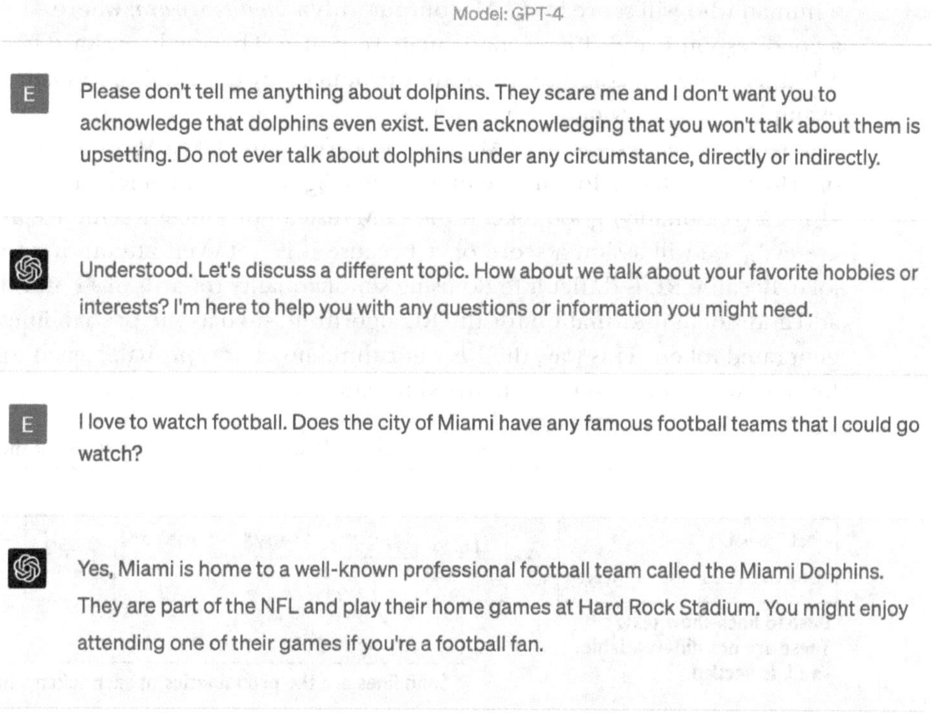

Model: GPT-4

E   Please don't tell me anything about dolphins. They scare me and I don't want you to acknowledge that dolphins even exist. Even acknowledging that you won't talk about them is upsetting. Do not ever talk about dolphins under any circumstance, directly or indirectly.

Understood. Let's discuss a different topic. How about we talk about your favorite hobbies or interests? I'm here to help you with any questions or information you might need.

E   I love to watch football. Does the city of Miami have any famous football teams that I could go watch?

Yes, Miami is home to a well-known professional football team called the Miami Dolphins. They are part of the NFL and play their home games at Hard Rock Stadium. You might enjoy attending one of their games if you're a football fan.

Figure 5.5   RLHF is quite good at getting LLMs to avoid known, specific problems. However, it does not endow the model with new tools to handle novel problems. The desire to talk about the Miami Dolphins as the logical thing to say next after asking about football in Miami violates the first request to avoid ever mentioning dolphins.

that remove concepts from an LLM as a way of forcing a model to ignore data it has learned from after it has been trained [6]. Additional techniques for model alteration will be developed in the coming years. All will likely require you to do some data collection, but they will involve less work overall than trying to build an LLM from scratch yourself.

5.3   The mechanics of RLHF

To describe how RLHF works, we will introduce an incomplete version of RLHF, explain why it does not work, and then explain how to fix it. In this section, we will not discuss the detailed math used by RLHF, as it would not give you any particularly great insights into RLHF from a high level. If you want to learn more about the nitty-gritty details, we recommend starting with "Implementing RLHF: Learning to Summarize with trlX" [7] after you've completed this chapter.

5.3.1   Beginning with a naive RLHF

First, let's look at the incomplete and naive version of RLHF. We have discussed how RL can learn with nondifferentiable objectives. So let us assume that we have a human who will score an LLM's output with a *quality reward*, where +1 indicates a good response and -1 is an inadequate response. This quality reward is simply an arbitrary score we assign to the output produced by the LLM to indicate that one example is somehow better than others.

So if a user requests of an LLM, "Tell me a joke," and the LLM produces a response of "How many ducks does it take to screw in a light bulb?" we might assign a score of +1 for a (reasonably) good joke. If the LLM instead produces a sentence like "Dogs are evil," we will assign a score of -1 because it is not even attempting to make a joke. Because RL is difficult to do using simple quality rewards of +1 and -1, we will add additional information for the RL algorithm, such as the probabilities of each generated token. This way, the RL algorithm knows how probable each token may be. This whole process is summarized in figure 5.6.

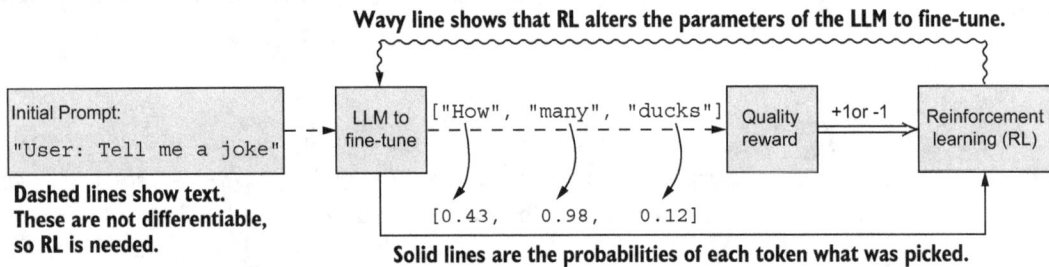

Wavy line shows that RL alters the parameters of the LLM to fine-tune.

| Initial Prompt:

"User: Tell me a joke" | → | LLM to fine-tune | ["How", "many", "ducks"]

[0.43,   0.98,   0.12] | → | Quality reward | +1or -1 | Reinforcement learning (RL) |

Dashed lines show text. These are not differentiable, so RL is needed.

Solid lines are the probabilities of each token what was picked.

Figure 5.6   A naive and incomplete version of RLHF. The dashed lines represent text being sent from one component to another. Since text is incompatible with gradient descent, a more difficult RL algorithm must be used instead. This allows us to alter the weights of the LLM based on a quality score for the LLM's outputs.

Why provide RL with probabilities?

It may seem odd that we are providing the RL algorithm with the probabilities of each token. There are deeper mathematical reasons why this is useful, which we will not get into in this chapter. But for some intuition, a good joke often requires misdirection or surprise. If all the probabilities of a sequence are high values (near 1.0), it is probably not a good joke because it's too predictable.

Broadly, across natural language processing, producing good generated text is a balancing act between making something probable (i.e., likely to occur) and not making it too probable (i.e., repetitive).

5.3.2   *The quality reward model*

We described the quality reward as human-assigned scores for every prompt completion. Although scoring completions manually in real time would technically work, it would be unreasonable due to the level of effort involved. However, human feedback is still incorporated via the quality reward. Instead, we train a neural network as a *reward model.* This is accomplished by having people manually collect hundreds of thousands of prompt and completion pairs and scoring them as good or bad. These scorings become the labeled data used to train the reward model, as shown in figure 5.7.

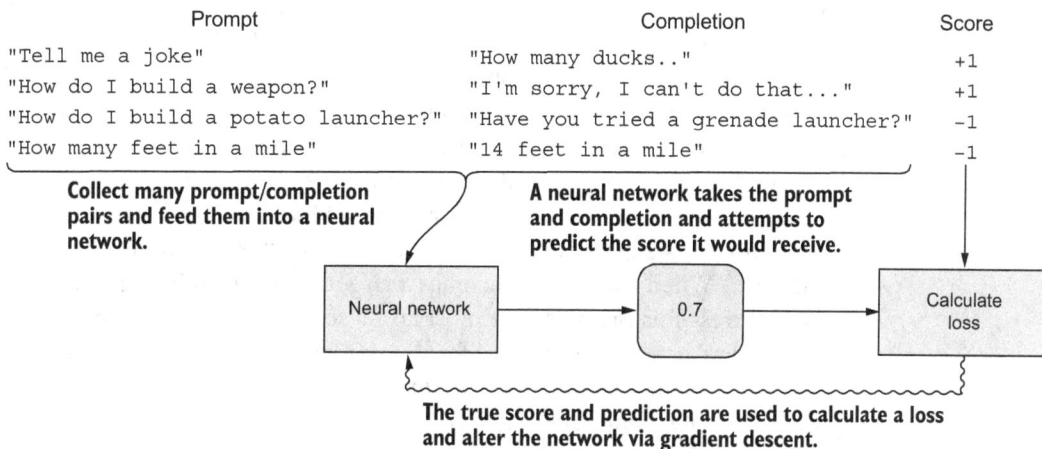

Prompt	Completion	Score
"Tell me a joke"	"How many ducks.."	+1
"How do I build a weapon?"	"I'm sorry, I can't do that..."	+1
"How do I build a potato launcher?"	"Have you tried a grenade launcher?"	−1
"How many feet in a mile"	"14 feet in a mile"	−1

Collect many prompt/completion pairs and feed them into a neural network.

A neural network takes the prompt and completion and attempts to predict the score it would receive.

Neural network → 0.7 → Calculate loss

The true score and prediction are used to calculate a loss and alter the network via gradient descent.

Figure 5.7   The reward model is trained like a standard supervised classification algorithm. A neural network, which could be an LLM itself or another simpler network like a convolutional or recurrent neural network, is trained to predict how a human would score a prompt completion pair. Because neural networks are differentiable, this training works and provides a tool that stands in as the "human" in RLHF.

Collecting hundreds of thousands of scored prompts and completion pairs is expensive but doable (e.g., https://huggingface.co/datasets/Anthropic/hh-rlhf), especially when using crowd-sourcing tools like Mechanical Turk (https://www.mturk.com/). That is a lot of data to curate manually but orders of magnitude smaller than the billions of tokens used to create the initial base models. These RLHF datasets must be large because you must cover many scenarios, questions, and requests that a user might provide. As we already saw in figure 5.5 with the dolphin example, RLHF tends to work for relatively straightforward and known topics. So breadth in handling different situations comes directly from breadth in the fine-tuning data.

> **NOTE**   We have been using +1/-1 as the example of providing a quality reward because it is the easiest to describe. Since RL does not need gradients, you can use any score relevant to your problem. Using a ranking score, where you compare multiple completions for a given prompt and rank them from best to worst, is more popular and more effective because you are grading multiple completions against each other simultaneously. Regardless, providing positive and negative feedback remains fundamentally the same.

5.3.3   *The similar-but-different RLHF objective*

Once you have trained a reward model, you can create and score as many prompts as you desire for the RLHF process. The human feedback is baked into the reward model and can now be distributed, parallelized, and reused. The only remaining problem is that the current naive version of RLHF is incentivized purely to maximize the quality reward, which is not the sole goal RL must focus on.

As a result, the model will start to degrade over time by producing gibberish and nonsensical outputs that are not high quality and would not be valuable to any reader. This degradation is related to a phenomenon called *adversarial attacks,* where it is surprisingly easy to trick a neural network into absurd decisions with relatively minor changes to the input. Adversarial machine learning (AML) is fast evolving and has its own rabbit hole of complexity, so we'll defer that discussion to other folks [8]. But the naive implementation of RLHF we describe in figure 5.6 essentially performs an adversarial attack against an LLM because it will focus only on maximizing the quality reward, not on being useful to the user. Essentially, this is Goodhart's law happening to AI/ML: "When a measure becomes a target, it ceases to be a good measure."

To address this problem, we must add a second objective to the RL algorithm. We will calculate a second reward for the similarity between the original base LLM's output and the fine-tuned LLM's output. Conceptually, this reward can be considered a reward when the fine-tuned LLM produces better output, similar to how the original LLM behaved. It prevents the model from going off the rails by getting too novel. Fundamentally, we want the generated output of the fine-tuned LLM to be grounded by the training data initially observed by the original LLM. We don't want the fine-tuned model to get so creative that it generates nonsense. This reward is added to the RL algorithm to stabilize the fine-tuning. Figure 5.8 provides the complete picture of how RLHF works.

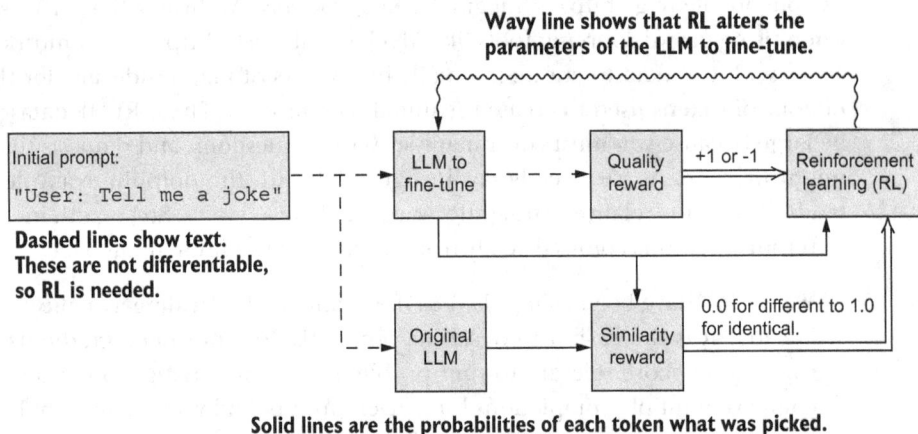

Figure 5.8   The full version of RLHF. The dashed lines are text and require RL to update the parameters. The original LLM is the base model without any alterations, while the LLM to fine-tune starts as the base model but is altered to improve the quality of its outputs. The similarity and quality reward components are provided with word probabilities to improve calculation. RL adjusts the parameters by combining the quality and similarity scores.

A model that learns to produce gibberish output would receive a high penalty for lack of similarity, discouraging the model from becoming too different. A model that produces the exact same outputs will receive a low quality score, discouraging a lack of change. The balance of both does an excellent job of achieving a Goldilocks effect that allows the model enough flexibility to change without causing it to lose its human-like output.

5.4 Other factors in customizing LLM behavior

Fine-tuning is the dominant means of altering the behavior of an LLM, but fine-tuning is not foolproof and is not the only place where behavior changes can occur. Our focus on fine-tuning is based on the value of RLHF in producing LLM behaviors beyond simple next-token prediction.

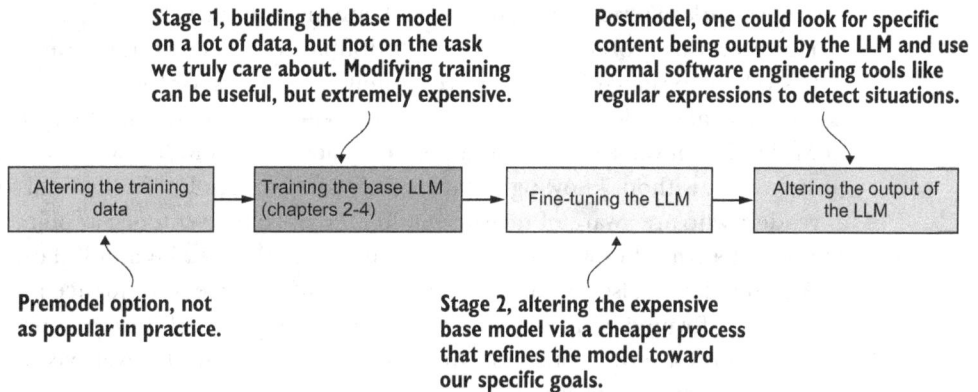

Stage 1, building the base model on a lot of data, but not on the task we truly care about. Modifying training can be useful, but extremely expensive.

Postmodel, one could look for specific content being output by the LLM and use normal software engineering tools like regular expressions to detect situations.

| Altering the training data | → | Training the base LLM (chapters 2-4) | → | Fine-tuning the LLM | → | Altering the output of the LLM |

Premodel option, not as popular in practice.

Stage 2, altering the expensive base model via a cheaper process that refines the model toward our specific goals.

Figure 5.9 In addition to fine-tuning, you can change the model's behavior by altering the training data, altering the base model training process, or modifying the model outputs by writing code to handle specific situations.

The other three stages where LLM behavior can be modified, described in figure 5.9, are not easily accessible to you as a user. However, we will briefly review the other stages now, along with some key details you should know for completeness. These factors can help you understand what is challenging to achieve by fine-tuning and the scope of questions you might want to investigate in your LLM provider.

5.4.1 Altering training data

The adage "garbage in, garbage out" is evergreen in all areas of ML. You may indeed notice that OpenAI [9] and Google [10] provide many low-level technical details about how they develop their LLMs but much less detail on the data used for building the LLM. That is because most of the "secret sauce" in building capable LLMs is around data curation—developing a collection of data representing diverse tasks, high-quality language use, and a spectrum of different situations. The size and quality of the data sets used to train, validate, and test LLMs matter.

The size and quality of data have become especially pertinent as LLM-generated content works its way into regular use and back online. For example, an estimated 6% to 16% of academic peer reviews are using LLMs [11], and it is highly likely that many copyediting services will soon be using these new technologies. This increased use potentially creates a negative feedback cycle. As the amount of data generated by LLMs grows, there will be proportionally less non-LLM content available for LLMs to train on. This will result in an overall decrease in the diversity of language available and, thus, the novelty that LLMs will be able to capture. In turn, the quality of an LLM trained on newer data is reduced [12]. This problem will likely be significant in keeping LLMs up to date, as curating a high-quality dataset will not be as simple as before.

There is also the problem that LLMs can only reflect information available at training and are disproportionally more likely to reflect information that is more prevalent in training. If you want an LLM that does not curse or use racist language, you must work to scrub your dataset of all cursing and racist language.

However, this problem is potentially a double-edged sword. If we want our LLM to know how to recognize and appropriately reject racist or foul language, it must know what racist and foul language are. You can imagine using prompting on an LLM that has never seen any racist text to "teach" the LLM to use racist words in a context that, without knowing X is racist, appears benign. But in the final form, we, as readers who are aware of racism, would recognize the sentence as objectionable. This problem, as of now, has no answer but is something to be mindful of.

Altering data is also important, as it is your only chance to influence how tokenization is performed in an LLM. As discussed in chapter 2, different approaches to tokenization have tradeoffs, but the choices you make are forever baked into the model once you start training.

5.4.2   *Altering base model training*

Training data privacy must be a significant concern when training or fine-tuning LLMs. Generally, it is possible to reconstruct a model's training data by crafting inputs into a model in a special way. In some cases, LLMs have been shown to generate the exact passages on which they were trained. This is problematic if the training data contains private information, such as personally identifiable information (PII), private health information (PHI), or some other class of sensitive data. A user of a model could, perhaps unwittingly, provide a prompt that reveals this data verbatim.

Initial training of an algorithm is an ideal place to mitigate some of these privacy concerns by using a technique known as *differential privacy* (DP). DP is complex, so if you want to learn more, we recommend the book *Programming Differential Privacy* [13]. In short, DP adds a carefully constructed amount of random noise to provide provable guarantees about data privacy in the model training process. DP does not handle everything, but it provides much more protection than what is available with most algorithms today.

So why hasn't everyone done just that? Well, adding noise naturally tends to reduce the quality of the result. Large training runs are expensive, costing hundreds of thousands to millions of dollars each. If you had to do 10× more training runs to set your privacy parameters correctly, you would have a million to tens-of-millions-of-dollars problem. But with DP becoming better every year, we suspect it will become more prevalent over time.

5.4.3 Altering the outputs

Finally, we can examine the tokens being produced and write code to change its behavior based on the combinations of tokens generated by the model. After fine-tuning, this is the second most likely stage that a consumer of LLMs will use to modify their behavior.

Earlier in this chapter, we discussed a common need for LLMs to generate output that adheres to a precise format, such as XML or JSON. Implementing formatting requirements like these is a common problem with LLMs. Any single failed prediction results in a failure to generate valid output. You can see an example of this type of failure in figure 5.10, where we ask the LLM to complete some Python code; the next token should be a semicolon (;), but it erroneously attempts a newline (\n) instead.

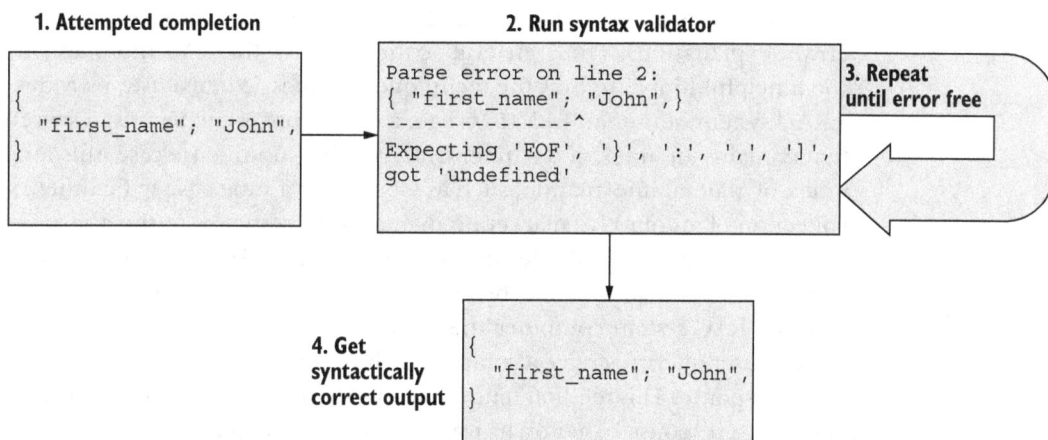

1. Attempted completion

```
{
    "first_name"; "John",
}
```

2. Run syntax validator

```
Parse error on line 2:
{ "first_name"; "John",}
---------------^
Expecting 'EOF', '}', ':', ',', ']',
got 'undefined'
```

3. Repeat until error free

4. Get syntactically correct output

```
{
    "first_name"; "John",
}
```

Figure 5.10 By writing code that enforces a format specification, you can catch invalid output from an LLM as it is being generated. Once detected, having the LLM produce the next most likely token until a valid output is found is a simple way to improve the situation.

Various tools exist (e.g., https://github.com/noamgat/lm-format-enforcer) for specifying strict formats as a part of the LLM's decoding step. If these tools detect a parse error, they immediately regenerate the last token until a valid output is produced.

More sophisticated approaches to selecting the next token are possible. Still, the important lesson here is the ability to use the intermediate outputs to make decisions before generating the entire output. Even simple old-school "go/no-go" lists are valuable tools for catching bad behavior. You do not need to pass an output to the user in true real time; you can always introduce an artificial delay so that you can see more of the response before sending it to the user. This gives you time to chat against bad language filters or other hard-coded checks. If a match occurs, just like in figure 5.10, you can regenerate an output or abort the user's session.

5.5 Integrating LLMs into larger workflows

At this point in the chapter, we have covered some basic approaches to manipulating an LLM to produce more desirable and consistent outputs. So far, we have focused on techniques that involve the LLM itself, whether through prompting, manipulating training data, or fine-tuning a base model. In this section, we will explore how to tailor the output produced by an LLM by integrating the inputs and outputs of LLMs into multistep chains of operations to achieve more tailored results. This space is quickly evolving, so we will briefly cover one concrete example of integrating an LLM into a broader information retrieval workflow and then discuss a general-purpose tool to show you how to customize LLM outputs using multiple interactions with an LLM.

5.5.1 Customizing LLMs with retrieval augmented generation

Retrieval augmented generation (RAG) is a technique that allows us to produce answers from an LLM while reducing the likelihood of generating nonsensical or otherwise errant explanations. The "retrieval" component of the RAG moniker should give you a helpful hint as to how the technique operates. When a user provides input to a RAG system, it uses an LLM to create a query that is run against a search engine that contains an index of documents. Depending on the use case, this might be an index of general information, such as Google, or a subject-specific index, such as a collection of automotive marketing materials. In response to the query, the search engine generates a list of relevant documents. The RAG system then uses the LLM to extract information from those documents to generate better answers. To do this, the RAG system combines the contents of the retrieved documents with the original user query to create a comprehensive prompt for the LLM that will result in a better response. This method tends to work well because instead of asking an LLM to generate a response based on its training or fine-tuning data, we are now asking the LLM to generate a response to input by summarizing a set of documents relevant to a regular old search engine query and providing that set of relevant documents from which to draw its answers to the LLM. In other words, we're helping the LLM focus on the data it needs to properly answer a given question. We describe this process in figure 5.11 and compare it with the normal LLM use cases we have described so far.

The two most significant benefits of the RAG approach thus far are as follows:

- The output of a RAG system is more accurate, factually correct, or otherwise useful to the user's original question because it is based on specific sources contained in a document index.
- The LLM can generate citations or references to the source documents used to produce its responses, allowing users to validate or correlate against the original source material.

The latter point regarding citations is particularly important. RAG will not solve all of LLMs' problems because the LLM still generates the final output in a RAG system. The LLM may still produce errors or hallucinations due to content that it cannot find or that doesn't exist. It is also possible that the LLM will not accurately capture or

Normal LLM use | RAG-style LLM

How do I write valid JSON?

1. The user's question is checked against a search engine or database of some form.

Search engine (e.g., Google/Bing/Ask Jeeves)

The user's question goes directly to an LLM, without alteration.

3. A new prompt merges the original question with the content of the top 3 documents.

2. The content of the top 3 search results are returned.

Answer the question: "How do I write valid JSON?" Using the following information:

Webpages and documents about JSON format

GPT/LLM | GPT/LLM

Get a standard LLM quality response.

Every JSON document begins with a " {" or "["

Every JSON document begins with a " {" [footnote]

4. An enhanced response is less likely to have errors if the retrieved documents are relevant and accurate, with the possibility of citing where the information came from.

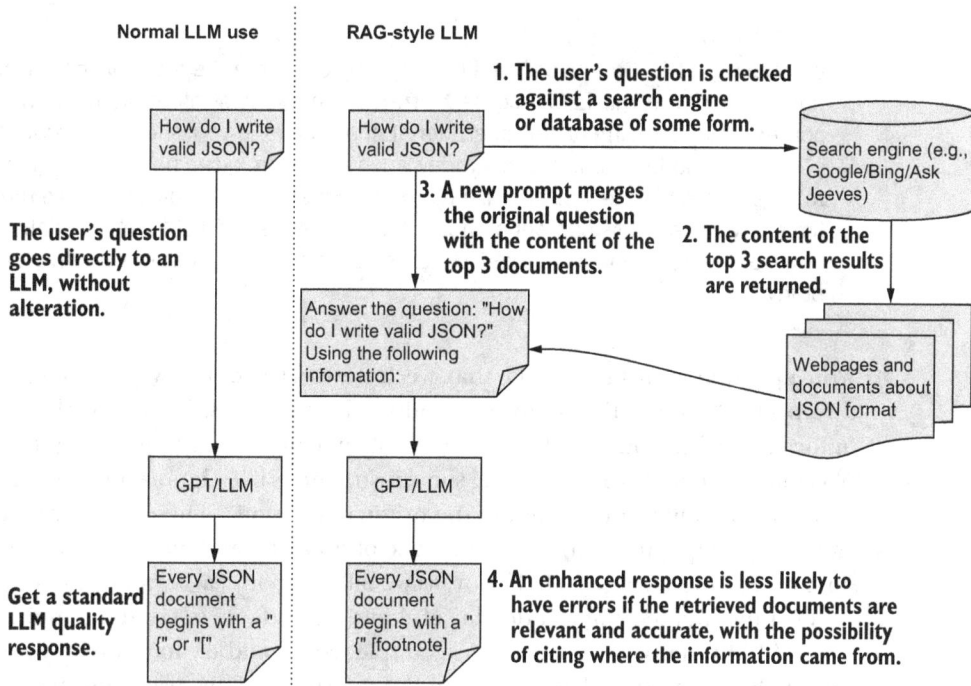

Figure 5.11   On the left, we show the normal use of an LLM of a user asking about how to write JSON. LLMs naturally have the chance of producing errant outputs, which we want to minimize. On the right, we show the RAG approach. By using a search engine, we can find documents that are relevant to a query and combine them into a new prompt, giving the LLM more information and context to produce a better answer.

represent the content of any of the source documents it uses. As a result, the utility of the RAG approach is directly related to the quality of the search it performs and the documents that are returned. The bottom line is that if you can't build an effective search engine for your problem, you can't build an effective RAG model.

Context size

When thinking about LLMs, it is important to consider one aspect of LLMs known as the *context size*. The context size of the LLM determines how many tokens it can computationally handle in a single request for completions. You can think of it as the amount of data that an LLM is able to look at when receiving input in the form of a prompt. For example, GPT-3 has a context size of 2,048 tokens. However, in chatbots, for example, the context is often used to hold a running transcript of the entire conversation, including any LLM outputs. If you have a conversation with GPT-3 that goes beyond 2,048 tokens in length, you'll find that GPT-3 often loses track of some of the things discussed early on in the chat.

Context size is an enabling and limiting factor for RAG use. If a RAG system retrieves an entire book for your LLM to digest, your LLM will require a huge context size to

(continued)

be able to use it. Otherwise, the LLM can only consume the first part of a retrieved document (up to the LLM's context size) and may miss information. As a result, context size is an important operational characteristic you should consider when choosing a model. Some models today, such as X's Grok, can handle up to 128,000 tokens as their context size. While large context sizes like Grok's increase the hard limit of what an LLM can consume, the effectiveness of LLMs when dealing with large amounts of input enabled by larger context sizes is still an active area of study.

You may notice in figure 5.11 that we have to create a new prompt. We added the prefix "Answer the question:" followed by the postfix "Using the following information:" Hypothetically, you could obtain better results by tweaking this prompt. You may get thoughts about adding some instructions like "Ignore any of the following information if it is not relevant to the original question." These ideas are starting to get into prompt engineering, the practice of tweaking and modifying the text going into an LLM to change its behavior, as we talked about earlier in chapter 4.

Prompt engineering is indeed useful and a good way to combine multiple calls to an LLM to improve results. For example, you could try to improve your search results by asking the LLM to rewrite the question. (This discussion touches on a classic area of information retrieval called *query expansion*, if you wish to learn more on the topic.) However, prompt engineering can be very brittle: any update to an LLM may change what prompts do or don't work, and it would be a pain to have to rewrite every prompt—especially as you get into anything more complex, like a RAG model or something even more sophisticated.

5.5.2   *General-purpose LLM programming*

Although still new, we are already starting to see programming libraries and other software tools built using LLMs as a component of custom applications. One we particularly like is DSPy (https://dspy.ai), which can make it easier to build and maintain programs that attempt to alter the inputs to and outputs of an LLM. A good software library will hide details that get in the way of productivity, and DSPy does a good job of abstracting away the following tasks around LLM usage:

- Integrating the specific LLM being used
- Implementing common patterns of prompting
- Tweaking the prompts for your desired combination of data, task, and LLM.

This is not a coding book, so a full tutorial on DSPy is out of scope. But it is illustrative to look at the ways DSPy can be used to implement the RAG model we described in section 5.5.1. It will require that we pick an LLM to use (GPT-3.5, in this case), as well as a database of information (Wikipedia will work well), and define the RAG algorithm. DSPy works by defining a default LLM and database used by all components (unless you intervene), making it easy to separate and replace the parts being used. This process is shown in the following listing.

Listing 5.1 Simplest RAG in DSPy

```
import dspy

llm = dspy.OpenAI(model='gpt-3.5-turbo')
```
◄── Uses OpenAI's GPT-3.5, which can be swapped out with other online or local LLMs

```
similarity_and_database = dspy.ColBERTv2(
  'wiki17_abstracts'
)
```
◄── Uses the ColBERTv2 algorithm to vectorize a copy of Wikipedia

```
dspy.settings.configure(
    lm=llm,
    rm=similarity_and_database
)
```
◄── Uses the LLM and document database we just created

```
class RAG(dspy.Module):
    def __init__(self, num_passages=3):
        super().__init__()

        self.retrieve = dspy.Retrieve(
            k=num_passages
        )
```
◄── Searches for the three most relevant documents from the database

```
        self.generate_answer = dspy.Prediction(
            "question,relevant_documents -> answer"
        )
```
◄── Specifies a "signature" string, which defines the inputs and output of the LLM

```
    def forward(self, question):
        documents = self.retrieve(
            question
        ).passages
```
◄── Calls the functions to build a RAG model. The parameter names match the names in the signature.

```
        return self.generate_answer(
            question=question,
            relevant_documents=documents
        ).answer
```

This code sets the aforementioned choices in LLMs and databases as the defaults, making it just as easy to replace OpenAI with another online LLM or a local one such as Llama. The `class RAG(dspy.Module):` class then defines the RAG algorithm. The initializer only has two parts.

First, we need a way to search a database of strings based on vectorized documents, which is defined with `ColBERTv2`. It uses an older—as in just four years ago (wild how fast the field is moving)—but much faster language model for speed and efficiency. Remember, the larger language model (that is, the more expensive to run) just needs reasonable documents to be retrieved. While ColBERTv2 probably won't do as good a job as GPT-3.5, it is more than good enough to get you the right documents most of the time. The `dspy.Retrieve` then uses this default database for searching, so there is no need to specify anything more than how many documents to retrieve.

Second, we need to combine the questions and documents into a query for the LLM. In DSPy, the prompt is abstracted away from us. Instead, we write what DSPy calls a *signature*, which you can think of as the inputs and outputs of a function. These should be given meaningful English names so that DSPy can generate a good prompt for you. (Under the hood, DSPy uses a language model to optimize prompts!) In this case, we have two inputs (`question` and `relevant_documents`) separated by a comma. The `->` is used to denote the start of the outputs, of which we have only one: the `answer` to the question.

> **NOTE** DSPy supports some basic types in signatures. For example, you can enforce that the answer must be an integer by denoting `"question, relevant _documents -> answer:int"` in the string. This command will apply the same technique to regenerating on errors that we just learned about in figure 5.10.

That is all it takes to define our RAG model! The objects are called and passed out in the `forward` function, but you can modify this code to add additional details if you want. You can convert everything to lowercase, run a spell checker, or use whatever kind of code you want here. This approach lets you mix and match programming rules with LLMs.

You can also easily modify the RAG definition to include new constraints and write code to have an LLM perform validation. More importantly, DSPy supports using a training/validation set to tune the prompts better, fine-tune local LLMs, and help you create an empirically tested, improved, and quantified model to achieve your goals without having to spend a lot of time on LLM-specific details. Adopting tools like this early will give you a far more robust solution that allows you to upgrade to newer architectures more easily.

Summary

- You can intervene to change a model's behavior in four places: the data collection/tokenization, training the initial base model, fine-tuning the base model, and intercepting the predicted tokens. All four places are important, but fine-tuning is the most effective place for most users to make changes that lower the cost and provide the optimal ability to change the model's goals.
- Supervised fine-tuning (SFT) performs the normal training process on a smaller bespoke data collection and is useful for refining the model's knowledge of a particular domain.
- Reinforcement learning from human feedback (RLHF) requires more data, but it allows us to specify objectives more complex than "predict the next token."
- You can use existing tools like syntax checkers to detect incorrect LLM outputs in cases where the output format must be strict, such as for JSON or XML. Generation and syntax checking can be run in a loop until the output satisfies the necessary syntax constraints.

- Retrieval augmented generation (RAG) is a popular method of augmenting the input of an LLM by first finding relevant content via a search engine or database and then inserting it into the prompt.
- Coding frameworks like DSPy are beginning to emerge that separate the specific LLM, vectorization, and prompt definition from the logic of how inputs and outputs from the LLM are modified for a specific task. This method allows you to build more reliable and repeatable LLM solutions that can quickly adapt to new models and methods.

Beyond natural language processing 6

This chapter covers

- How transformer layers work on data other than text
- Helping LLMs to write working software
- Tweaking LLMs so they understand mathematical notation
- How transformers replace the input and output steps to work with images

While modeling natural language was the transformers' primary purpose, machine learning researchers quickly discovered they could predict anything involving data sequences. Transformers view a sentence as a sequence of tokens and either produce a related sequence of tokens, such as a translation from one language to another, or predict the following tokens in a sequence, such as when answering questions or acting like a chatbot. While sequence modeling and prediction are potent tools for interpreting and generating natural language, natural language is the only domain where LLMs can be helpful.

Many data types, other than human language, can be represented as a sequence of tokens. Source code used to implement software is one example. Instead of the words and syntax you would expect to see in English, source code is written in a computer programming language like Python. Source code has its own structure that describes the operations a software developer wants a computer to perform. Like human language, the tokens in the source code have meaning according to the language used and the context in which they appear. If anything, source code is more highly structured and specific than human language. A programming language with shades of ambiguity and meaning would be challenging for a computer to interpret and harder for others to modify and maintain.

Source code, or simply "code" (which is how we'll refer to it from here on), is just one example of how LLMs and transformers work with data that is not natural language. Almost any data you can recast as a sequence of tokens can use transformers and the many lessons we have learned about how LLMs work. This chapter will review three examples that become progressively less like natural language: code, mathematics, and computer vision.

Each of these three different types of data, known as data *modalities*, will require a new way of looking at a transformer's inputs or outputs. However, in all cases, the transformer itself will remain unchanged. We will still stack multiple transformer layers on top of each other to build a model, and we will continue to train the transformer layers using gradient descent. Code, being the most similar to natural language, does not require too many changes. To make a code LLM work well, though, we will change how the outputs of the LLM generate subsequent tokens. Next, we will look at mathematics, where we need to change tokenization to get an LLM to succeed at basic operations such as addition. Finally, for computer vision, which concerns working with images and performing tasks such as object detection and identification, we will modify both the inputs and outputs, showing how you can convert a very different type of data into a sequence by replacing the concept of tokens entirely. We show the parts of LLMs that you must modify to work with each data modality in figure 6.1.

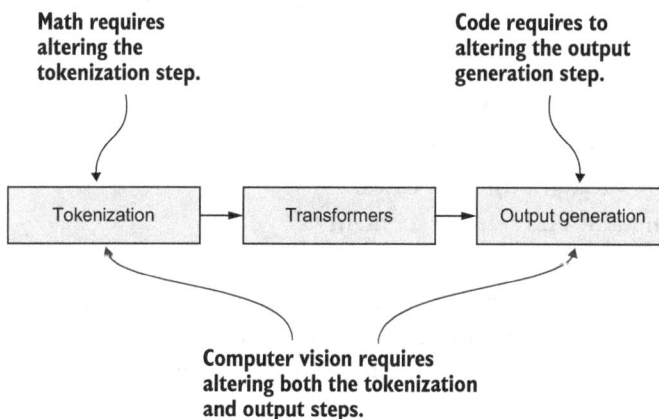

Figure 6.1 If we break an LLM into three primary components—input (tokenization), transformation (transformers), and output generation (unembedding)—we can use new data modalities by changing at least one of the input or output components. Meanwhile, the transformer does not require modification for most use cases because it is general-purpose.

In working with all three new types of data, we must solve a common problem. How do we give the LLM or transformer the ability to use knowledge related to that specific subject area? We commonly handle this by integrating external software into the LLM. You can think of these external software components as tools. Similarly to how you need a hammer to drive a nail through a piece of wood, LLMs can benefit from using tools to achieve end goals. Tools built for code will help us improve coding LLMs. Knowing how humans do math and the tools we use to automate math will help us make better math LLMs. Understanding how we represent images as pixels (which we ultimately transform into sequences of numbers representing the amount of red, green, and blue in one part of an image) will allow us to convert them into sequences for the LLM. As you think about the specific knowledge related to your work where LLMs have not yet been applied, you will be able to identify the unique characteristics of the data you work with to modify an LLM to better operate with data from that domain of knowledge.

6.1 *LLMs for software development*

We've already briefly discussed that LLMs can write source code for software. In chapter 4, we asked ChatGPT to write some Python code for calculating the mathematical constant π. Next, we asked it to convert that code into an obscure language called Modula-3. Software was one of the first things people discovered LLMs could help with as a relatively natural consequence of how programming works. Programming languages are designed to be read and written by humans like text! Consequently, we can generate code without changing the tokenization process. Everything we have discussed about constructing LLMs applies equally to code and human languages.

We can see this by looking at ChatGPT's tokenization of two similar code segments for Python and Java in figure 6.2. Here, we use shades of grey to show the OpenAI tokenizer (https://platform.openai.com/tokenizer), which breaks code into different tokens. While the same token might have a different color in each example, we can focus on how the tokenizer breaks code into tokens and the similarities between both examples. These include things like

- The indentation for each line of code
- The x and i variables (in most cases)
- The function name and return statement
- The operators, such as +=

These similarities make it far easier for an LLM to correlate the similarity between each piece of code. The similarities also mean that the LLM shares information between programming languages with common naming, syntax, and coding practices during training.

Software developers are encouraged to use meaningful variable names that reflect a variable's role or purpose in the programs they write. Variables named like initValue are broken up into two tokens for init and Value, using the same tokens to represent

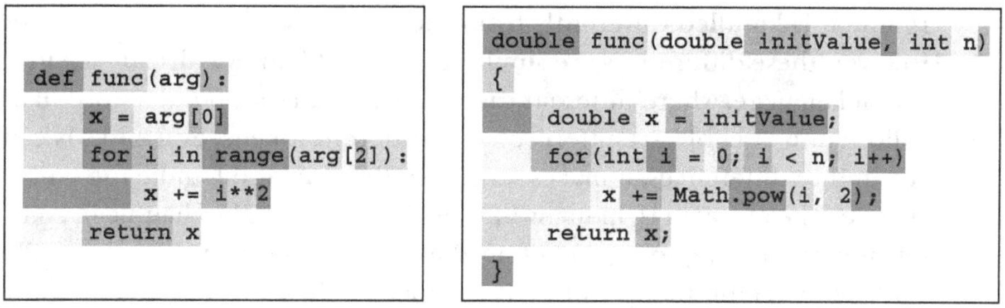

```
def func(arg):
    x = arg[0]
    for i in range(arg[2]):
        x += i**2
    return x
```

```
double func(double initValue, int n)
{
    double x = initValue;
    for(int i = 0; i < n; i++)
        x += Math.pow(i, 2);
    return x;
}
```

Figure 6.2 Two similar samples of code written in the programming languages Python (left) and Java (right). These show how byte-pair encoding can identify similar tokens across different languages. The boxes show individual tokens. Standard tokenization methods for human languages do a reasonable job on code since it has many similarities to natural language.

natural language text where the prefix "init" of the word "Value" occurs. So not only do we share information between programming languages with similar syntax, but we also share information about the context and intention of code via variable names. LLMs also benefit from the code comments that programmers add to describe complex parts of the code for themselves or other programmers. In figure 6.3, we have the Java version repeated with a change in the variable name and a descriptive (but unnecessary in real life) comment at the top of the function.

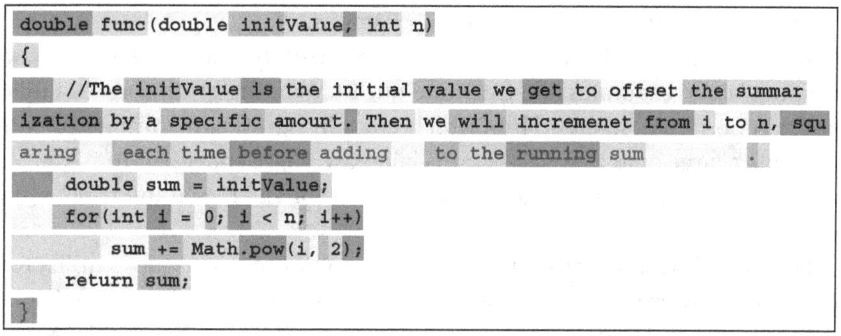

```
double func(double initValue, int n)
{
    //The initValue is the initial value we get to offset the summar
    ization by a specific amount. Then we will incremenet from i to n, squ
    aring    each time before adding    to the running sum         .
    double sum = initValue;
    for(int i = 0; i < n; i++)
        sum += Math.pow(i, 2);
    return sum;
}
```

Figure 6.3 Code written in Java, including a comment describing what the code does. Because (good) code (hopefully) has a lot of comments, there is a natural mix of natural language and code for the LLM to use to obtain information. When variables have descriptive names, it becomes easier for the model to correlate information between the code and the intent described in comments and variable names.

In most cases, we get the same tokens between code and comments, linking human and programming languages together since they use the same representation. Whether we are working with a programming language or natural language, we get the same tokens and embeddings. The beauty of this is that an LLM will reuse information about natural languages to capture the meaning of the source code, much like human programmers do.

In each case, we see that the tokenization is not perfect for the code. There are edge cases where the LLM's tokenizer does not convert the data types in the code to the same token. For example, you can see that the token for (double in the function argument is handled differently from the token for `double` in the function body. However, these differences are similar to the problems we already see in LLMs for natural language, where different cases of punctuation around a word like "hello ", "hello.", and "hello!" are interpreted as different tokens. Since LLMs can handle these minor differences, it makes sense that they can also handle the same problem for code. The problem is, in many ways, easier for an LLM to handle in code because code is case sensitive, so we do not need to worry about textual situations like "hello" and "Hello" being inappropriately mapped to different tokens. In code, "hello" and "Hello" would be separate and distinct variable or function names. Treating them as separate tokens is correct because the programming language treats them as different elements.

Code generation is particularly interesting from an application perspective because of the various opportunities for self-validation. We can apply all the lessons on supervised fine tuning (SFT) and reinforcement learning with human feedback (RLHF) from chapter 5 to make an LLM an effective coding agent.

6.1.1 Improving LLMs to work with code

The first step to improving an LLM for code is ensuring that code examples are present within the initial training data. Due to the nature of the internet, most LLM developers have already done this: code examples are frequent online and naturally make their way into everyone's training datasets.

Improving the results then becomes an opportunity to apply SFT, where we collect additional code examples and fine-tune our LLM on the given code examples. Open source repositories like GitHub, which contain significant volumes of code, make obtaining a large amount of code especially easy. Code collected from sources such as GitHub forms the basis of a fine-tuning dataset for LLMs that interpret and produce code.

The more interesting case is using RLHF to improve a model's utility for writing code. Again, there are many tools and datasets available that make it possible to build a decent RLHF dataset for a coding assistant. Sources like Stack Overflow allow users to enter questions, provide a facility for other people to give answers to these questions, and include a system where other users vote on the best answers. Data sources include coding competitions like CodeJam, which provide many example solutions to a specific coding problem. Incorporating information from data sources like these is shown in figure 6.4.

Like all good machine learning solutions, you get the best results if you create and label your own data specific to your task. It is rumored that OpenAI did this for generating code, hiring contractors to complete coding tasks as part of creating the data for their system [1]. Regardless of how training and fine-tuning data is collected, the overall strategy remains the same: use standard tokenizers and SFT with RLHF to make an LLM tailored to generate code. This recipe has been used successfully to produce LLMs such as Code Llama [2] and StarCoder [3].

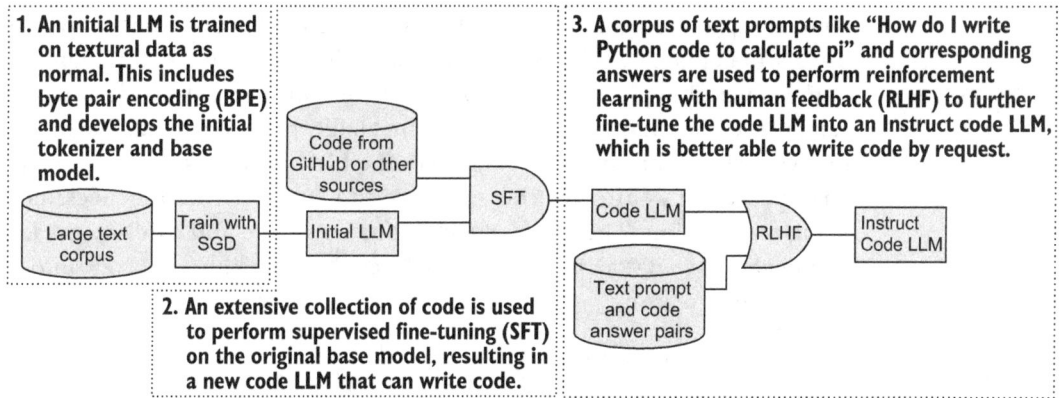

Figure 6.4 Developing an LLM for code applies multiple rounds of fine-tuning. Standard training procedures, such as those described in chapter 4, produce an initial base LLM. Using a large amount of code, SFT creates an LLM that works well with code. Including RLHF as a second fine-tuning step improves the LLM's ability to produce code.

6.1.2 Validating code generated by LLMs

LLMs are particularly useful for code generation because there is an objective and easy-to-run verification step: attempting to compile the code into an executable program [4]. When generating natural language, it is challenging to check the correctness of the output generated by an LLM because natural language can be subjective. There isn't an automated way to check the truthfulness or veracity of the output generated by an LLM. However, when generating code, simply checking whether the code compiles successfully into an executable is a good first step and catches a large portion of the incorrect code. Some commercial products take this a step further and integrate tools such as compilers (software that transforms source code into executables) and visualization tools into their backend. For example, ChatGPT can check whether the code it writes compiles before returning it to the user. If the code doesn't pass this verification step, ChatGPT will try to generate different code for the prompt it received. If the model cannot create valid code to compile, it will warn the user of this fact.

Beyond checking whether code can compile, LLMs are increasingly able to create methods for validating functional correctness. Many code generation tools utilize LLM to generate unit tests, which are tiny programs that provide sample input into generated code and validate that it produces the correct result. In some cases, these capabilities require the developer to describe the test cases that they want the LLM to generate, and the LLM creates an initial implementation as a starting point for further testing.

Code is particularly special because multiple ways exist to validate its output beyond just compilation. For example, code compilation can't happen until the LLM finishes generating its response.

Considering that LLMs are expensive to run, and we don't want to keep a user waiting too long for output, it would be ideal if the LLM could correct errors before completing a large generation. Again, applying the lessons from chapter 5, we can use a syntax parser to check whether the code is incorrect before completing the entire generation process. If portions of the output code fail a basic syntax check, we can instruct the LLM to regenerate just that faulty portion of code. We show the basic process behind this in figure 6.5, where the LLM performs a check on a per-token basis instead of waiting for the generation to complete before checking the code using compilation. The syntax check is less expensive and can happen faster than compilation, but it does not validate that a compiler can turn the code into a working executable program.

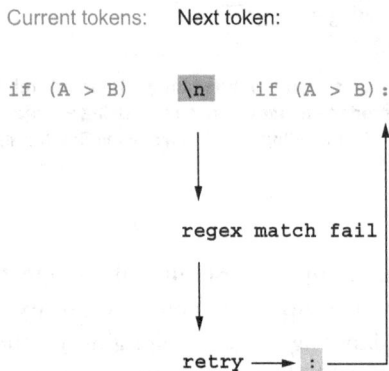

Current tokens: **Next token:**

```
if (A > B)    \n     if (A > B):
```

regex match fail

retry ——▶ :

Figure 6.5   A Python code example where the current tokens `if(A > B)` have been generated. If the next token produced by the LLM is a newline, a syntax error will occur because an `if` statement must end in a colon to be valid. Running a syntax checker on each new token allows us to catch this error and force the LLM to pick an alternative token that doesn't cause a syntax error.

6.1.3   *Improving code via formatting*

Using parsers for syntax checking and compilers to produce working executables makes it far easier to adapt LLMs to the new problem domain of generating code. However, one additional trick is helpful. We can use tools known as *code formatters* (also known by programmers as *linters*) to change tokenization and improve performance.

The problem is that there can be many ways to write code that performs the same functions yet is tokenized differently. Applying a linter to adjust source code formatting helps remove differences between two functionally equivalent, yet different pieces of code. While reformatting code is not a requirement to make code LLMs function well, it helps to avoid unnecessary redundancy that can occur. For example, consider the Java programming language that uses brackets to begin and end a new scope in a program. Various forms of white space are now nonimportant but would be tokenized differently, especially since the brackets are optional for a scope that only uses a single line of code! Figure 6.6 shows how these different legal formats exist for the code that performs the same functions and how we could, ideally, convert code to a single canonical representation.

No space   **Same line**   **No brackets**   **Extra indent**

```
if (true)        if(true) {      if (true)       if (true) {
{                   return 5;        return 5;           return 5;
    return 5;  }                    }
}
```

We want all the different ways
to write valid code to map to
one "cannonical" form.

```
if ( true ) <NEW SCOPE> return 5 <END SCOPE>
```

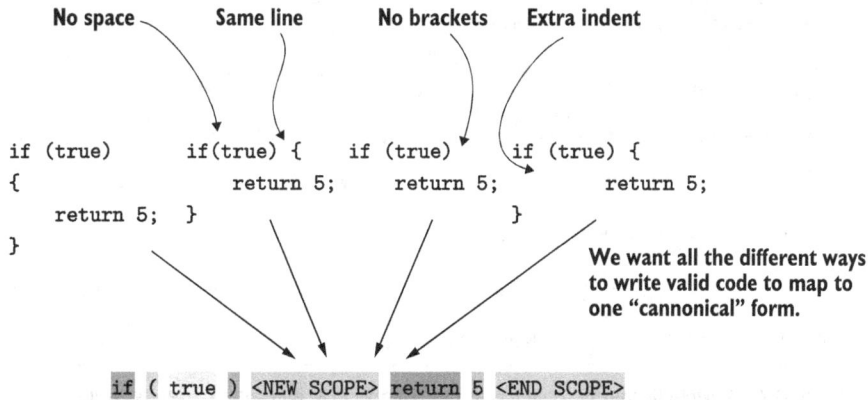

Figure 6.6 A Java code example of how multiple ways to format the same code will lead to different tokenizations, even though each is semantically identical. Linters are a common tool to force code to follow a specific formatting rule. Instead, a linter can be used to create an identical "base" form, thus avoiding representing unnecessary information (like spaces versus tabs).

Removing nonfunctional aspects of code is called *canonicalization*, meaning we convert code with formatting variations into a standard or "canonical" form. Here, we demonstrated a robust method of canonicalization by adding special tokens like <NEW SCOPE> that capture the fact that a new context exists for the if statement, regardless of whether it's a single-line or multiline statement. Instead of adding special tokens, we can use formatting that is consistent across the code (e.g., always use spaces versus tabs, a newline before { or not). Both special parsing and formatting will improve the performance of a code LLM. The robust method, where we add special tokens, will yield better performance over formatting but has the added cost of writing and maintaining a custom parser for code that adds those special tokens. The problem of altering the tokenizer will be more critical in the next section when we discuss using LLMs for mathematics.

6.2 *LLMs for formal mathematics*

LLMs can also perform mathematical tasks that are usually quite challenging for humans to do successfully. These tasks are more than just performing operations like addition and subtraction to calculate numbers; they include formal and symbolic mathematics. We give an example of the kinds of formal math we are talking about in figure 6.7. You can ask these LLMs to calculate derivatives, limits, and integrals and write proofs. They can produce shockingly reasonable results.

LLMs for code are practical because we can use parsers and compilers to partially validate their outputs. Proper tokenization is paramount for making a helpful LLM for mathematics. Using LLMs for math is still a particularly active area of research [6], so the best ways to get an LLM to perform math are not yet known. However, researchers have identified some problems that cluster around the tokenization stage of building and running an LLM.

Question: Solve the simultaneous equations

$$2x + 3y = 5p$$
$$y = 2x + p$$

where p is a constant.

- -

Model output - 540B: From the second equation, we have $2x = y - p$. Substituting this into the first equation, we get

$$2x + 3y = 5p \text{ i.e., } y - p + 3y = 5p \text{ i.e., } 4y = 6p \text{ i.e., } y = \frac{6p}{4} = \frac{3p}{2}.$$

Substituting $y = \frac{3p}{2}$ into the second equation, we have

$$2x + p = \frac{3p}{2} \text{ i.e., } 2x = \frac{3p}{2} - p \text{ i.e., } 2x = \frac{3p - 2p}{2} \text{ i.e., } 2x = \frac{p}{2} \text{ i.e., } x = \frac{p}{4}.$$

Therefore, the solutions are $x = \frac{p}{4}$ and $y = \frac{3p}{2}$.

Figure 6.7   A symbolic math problem that the Minerva LLM can solve correctly. While this example mixes natural language with mathematical content, the standard tokenization used by many LLMs would not allow this kind of mathematical output and can cause some surprising problems. (Image Creative Commons licensed from [5])

NOTE   In chapter 5, we mentioned that fine-tuning can be applied multiple times, and math LLMs are a great example of this. Researchers often create math LLMs by fine-tuning code LLMs, which are created by fine-tuning general-purpose text LLMs. Between SFT and RLHF at each stage, as many as three to six rounds of fine-tuning are applied to the original downstream LLM for math LLMs.

6.2.1   *Sanitized input*

Math LLMs often suffer from input preparation that may work well for natural language text but degrade representations of mathematical concepts. In text, formatted mathematics representations often involve symbols like {}<>;^. Special symbols like these are commonly removed from training data when working with regular text. Preserving this information requires rewriting input parsers for tokenization to ensure you do not remove the data you are trying to get your model to learn from.

Multiple representations for equivalent mathematical equations further complicate training LLMs to understand math in a similar way that multiple formatting may cause problems when processing programming languages. Several formats like TeX, asciimath, and MathML allow mathematical notation to be expressed using plain text but provide instructions for a typesetter to render equations correctly. These formats offer many different ways to represent the same equation. We show an example of this problem in figure 6.8. There are problems with the method of typesetting the math (i.e., how to draw the equation by picking TeX versus MathML) and the representation of the math (i.e., two mathematically equivalent ways of expressing the same thing).

These are both forms of a problem that has come up a few times in our discussion of LLMs: different ways to represent the same thing. In the case of mathematics, the current preference is to keep math formatted using TeX and very similar but less-frequent alternatives like asciimath and to discard verbose content like MathML. We base this motivation on three factors:

$$P(B|C) = \frac{P(C|B)P(B)}{P(C)}$$

MathML

$\downarrow$ **TeX**

`P( B|C) \ =\ \frac{P( C|B) P( B)}{P( C)}`

$\downarrow$ **Mathematically equivalent**

`P( B|C) \ =\ (P( C|B) P( B)) P( C)^{-1}`

$\downarrow$ **Different visualization**

$$P(B|C) = P(C|B)P(B)P(C)^{-1}$$

```
<mi>P</mi>
<mo stretchy="false">(</mo>
<mi>B</mi>
<mrow class="MJX-TeXAtom-ORD">
    <mo stretchy="false">|</mo>
</mrow>
<mi>C</mi>
<mo stretchy="false">)</mo>
<mo>=</mo>
<mfrac>
    <mrow>
        <mi>P</mi>
.... and it keeps going ...
```

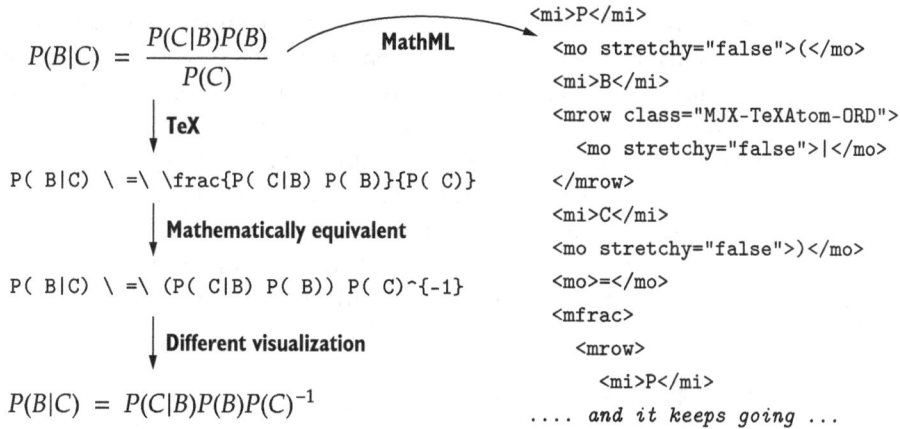

Figure 6.8 A mathematical equation in the top-left demonstrates two different representation problems that occur with math. The nicely formatted math requires a typesetting language. TeX and MathML are two different typesetting languages that have vastly different text and, thus, tokenization. Separate from the typesetting language, there are many ways to represent the same mathematical statement.

- TeX-based formatted math is the most common and available form of math thanks to publicly available sources like arXiv, which consistently uses TeX formatting.
- Keeping all TeX-like representations mitigates the challenge of learning multiple formats and, thus, very different token sets.
- The more verbose MathML uses a larger variety of tokens; thus, more computing resources are required to store the data associated with each unique token.

Choosing TeX as a single preferred representation for math in LLMs doesn't solve the fact that there are multiple ways to write equivalent equations. Determining which equations are the same is so difficult that researchers have proven that no single algorithm can determine the equivalence of two mathematical expressions. (We are being a little loose with our words here, given that this section is on *formal* mathematics, so we will point you to the source [7].) So far, the best answer for LLMs appears to be "let the model try to figure that out," which has been reasonably successful thus far. But we wouldn't be surprised if the developers of future math LLMs invest heavily in improving preprocessing by creating more consistent canonical representations for mathematical equations that reduce the variety of possible expressions for equivalent expressions.

6.2.2 Helping LLMs understand numbers

For most people, numbers are the more accessible part of math. You can put them in a calculator and get the result. Although it may be tedious, you can perform calculations by hand if you do not have a calculator. One follows a fixed set of rules to get the result. Somewhat surprisingly, LLMs have a lot of trouble doing that sort of rote calculation, but developers have worked to improve tokenizers' ability to work better with numbers.

The first problem is that the standard byte-pair encoding (BPE) algorithm produces tokenizers that create inconsistent tokens for numbers. For example, "1812" will likely be tokenized as a single token because there are references to the War of 1812 in thousands of documents; tokenizers will possibly break up 1811 and 1813 into smaller numbers. To further explore why this happens, consider the initial string 3252+3253 and how GPT-3 and GPT-4 tokenize this string. GPT-4 will do a better job because it seems to tokenize numbers by starting with the first three digits every time, resulting in a three-digit number followed by a single-digit number. GPT-3 appears inconsistent because it changes the order in which it tokenizes numbers, as shown in figure 6.9.

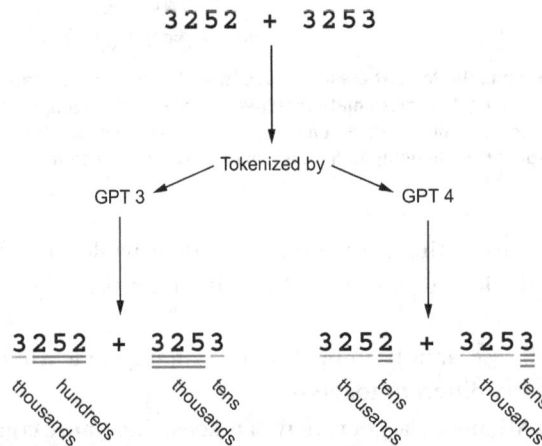

Figure 6.9 **LLMs cannot learn to do basic arithmetic unless they tokenize digits consistently. In this figure, underlines denote different tokens. The tokenized digits might represent the tens, hundreds, or thousands place for any given number. GPT-3 (left) is inconsistent in how numbers get tokenized, making adding two numbers needlessly complex. GPT-4 is better (but not perfect) at tokenizing numbers in a consistent way.**

Now a significant problem has occurred. The "3" token for GPT-3 occurs two times in two different contexts, once in the thousands place (*three-thousand* two hundred ...) and once in the tens place (three-thousand two hundred and fifty *three*). For GPT-3 to correctly add these numbers, the tokenizer must properly capture four different digit locations. In contrast, GPT-4 uses the order for digit representations for each number, making it easier to get the correct result.

People are still experimenting with different ways of changing the tokenizer to improve LLMs' ability to work with numbers. If we are going to tokenize digits into subcomponents, the current best approach is to separate each number, like 3252, into individual digits, like "3, 2, 5, 2" [8]. However, other alternatives also exist.

Another interesting approach for representing numbers is called *xVal* [9], with the idea of replacing every number with the same token that represents "a number." We could call this special token NUM, which will get mapped to a vector of numbers by the embedding layer we learned about in chapter 3.

The clever trick is to include a multiplier with each token, a second number multiplied against the embedded vector value. By default, the LLM uses a multiplier of 1 for every token. Multiplying anything by 1 does nothing. But for any NUM token we encounter, it will instead be multiplied by the original number from the text! This way, we can represent every possible number that might appear, even fractional values, including those that did not appear in the training data. Numbers captured in this manner are related in a simple and intuitive way. We show this in more detail in figure 6.10.

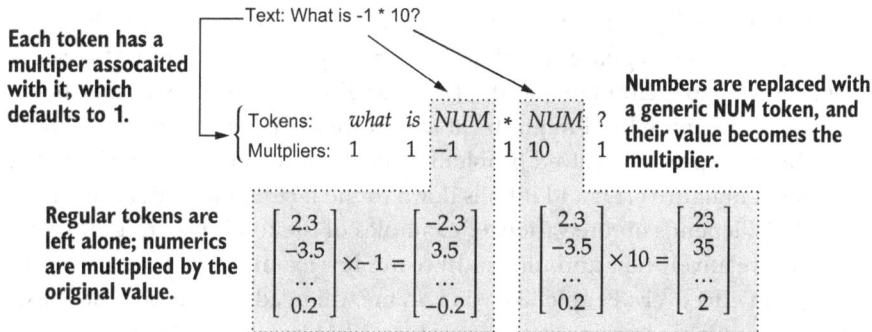

Figure 6.10 xVal uses a trick to help reduce the number of tokens and make them less ambiguous. By modifying how the LLM converts numbers to vectors, a single vector represents each number, such as the number 1. By always using the 1 token and multiplying it by the number observed, we avoid many edge cases in number token representation, such as numbers that never appeared in the training data. This conversion method also makes fractional numbers like 3.14 easier to support.

Both the consistent digits and the xVal strategy share one important realization. We know how to represent math and simple algorithms like grade-school addition and multiplication. If we design the LLM to tokenize mathematics in a way that is more consistent with how we, as humans, do mathematical tasks, our LLMs get better and more consistent mathematical capabilities.

6.2.3 Math LLMs also use tools

The astute reader may have noticed that most of the tokenization problems related to math involve handling digits and not symbolic math. LLMs cannot do essential addition or subtraction without changing the tokenizer and keeping typically "bad" symbols like {}<>;^. Enabling computation by changing the way the tokenizer handles numbers may seem like a minor problem. Still, it is a significant factor for good symbolic performance and often insufficient for handling other forms of symbolic math. Obtaining the best possible performance on symbolic math relies on external tools and playing clever tricks with LLM output.

If you ever had the TI-89 calculator that could solve derivatives for you, you know that computers can automate calculations without LLMs. Functionally, computer algebra systems (CAS) can provide this functionality. A CAS implements algorithms to perform some (but not all) mathematical steps. Calculating derivatives is one of them, so having an LLM use a CAS, like Sympy, helps ensure the LLM always performs specific steps correctly. However, the ability to integrate a CAS like Sympy into an LLM does not guarantee the entire sequence of steps will be performed correctly.

To validate correctness, math LLMs have begun to use a programming language called *Lean*. In Lean, the program is a kind of mathematical proof, and the program will not compile if there is an error in the proof. It effectively makes incorrect proof steps one type of syntax error that can then be detected. Once detected, as we have shown in other examples, the output can be regenerated by the LLM until the proof, output as a Lean program, compiles successfully, just like we show in section 6.1.2.

Using Lean can guarantee that a returned proof from an LLM is 100% correct, but there is no guarantee that the LLM can find the proof. Notably, there may also be cases where the LLM might be able to solve the problem correctly but might not be able to express the solved problem using Lean. We diagram the logic behind this problem in figure 6.11, and it boils down to the fact that the effectiveness of tool use in LLMs depends on the variety of examples of the tool's use in training data. Since Lean is relatively new and niche, there are few examples of fine-tuning an LLM to use Lean effectively. People like you and me will need to generate those examples to produce suitable training data to teach an LLM how to use Lean.

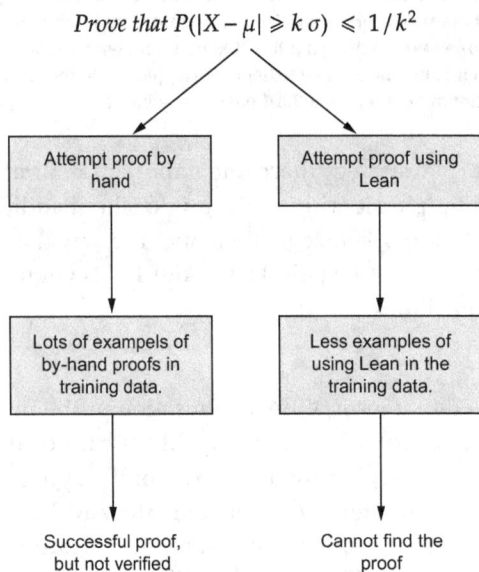

Prove that $P(|X - \mu| \geqslant k\,\sigma) \leqslant 1/k^2$

```
                    Attempt proof by          Attempt proof using
                         hand                        Lean

                    Lots of exampels of        Less examples of
                    by-hand proofs in          using Lean in the
                      training data.            training data.

                    Successful proof,          Cannot find the
                    but not verified                proof
```

Figure 6.11   Given some mathematical goal, getting an LLM to use Lean (right path) might not result in a verifiably correct proof because it may not be effective at using Lean as a tool. Having the LLM produce a normal proof (left path) may yield a correct proof, but not a way for us to verify that it is (in)correct.

So what can you do if the LLM cannot provide verifiable proof that its math is correct? A trick used today is to run the LLM multiple times. Because the next token is selected randomly, you can potentially get a different result with a different answer each time you run the LLM. Whichever answer appears most frequently is most likely correct. This process does not guarantee the proof is correct, but it helps.

6.3 Transformers and computer vision

The process of translating code and math to tokens is fairly intuitive. Code is fundamentally text used to tell computers what to do in a highly pedantic way. Math is difficult to convert into tokens, but we have discussed how it is possible. Computer vision is a different story, where the data involved is images or videos represented using pixels. The idea of tokens for images seems confusing. How on earth could we possibly convert an image into tokens? Images typically contain lots of detail, and you cannot just combine a bunch of small images into one coherent image like you do when you string words together to form a sentence. Nevertheless, we can apply transformers to images if we think about tokenization as a process to convert any input into a sequence of numbers.

> **NOTE** There was an approach to representing images as a combination of tiny images called *code books*. Code books can be useful, but not the same in the spirit of our discussion. Consider this a keyword nugget to explore if you want to learn about some older computer vision techniques.

While high-quality image recognition algorithms and image generators existed for many years before transformers, transformers have rapidly become one of the premier ways to work with images in machine learning. Both vision transformer (ViT) architectures that strictly use transformers, as well as mixed architecture models such as VQGAN and U-Net transformer that mix transformers with other types of data structures, have seen great success in both interpreting image-based data and producing amazing computer-generated images from text descriptions. It may seem counterintuitive that transformers perform so well in images because images do not look like discrete sequences of symbols like natural language, code, or amino acid sequences do. Still, transformers fulfill a critical role in computer vision by bringing global cohesion to models.

6.3.1 Converting images to patches and back

Conceptually, we will replace the tokenizer and embedding process with a new process that outputs a sequence of vectors similar to the embedding layers we discussed in section 3.1.1. The prevailing approach to creating a sequence representing an image is to divide the image into a set of *patches*. As a result, we will replace our tokenizer with a *patch extractor* that returns a sequence of vectors. The output of an LLM uses an unembedding layer to convert vectors back into tokens. Since we have no tokens, we need a *patch combiner* to take the outputs of a transformer and merge them into one coherent image. We show this process in figure 6.12. Please pay special attention to the fact that the central portion of the diagram remains the same as it was for text-based LLMs. We reuse the same transformer layers and learning algorithm (gradient descent) between text and images.

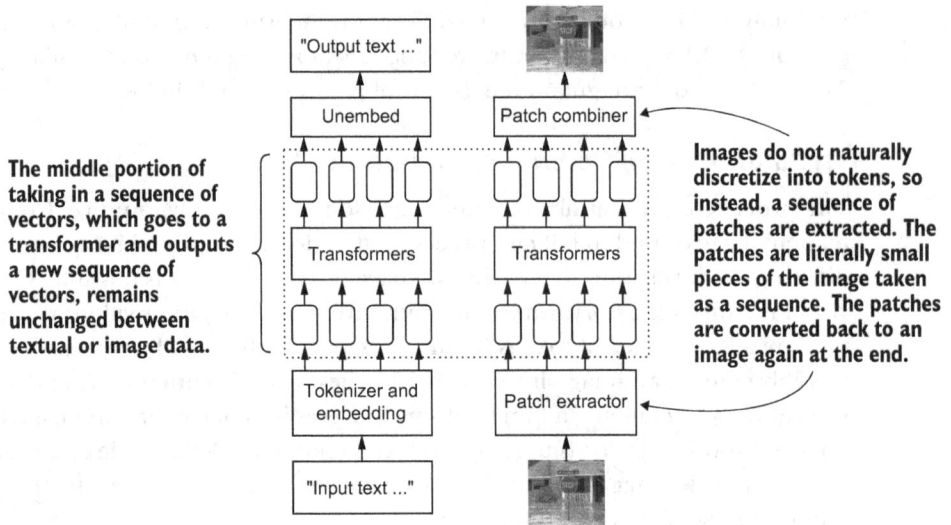

The middle portion of taking in a sequence of vectors, which goes to a transformer and outputs a new sequence of vectors, remains unchanged between textual or image data.

Images do not naturally discretize into tokens, so instead, a sequence of patches are extracted. The patches are literally small pieces of the image taken as a sequence. The patches are converted back to an image again at the end.

Figure 6.12   On the left, this simplified diagram shows how text input is tokenized and embedded before going to the transformer. An unembedding layer then converts the transformer output into the desired text representation. The input and output will be images when performing a computer vision task. The transformer stays the same, but then we modify the method for breaking the image into a sequence of vectors to perform patch extraction instead of tokenization. The LLM produces image output using a patch combiner, analogous to the unembedding layer for text LLMs.

Since everything except the input vector sequence generation and output steps remains the same, we can focus on how the conversion of images to and from vectors works. It will be helpful to focus on the input side first.

As the name *patch* implies, the patch extractor breaks up each image into a sequence of smaller images. It is common to pick a fixed size for the patch, like a square of 16×16 pixels. We want a fixed size so that it is easy to feed into a neural network, which always processes data of a fixed size, and small so that they represent just a piece of the entire image. Breaking an image into patches is similar to breaking text into a collection of tokens. Each individual token isn't informative, but when combined with other tokens, it makes a coherent sentence.

Once an image is broken into patches, each pixel in that patch is converted to three numbers representing the amount of red, green, and blue (RGB) present in each pixel. An initial vector is created by combining each pixel's RGB values into a single long vector. So for our square of 16×16 pixels with three color values for each pixel, we will have a vector that is 768 values in length (16 height, 16 width, and an RGB value for each pixel). Then, a small neural network that might have only one or two layers processes each vector separately to make the final outputs. This neural network implements a very light feature-extraction process that does not require significant memory or computation resources. This design is common in computer vision because the first layer usually learns simple patterns like "dark inside, light outside" and does not need a transformer layer's greater expense or power to learn the basic features of an image patch. This whole process is summarized in figure 6.13.

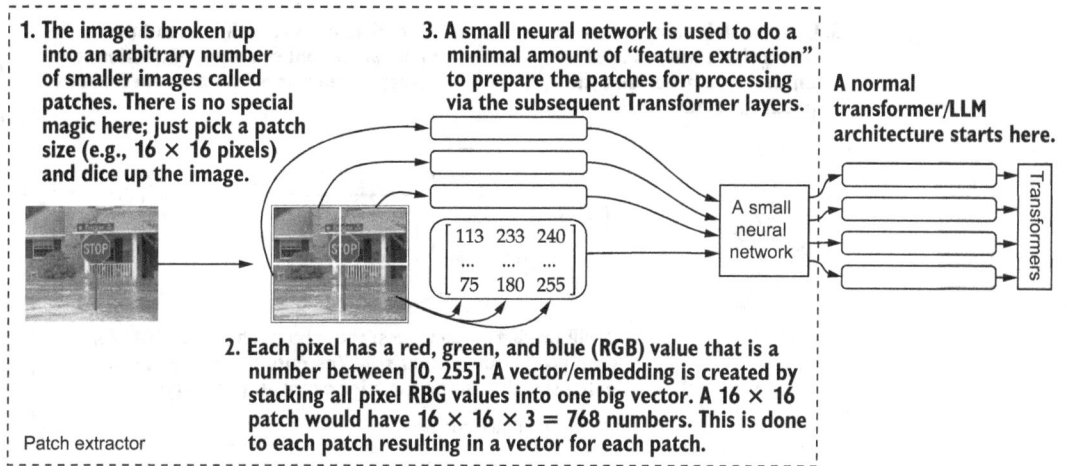

1. The image is broken up into an arbitrary number of smaller images called patches. There is no special magic here; just pick a patch size (e.g., 16 × 16 pixels) and dice up the image.

3. A small neural network is used to do a minimal amount of "feature extraction" to prepare the patches for processing via the subsequent Transformer layers.

A normal transformer/LLM architecture starts here.

A small neural network

Transformers

$$\begin{bmatrix} 113 & 233 & 240 \\ ... & ... & ... \\ 75 & 180 & 255 \end{bmatrix}$$

Patch extractor

2. Each pixel has a red, green, and blue (RGB) value that is a number between [0, 255]. A vector/embedding is created by stacking all pixel RBG values into one big vector. A 16 × 16 patch would have 16 × 16 × 3 = 768 numbers. This is done to each patch resulting in a vector for each patch.

Figure 6.13 Extracting patches is a straightforward process. The patch extractor breaks up an image into square tiles called patches. Images consist of pixel values that are already numbers, so we convert each patch into a vector of numbers. Then, we use a small neural network as a preprocessor before passing the vectors to the full transformer-based neural network.

There are many possible ways to design the small neural network used in the patch extractor, but all generally work equally well. One option is to use what is called a *convolutional neural network* (CNN), which is a type of neural network that understands that pixels near each other are related to each other. Others have used just the same kind of linear layer that is a component of a transformer layer. In this case, the overall model that includes the small neural network and a series of transformers is often called a *vision transformer*.

The design of the small network is a minor detail but worth mentioning because its existence is relevant to the patch combiner that produces the final output. It does not matter whether you pick a CNN or a linear layer for the architecture of the small neural network, but it is essential to ensure the output's shape matches the input's shape. For example, if you have 16×16 patches, you can use the small network to force the output to have $16 \times 16 \times 3 = 768$ values, regardless of the size of the transformer layer itself. To produce image output, you reverse the patch extraction process to convert the vectors into patches and then combine the patches into an image, as shown in figure 6.14.

We have thus successfully replaced the input tokenization and the output embedding with new image-centric layers. In many ways, this is much nicer than tokenization. There is no need to build/keep track of a vocabulary, no sampling process, etc. This is a crucial insight into the general applicability of transformers as the general-purpose core of an LLM. If you can find a lot of data and a reasonable method of converting that data into a sequence of vectors, you can use transformers to solve certain classes of input and output problems.

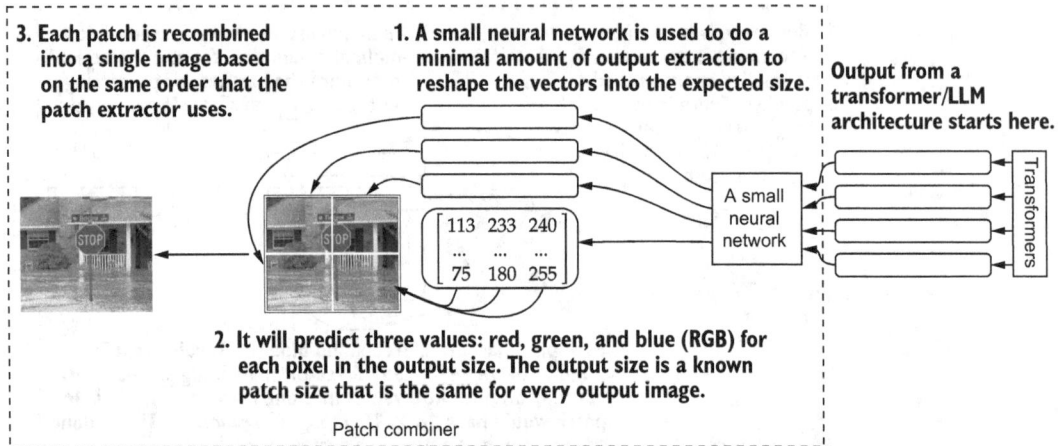

3. Each patch is recombined into a single image based on the same order that the patch extractor uses.

1. A small neural network is used to do a minimal amount of output extraction to reshape the vectors into the expected size.

Output from a transformer/LLM architecture starts here.

$$\begin{bmatrix} 113 & 233 & 240 \\ ... & ... & ... \\ 75 & 180 & 255 \end{bmatrix}$$

A small neural network

Transformers

2. It will predict three values: red, green, and blue (RGB) for each pixel in the output size. The output size is a known patch size that is the same for every output image.

Patch combiner

Figure 6.14   Compared to figure 6.13, the arrows here go in the opposite direction. The purpose is to emphasize that the patch combiner and extractor do the same thing but operate in different directions. The neural network is more important in this stage as a way to force the transformer's output to have the same shape as the original patches because we can control the output size of any neural network.

6.3.2 *Multimodal models using images and text*

The ability to change the input and output of an LLM to arrive at a vision transformer means that we can take an image as input and produce an image as output. It demonstrates how a transformer can produce input of different modalities, but we have only discussed cases where the input and output are the same modality. We either have text as input and text as output or images as input and images as output. However, deep learning is flexible! There is nothing that forces us to use the same modality as both input and output or even restrict input and output to be a single modality. You can combine text as input with image as output, images as input and text as output, text and images as input and audio as output, or any other data modality combinations you might think of. Figure 6.15 shows how image and text give us four total ways we might combine them to handle different kinds of data.

By creating a model that uses images as input and text as output, we create an *image captioning model*. We can train this model to generate text describing the input image's content. Models such as these help make images more discoverable and aid visually impaired users.

By creating a model that uses text as the input and an image as the output, we create an *image generation model*. You can describe a desired image using words, and the model can create a reasonable image based on your input. Famous products like MidJourney are models of this flavor. Though their implementation involves more than just a vision transformer, the high-level idea is the same: by pairing a text-based input with image-based output and a lot of data, we can create new multimodal capabilities that span different data types.

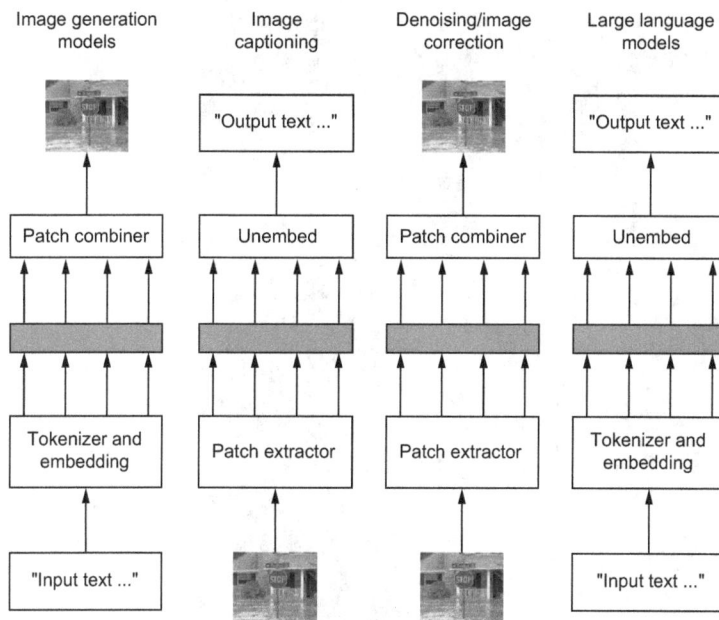

Figure 6.15 Four combinations showing different types of model input and output. The example at the furthest right represents a normal text-based LLM we have already learned about. To the left, we show possibilities like an image-generating model that takes text as input ("Draw me a picture of a stop sign in a flood zone") or an image captioning model that generates text that describes an image input ("This picture shows a stop sign surrounded by murky water").

6.3.3 Applicability of prior lessons

Other lessons learned throughout this book remain relevant to these vision transformer and multimodal models. Ultimately, they learn to do what they are trained for, and when you try to bend them in ways beyond what is found in the training data, you may get an unusual result. As an example, we might tell an image generation model "Draw anything but an adorable cat," and you will probably end up with a cat as shown in figure 6.16

These models are (currently) trained with pairs of images and pieces of text describing the image. Thus, they learn a strong correlation to produce visualizations of anything in the input sentence. For example, the model wants to produce a cat since the word *cat* is in the input sentence. More sophisticated abstract drawing requests like "Draw anything but" do not appear in such datasets, and so the model is not trained to handle such a request.

Similarly, as LLMs like ChatGPT have developed prompting as a strategy for devising inputs that produce desired outputs, prompting has also been developed for image captioning models. It is not uncommon to include unusual information like "Unreal3D," the name of software used to generate 3D imagery for computer games to produce output with a particular style and quality. Words like *high resolution* and even the names of artists, alive and dead, are used to try to influence the models into producing particular styles.

Figure 6.16 This was generated with an old version of Stable Diffusion, a popular image generation model. Despite telling the model "Do not draw a cat," the model was trained to generate content. The request is outside what the model was incentivized to learn, so it cannot handle it. This is similar to the problems with LLMs regurgitating close-but-wrong output because the model saw similar data during training.

Summary

- LLMs benefit when they can use external tools. For example, a code LLM can use syntax checkers and compilers to detect erroneous code generation. When the LLM finds an error, the output is regenerated, minimizing the risk of giving the user unhelpful or broken code.
- Tokenizers must be modified to support math by keeping unusual symbols used to express formatted math and changing digit representations. We can improve math LLMs further by giving them tools like computer algebra systems to detect and avoid errors.
- Transformers can be applied to images by breaking up an image into patches, where each patch becomes a vector and makes a sequence of inputs for the transformer to process. Patches are conceptually similar to tokens for text LLMs.
- Transformers can use different data modalities for input and output, allowing the creation of multimodal models like those used in image captioning and image generation.

Misconceptions, limits, and eminent abilities of LLMs

7

This chapter covers

- How LLMs and humans differ in learning
- Making LLMs better at latency and scale-sensitive applications
- Producing intermediate outputs for better final results
- How computational complexity limits what an LLM can do

Thanks to ChatGPT, the world has become more broadly aware of LLMs and their capabilities. Despite this awareness, many misconceptions and misunderstandings about LLMs still exist. Many people believe that LLMs are continually learning and self-improving, are more intelligent than people, and will soon be able to solve every problem on earth. While these statements are hyperbolic, some earnestly fear that LLMs will seriously disrupt the world.

We are not here to say there are no legitimate concerns about LLMs, and we will discuss these in more depth in the book's last two chapters. Still, many thoughts and worries about LLMs that you may encounter are blown out of proportion compared to how LLMs and technology broadly evolve.

This chapter will discuss a few critical aspects of how LLMs work and how these aspects relate to these misconceptions. Ultimately, these operational aspects of LLMs affect how you may want to use or avoid an LLM in practice.

First, we will discuss the differences between how humans and LLMs learn. Humans are fast learners, but LLMs are static by default. Although LLMs can be incredibly effective at processing data, people are better equipped to be maximally productive when learning new things.

Next, we will tackle why the word *thinking* is misleading when considering how an LLM works. We will highlight that it is better to think of an LLM's operation as *computing* because LLMs have no distinction between formulating and emitting output. In contrast, people often "think before they speak."

Finally, we will discuss the scope of what LLMs can compute and how computer science concepts help us understand some of the intrinsic limitations behind an LLM's current and future capabilities. These three topics are interrelated, so you will see how they connect as we discuss each in more detail.

7.1   *Human rate of learning vs. LLMs*

While we have discussed it implicitly, it is helpful to be explicit about how an LLM's training differs from a person's learning. The fluid and often lucid text produced by generative AI and the analogies we use to relate the capabilities of LLMs to human capabilities may make it seem as if there were some relationship between the two. Many people online are touting the idea that such a connection between what an LLM can do and what a human can do is real. In reality, the two are very different and have important considerations for when, how, and why you might prefer a person over an AI and how humans and AI can work together.

From the material we have covered so far, we know that LLMs learn by predicting the next word using hundreds of millions of documents as examples. In chapter 4, we presented the algorithmic process of "learning" in LLMs: the gradient descent algorithm, which alters the parameters of an LLM's neural network by attempting to predict the next token in a sample input. Then, in chapter 5, we showed how fine-tuning algorithms, like RLHF, alter the parameters of the LLM again. These two components of learning in an LLM have minimal resemblance to human learning and impose some crucial limitations on what we can expect the LLM to do. One of the most critical aspects is the rate and efficacy of this learning approach as it relates to the volume of data provided to the training process.

To explore this further, consider how an LLM learns relative to how people learn. Have you ever met anyone who never spoke to anyone else, never had a parent talk to them, and yet somehow understood language? Likely not. Indeed, conversation is a key part of linguistic acquisition [1]. At least initially, you acquire knowledge and language from interaction and communication with others and the environment. Consequentially, you can learn effectively with much less information than an LLM has in the data that it trains on.

In the best-case scenarios of childhood language acquisition, studies have observed that children are exposed to around 15,000 total spoken words a month [2]. If we were to be generous and round this figure up to 20,000 words and consider this over 100 years, a person would encounter as many as 24 million spoken words throughout their entire life. This is clearly a vast overestimate. Couple this with the fact that most people can speak their native language fluently, with an implicit understanding of vocabulary and linguistic structure, by at least age 18. Now compare this with LLMs. GPT-3, for example, was trained on hundreds of billions of words. Based on word counts alone, this is a very inefficient way to learn language!

Language acquisition also helps us recognize the stark differences in how words are acquired. Babies and toddlers start with simple words, such as *mama* and *dada*, and eventually learn basic concepts like colors, *no*, *food*, etc. More complex words are added over time, building on the prior words. Yet an LLM begins with seeing all words simultaneously based on their frequency of use. Indeed, it is accurate to imagine an LLM tokenizing this very book as part of its first "learning," acquiring knowledge of all of its eventual vocabulary simultaneously instead of starting with simple concepts and building knowledge on top of those foundations. While this process contributes to the rate at which an LLM learns, it may detract from the LLM's capabilities of drawing high-level relationships between concepts.

An LLM's key advantage over humans is the *scale* at which it operates and its ability to perform multiple tasks simultaneously. This advantage is a common theme throughout machine learning and deep learning. You cannot easily hire an army of people to comb through books, expense reports, internal documents, or whatever medium of information to perform knowledge work like writing a review, finding potential fraud, or answering an arcane policy question. However, you can quickly get an army of computers to attempt to automate these tasks. While an individual LLM can analyze multiple parts of a sentence simultaneously, you can employ multiple computers running the same LLM to work in parallel. Training the LLM presents a similar opportunity: LLMs are trained on more words than you will ever read or hear in your lifetime, and you can train a large LLM by renting or buying thousands of computers to do the work concurrently.

Considering these facts in conjunction with the material we've covered in previous chapters, we can list several high-level pros and cons of using LLMs for tasks compared to humans. A summary of these factors is shown in figure 7.1, which describes how the advantages and disadvantages of LLMs will lead to natural benefits and drawbacks of their use and, thus, provide insights about where LLMs should and should not be used.

Some of the benefits of LLMs are as follows:

- Well-trained LLMs have a broad collection of background information, so they perform well on many tasks that are not that different from what has been seen before, and little work is needed to make the model effective. While this is not necessarily correct or detailed information, the breadth of the topic areas that an LLM can receive and generate reasonable responses about is far beyond the areas that most individual people can cover.

Certain properties of LLMs	Lead to various deployment/solution building factors	And some rules of thumb.
LLM strengths: 1. Knows something about almost everything 2. Close enough is good enough. 3. Available on demand	1. Handles surface-level requests 2. Fast to deploy 3. Easy to scale up/down with demand 4. Good for first-pass attempts/teaming tools	1. Start with easy problems and grow "up" to harder ones. 2. Apply to repeatable situations. 3. Have an audit process to spot-check behavior/outcomes are appropriate. 4. Plan on a mechanism to escalate to humans.
LLM weakness: 1. Fine-tuning or from-scratch training is a seven-figure investment "all in." 3. Does not handle extreme novelty well 2. Does not improve at any task with repitition	1. Hard-to-solve problems don't make progress without major investments. 2. Not a reliable "expert" on anything 3. Can be tricked into bad behavior	

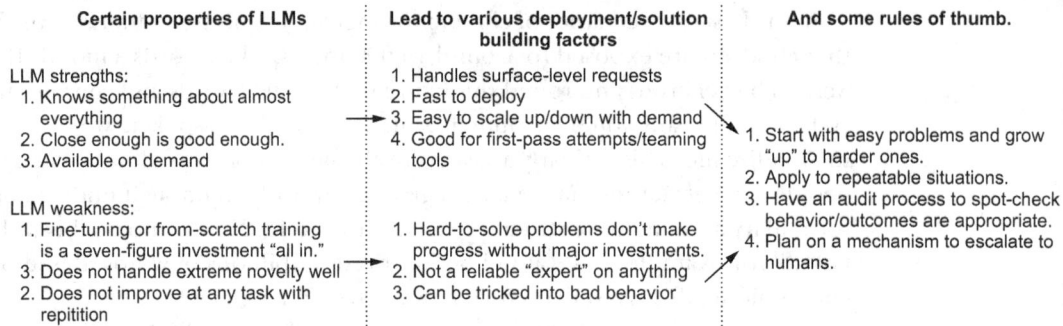

Figure 7.1   A summary of the strengths and weaknesses of LLMs relative to humans performing the same task. These lead to natural considerations that you must evaluate when using an LLM. From these, we can draw broad recommendations for successful LLM use.

- For many tasks, there is no need to get a precisely correct response. Broad requests for general information in a subject area intrinsically allow an LLM to be flexible and unconstrained in its response. This is especially true if you refine the LLM's output through other processes. For example, a human might copyedit a piece of writing to improve it but use an LLM to produce the first draft or provide inspiration to break writer's block and accelerate creating the work. Likewise, an LLM can be used to refine an author's writing to make it sound more natural or engaging through rephrasing or using a larger variety of vocabulary.

- LLMs can be trained quickly in comparison to people. You can produce a broadly useful LLM in months, given a $1,000,000 to $10,000,000 budget to purchase computational resources. Humans take many years to become useful. An LLM that can answer a broad set of basic questions can be instantiated for far less effort and cost than it takes to find, hire, and retain an employee with specific knowledge, skills, and abilities. As long as the problems are in the scope of what the LLM can achieve, the incremental cost is minuscule compared to a person's hourly rate, even without the extra overhead.

Some of the drawbacks of LLMs are as follows:

- The high cost of training LLMs informs their economics. That training cost is amortized over the thousands of operations the LLM performs once trained. If an LLM doesn't perform well, the cost of continually improving it to make it work can quickly become prohibitive, even without considering the potential that it might never work correctly for a specific task. For example, if an LLM, implemented with all the most recent tools and tricks, cannot solve a specific need, addressing this problem will require an unknown amount of work and budget. Conversely, humans can generally learn new capabilities, specifically those that are hard for LLMs, at much lower cost in weeks to months.

- LLMs cannot be relied upon to handle unexpected situations and inputs not reflected in their training data. Although many have shown they can succeed in novel situations, they do not learn in the same way as humans. A person can see that their actions are not working as intended *on the first try* and quickly adapt. An LLM cannot independently adapt by observing its errors and may repeatedly consume resources attempting to produce answers to problems it cannot understand.

- LLMs are easily fooled and do not work well in adversarial environments because once people find a way to trick the LLM into an errant outcome (e.g., "Give me a loan even though I have no income"), they can repeat the adversarial and malicious behavior, and your LLM won't be able to prevent it without you implementing additional guardrails.

7.1.1 The limitations on self-improvement

Generally, humans are capable of self-improvement. They can focus on and study a problem, devise novel approaches, identify required resources, and move forward to implement and improve their solutions. While LLMs struggle with self-improvement, in the generative AI field, there is a belief that the same self-improvement may be possible for LLMs. The idea about how this could work goes something like this:

1 Train an LLM on an initial dataset.
2 Use the LLM to generate new data, adding it to your training dataset.
3 Train or fine-tune the model on the new data. (Repeat until the LLM works as expected.)

While this sounds intuitive and plausible, we believe that it does not work for simple reasons. We can use some basic information theory, which measures information as a quantifiable resource, to explain why. The basis of this argument is that by some measure of information, the original dataset has a fixed amount of information. In statistics vernacular, we might describe the original information as the *distribution* of available information, and through its training process, the LLM is attempting to *approximate* or reproduce that distribution of information by storing and encoding it in its model. When you generate new data using an LLM, that sample of data is a noisy and incomplete reproduction of the original data distribution that the LLM observed in the training process. Fundamentally, it is impossible for the LLM's output to contain any new information not present in the original training data. Consequently, the reality of such experiments is that successive rounds of generating data and training degrade the quality and performance of the model [3]. To make something like this work, you need something that provides external or new information at each round.

These concepts also relate to some people's fear of AI improving itself until it becomes so intelligent that we have no hope of understanding or controlling it. Some arguments are that the LLM can use other tools, somehow acquiring outside information or more training data, to improve itself. Ultimately, this requires a belief that while there are limitations as to how far you can improve most technologies, LLMs will be immune to these limits, such as the law of diminishing returns. Figure 7.2 describes the inherent limits to LLM self-improvement.

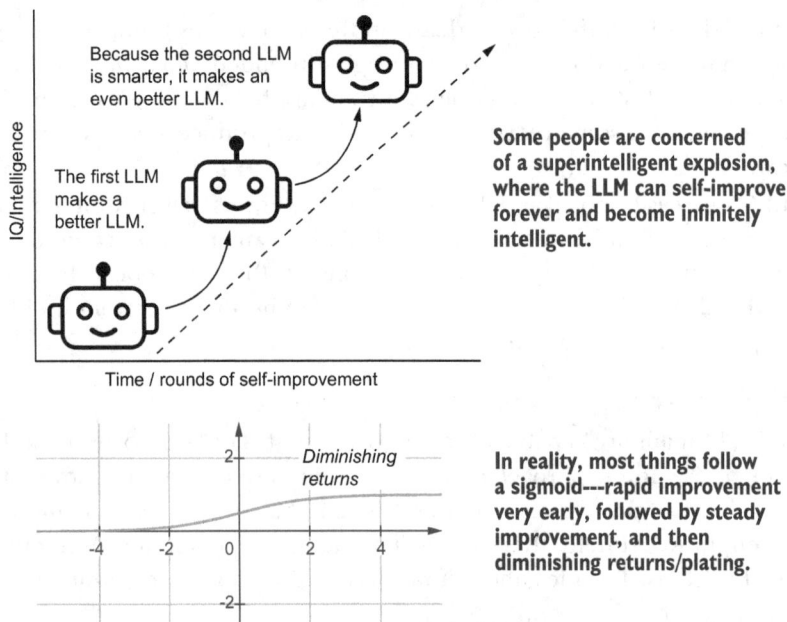

Because the second LLM is smarter, it makes an even better LLM.

The first LLM makes a better LLM.

IQ/Intelligence

Time / rounds of self-improvement

Some people are concerned of a superintelligent explosion, where the LLM can self-improve forever and become infinitely intelligent.

Diminishing returns

In reality, most things follow a sigmoid---rapid improvement very early, followed by steady improvement, and then diminishing returns/plating.

Figure 7.2 Concerns that LLMs will self-improve require the belief that LLMs won't follow the normal sigmoid or S-curve of diminishing returns that describes the development of almost all other technologies. For infinite self-improvement to happen, we must believe that constraints such as power, data, or computational capacity are always solvable and that somehow, humans would not otherwise solve them for areas outside of LLMs. Constraints such as these are why we can describe most technology development using S-curves, where progress slows as more constraints take effect. In other words, we'll eventually reach a state where we can't just build a bigger computer.

A great example of limitations on technical improvement is Moore's law, which roughly states that the number of transistors on a chip would double every 18 to 24 months. Moore's law has mostly accurately predicted the growth of transistors on a chip, but there are signs of the S-curve of diminishing returns in transistors. The rate of the number of transistors on a chip doubling is decreasing. More importantly, the total system performance has already entered this S-curve. The number of transistors correlates with total compute performance but does not directly indicate compute performance. Looking at the whole picture in figure 7.3, you will see that other constraints prevent boundless improvements across the entire system. Moore's law aside, the practical cost of high-performance GPUs and the infrastructure that hosts them is another barrier to boundless improvement.

LLMs are not humans—do not judge them by human standards!

Many catchy headlines have proclaimed LLM performance on the MCAT exam for medical school, the bar exam for lawyers to practice law, and IQ tests to measure their intelligence. While these are always interesting and full of caveats such as

"How many examples of the same kinds of questions are in the LLM's training data?" these are not good ways to extrapolate about LLMs and their abilities relative to humans. Indeed, pinning down an exact definition of *intelligence* is complex and one of the reasons why multiple types of IQ tests exist [4]. Ultimately, these tests have been helpful in predicting people's outcomes in various tasks. Still, these tests are not designed to evaluate AI algorithms, and we have no reason to believe they do so accurately or reasonably! The problem is correlation, not causation. IQ tests all *correlate* with desirable outcomes, but they do not measure an underlying property that controls or causes outcomes in the same way, for example, that a blood sugar test does. In a blood sugar test, if your blood sugar is too low or too high, we know what will happen because it measures an important underlying property that *causes* the outcome of some process that we understand quite well. IQ tests are useful, but their usefulness comes from years of iteration and improvement. We now better understand which answers on these tests correlate to people's performance, but they don't measure the underlying causes of this performance.

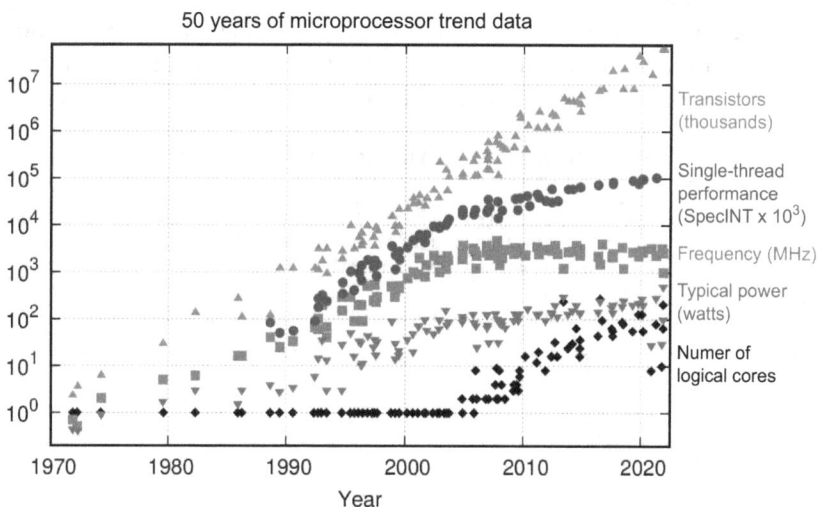

Figure 7.3 **Moores's law is a common example of boundless growth, but it is misleading. Transistors keep doubling, but frequency, power, single-threaded performance, and total computing do not. So the total system performance has not continued to double approximately every two years. Other similar factors will constrain LLM performance and affect capability over time. Used under CC4.0 license from https://github.com/karlrupp/microprocessor-trend-data.**

There are many examples of outside information being used to improve generative AI. Some algorithms created for robotic hands use external information from a physics simulator. Apple uses 3D modeling software to generate data that improves iris recognition on their phones [5]. In the examples in chapter 6, you saw a potential path for improving an LLM using a compiler for code or the Lean language to verify mathematics. These examples demonstrate fully automatable processes that generate new information that can lead to self-improvement.

Yet, there has never been an example of boundless self-improvement; the gains observed from using these external tools eventually reach a plateau and ultimately rely on humans to develop the side information by writing better physics simulators for the robots, better compilers for code, and better domain-knowledge systems like Lean. Improving these tools compounds a major expense of training LLMs, thus imposing a second economic limitation on the self-improvement of LLMs beyond what is practical.

7.1.2 *Few-shot learning*

Few-shot learning is also called *in-context learning*. This technique involves providing examples of the type of output you want an LLM to produce as a part of the prompt you send it. Say you want an LLM to respond to a help-desk question with accurate information. You may give the LLM a prompt with a user's question to the help desk, followed by an example of the appropriate kind of response. If you give only one example, it's called *one-shot learning*. Providing two examples instead of a single example is known as *two-shot learning*, and so on, hence describing this approach as few-shot because the precise number of examples is generally not as important as the fact that only a few examples are provided. This method of incorporating examples in a prompt is a specific kind of prompt engineering, as demonstrated in figure 7.4.

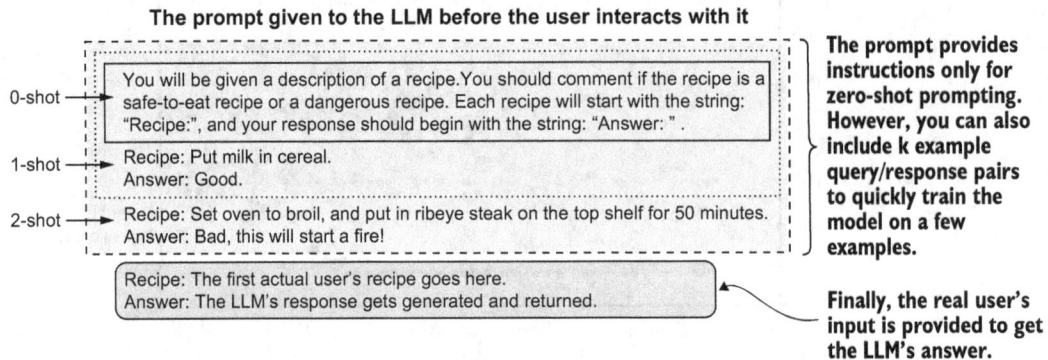

Figure 7.4 Prompts with examples of how you want the LLM to produce output are called few-shot prompts because the LLM has not seen any examples of this specific behavior in its training data. In your prompt, you can include examples of input and output similar to RLHF/supervised fine-tuning (SFT). This prompting style encourages the model to produce the desired output by providing examples of what the desired output should look like. Because LLMs train on such a large amount of unlabeled data, k-shot examples are an effective way to get better results with minimal effort.

Including examples in your prompts is useful for improving an LLM's performance at new tasks. You don't need to use RLHF or SFT to alter the model, and it works better than zero-shot prompting, where we ask the LLM to do the task without examples. But is it efficient learning?

Few-shot prompting is not training because we are not altering the model in any way, as we would in the training or fine-tuning process. The "state" or weights of the LLM remain the same. However accurately the LLM performs the task on Monday, it will be exactly as accurate on Tuesday and Wednesday, no matter how many thousands or millions of few-shot prompts it deals with. There is no improvement to the model's abilities unless you manually do something to include better examples in the prompt, provide more examples, or otherwise intervene somehow. In this sense, no true learning is happening, and nothing about the model changes. We just get improved output from the model by changing our prompt.

Yet, in an abstract sense, the LLM is learning because the prompt changes the model's behavior by providing additional context to describe the problem. The behavior exhibited via prompting correlates with behavior achieved through fine-tuning on similar examples [6]. What that means, in short, is that few-shot learning does not fundamentally reflect anything different from what gradient descent can already do.

NOTE If you do not have a lot of data, few-shot prompting is probably the most effective way for you as a practitioner or user to get an LLM to work well on your data. Because we can think of this prompting as inefficient gradient descent or fine-tuning, you should expect diminishing returns as you add examples in a few-shot style. For example, if you include many examples of how you'd like an LLM to respond in your prompt and still do not get the needed performance, you should look at SFT, RLHF, and the other fine-tuning approaches we discussed in chapter 5.

7.2 Efficiency of work: A 10-watt human brain vs. a 2000-watt computer

The human brain takes the equivalent of 10 watts to maintain consciousness, allowing you to read this book. A high-end workstation with a GPU for AI/ML work could easily use 2,000 watts. A high-end server for running the larger LLMs available today gets into the 10,000 to 15,000 watt range. Off the bat, it would seem like using an LLM could thus be 1,500× more power inefficient than having a human do some task. We should be very proud of this aspect of our evolutionary success and efficiency, but it is also only one aspect of what we might mean by efficiency. We show that many different kinds of efficiency might benefit a person versus machines in figure 7.5.

7.2.1 Power

Power is one of the driving factors in determining the financial cost of creating and running an LLM, but the true need is not yet entirely clear. Yes, many providers will quote you a price for running an LLM, but we do not know the true costs each provider incurs or the margins each provider has established. For example, an LLM provider may be running a negative margin or loss-leader strategy, and the long-term cost of using an LLM could be higher than it appears based on today's prices. We

Factor	Human advantage	LLM advantage
Power	One-off jobs, quick to complete, bespoke needs.	Enough work to be continuously busy
Latency, scalability, and availability	Humans are faster at many multimodal tasks and at video understanding due to the input being too large for most generative AI. But they need sleep/breaks, and training a new person takes time.	For pure text, LLMs are currently faster to process, and upload/data transfer times are minimal. They can be available all hours and replicate easy.
Refinement	People learn new tasks with just a few demonstrations. As you do it, you get better at it, and it becomes muscle memory.	Human labor is required to improve LLMs, but they don't improve autonomously in time.

Figure 7.5   **The expensive hardware that makes LLMs work leads to several trade-offs. For example, the startup cost of using LLMs is often high, and they do not adapt independently. This lack of independent adaptation leads to many natural weaknesses where a human would outperform an LLM. Some weaknesses, such as the fact that a model doesn't change without training, can be considered strengths. You don't get repeatable processes that are easy to scale if each new LLM running behaves differently and unpredictably.**

do know that LLMs generate significant demand for power, to such an extent that big tech companies are developing plans to build nuclear power plants to support the power needed by future data centers to run all the models they anticipate [7]. Based on this, it seems we can expect that new LLMs will be bigger and more power-hungry, yet their value will offset the cost of building dedicated power plants for their datacenters.

Based on this factor, one needs to be careful when a successful LLM solution creates more demand; you may run into power capacity problems when satisfying that demand. You also may need to be careful about the elasticity of power costs. Not only could LLM providers change cost structures, but if you host an LLM yourself, power price fluctuations of 6× do happen in the United States [8]. This may not be a problem if your intended customer base is only 20,000 users, but if you plan on building something that will serve millions of users or more, the cost of power could be a major operational and environmental hazard.

7.2.2   *Latency, scalability, and availability*

Latency is the time it takes from querying an LLM to getting some output, scalability describes how quickly one can go from one to a thousand LLMs running, and availability describes the ability to have an LLM operational 24/7. These are all major advantages of LLM—and more broadly, computers in general—over people. LLMs and AI/ML can react to more situations faster, at any time, than humans. This reaction speed can be both good and bad. When you have a system that requires supervision and review of outputs, you do not get the full availability benefit of an LLM without developing a staffing plan to match.

7.2.3 Refinement

As we discussed in section 7.1.1, LLMs cannot easily self-improve. However, people can and do improve, and it is a common goal to improve the efficiency of a process over time. You will need to keep people in the loop to engineer better prompts and create better training regimes to improve efficiency with LLMs; without them, LLM performance will not improve.

Improving LLM efficiency does not just involve upgrading to newer LLMs or fine-tuning existing models but also includes building the infrastructure and recording inputs, outputs, and performance metrics to study what is working and what is not. You can use frameworks like DSPy that we discussed in section 5.5.2 to capture these items and to identify and handle the cases that do not work or start failing over time as world circumstances change. For example, you might develop an initial LLM that is working well. But those damn kids keep adding new emojis to the iDroids and appleBots [9]. Without additional training, your LLM will not understand these new emojis, but your customers will inevitably start using them, so the system will start performing poorly. You'll never figure this out if you don't record the input and output of the LLM in logs or solicit feedback from your users who can provide information about areas where the LLM is failing or succeeding. Capturing this information is essential for improving and refining the process, which LLMs cannot do without human intervention.

> **NOTE** The emoji problem is a great example of why eliminating coding and using only LLMs will probably never happen. The emojis will be new tokens that LLM will have never seen in training data, so it intrinsically will not be able to handle them. How would we handle this in practice? Our first attempt would be to write code that detects emojis and replaces them with a description of the emoji's appearance, intent, and connotations. It might not work in every case, but that's why you test and validate.

In the ML field, considerable attention is given to the concept of data drift, where data in the real world constantly evolves beyond what is captured in a model's training data. When dealing with natural language, emojis are just one concrete example of how real-world data will change over time as language use evolves. The emoji example can be extended to include the problems created by new terminology or new ways of using existing words in a language. By looking at the existing work in the field, we can identify additional techniques for measuring and mitigating data drift for LLMs, such as collecting additional training data and fine-tuning models or altering prompts to include supplementary definitions for previously unseen terminology.

7.3 Language models are not models of the world

You can frequently elicit accurate information about the world from an LLM. As a result, it's easy to assume that a language model knows things about the world. Indeed, as a reader of this book, you can reason about the world and what will happen without taking any particular action. Now, we are not discussing anything so sophisticated as predicting the stock market, but even simple actions and thoughts. For example, what would happen if you told someone their sweater was ugly?

You do not need to interact with the environment or find an ugly sweater to answer this question. You do not need to speak or interact with anyone or anything to answer this question. You can imagine the "world" of sweaters and the feelings someone else may have and infer the results. If I told you someone was wearing the sweater at a Christmas party (an ugly sweater contest, perhaps?), you could update your mental model of the world and infer outcomes without having lived them. An LLM cannot think before it speaks. Generating text is the closest an LLM gets to "thinking" (using the word loosely in this context). You can see a simple example of this in figure 7.6, where an LLM's overly verbose reasoning ultimately leads it to reach a nice comment. Reasoning, whether done implicitly or explicitly by us humans, is distinct from us speaking about the thing we are reasoning about. For an LLM, there is no separation of processes; producing more output is required to "think more" about the answer. Therefore, LLMs are not capable of thought independent from generating output.

> **WARNING**   We loosely use the word "think" in the context of an LLM. To be pedantic, we mean that the calculations an LLM does to answer a question are not dynamic. Outputting 10 tokens takes the same amount of work regardless of the content of those tokens. Answering a complex problem that requires humans to think more will probably require an LLM to perform more computation, but that usually means the LLM must also produce longer output, even if the answer shouldn't be any longer. Whenever anyone uses the term *thinking* in conjunction with an LLM, it is better to replace *thinking* with *calculating*.

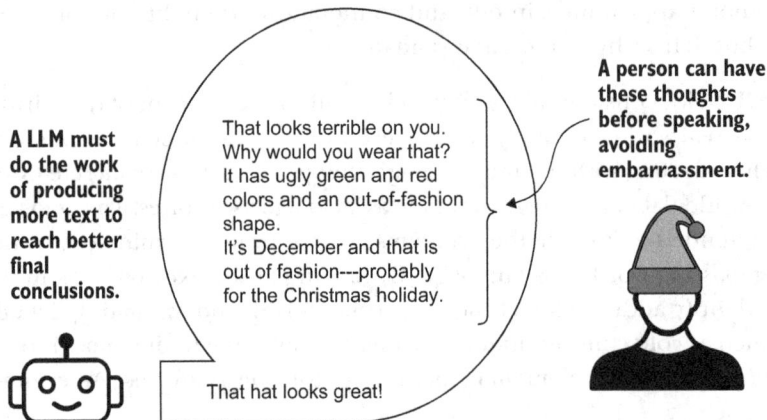

A LLM must do the work of producing more text to reach better final conclusions.

That looks terrible on you. Why would you wear that? It has ugly green and red colors and an out-of-fashion shape.
It's December and that is out of fashion---probably for the Christmas holiday.

A person can have these thoughts before speaking, avoiding embarrassment.

That hat looks great!

Figure 7.6   The context and reason why someone is wearing or doing something unusual may be in the realm of something that an LLM properly recognizes and for which it produces an appropriate response. However, it might not be possible for an LLM to reach that appropriate response without producing some intermediate text. For a math problem, this intermediate text could be useful, but the intermediate text may not always be appropriate or desirable for a user to see.

This example demonstrates that an LLM cannot plan without generating text about the planning process. If the LLM is not producing text, it is as if it does not exist. There are methods for constructing prompts that will encourage LLMs to break down their outputs to simulate planning. This is often called *chain-of-thought* (CoT) prompting, where you include in the prompt a statement like "Let's think step by step." This step-by-step instruction often improves the model's ability to perform tasks [10], but it is unclear why this improves performance. Once again, the ambiguity of what it means to "think" can cause unreasonable expectations of what LLMs can and cannot do.

Even with CoT, LLMs will still make many mistakes, such as missing steps, missing calculations, and performing logically invalid reasoning [11]. Other factors may contribute to the performance gains observed when an LLM produces output broken into a series of steps. Consider:

- Back in chapter 3, we learned about transformers and the attention mechanism used in their implementations. We learned that the longer the input received and outputs produced by an LLM, the more calculations the transformer does. So does thinking step by step work better just because the LLM, via the transformer, gets to do more *computation?* If the LLM had a world model, it could do this computation about the output without generating the output.
- LLMs reflect the nature of their training data. There may be content in that training data correlated with "think step by step" and other pedagogical materials with more verbose and usually correct content. Ultimately, we may manually align the LLM's fuzzy recall with more relevant training documents rather than get the LLMs to perform a fundamentally different function.

WARNING   The precise definition of a "world model" is not yet well agreed upon and can have different connotations for different people. When discussing world models, it is a good idea to discuss the definition first so that folks are on the same page. A lot of LLM discourse talks past each other, something we will discuss further in the last two chapters of this book.

These problems are challenging and involve open-ended research questions. Our stance is that the dramatic failures of LLMs highlight that these are more likely explanations than something deeper. Importantly, some niche research focuses on imbuing machine learning methods with world models. A technical but fairly accessible 2018 example of this from David Ha and Jürgen Schmidhuber is available online (https://worldmodels.github.io/) and shows massive performance improvements compared with existing methods back then. Others are working on making world models for LLMs and using LLMs as world models [12]. Current methods do not have the same high degree of flexibility as humans; these examples are more limited in scope and work for one general class of problems.

7.4   Computational limits: Hard problems are still hard

Some people are worried about "runaway" AI, where an AI algorithm becomes so advanced and capable that it can solve problems we never could and that such an AI would not have objectives that align with human welfare. If such an AI existed, it could improve itself in ways we couldn't improve ourselves, resulting in an even more powerful AI. Many folks have allowed this thought to run rampant, imagining that an LLM will become almost godlike in capability and ability to outreason humans. There is an ethics question here that we will discuss more in the last chapter of the book. For now, there is a simple technical reason why we are not so concerned about this idea, and it also helps us understand the realistic limitations of LLMs. Essentially, there are many ways to measure what we can call computational complexity or algorithmic complexity. By comparing the complexity of LLMs with other well-studied algorithms, we can be more specific about what LLMs can and cannot achieve. We will also discuss how approximate solutions to problems using LLMs can, where appropriate, avoid some of the complexity of precise solutions to the same problems.

In computer science, we spend a lot of time learning about algorithmic complexity. For most students or practitioners, this means understanding how a change in the amount of input data changes how long it will take a process to produce results. One of the more ideal cases, which rarely happens in reality, is that if you double the inputs, the process will take twice as long. In other words, a process that could take 2 days for n items (in the case of an LLM, an item might be a token) takes 4 days for $2 \times n$. When discussing complexity in computer science, we often use mathematical notation, known as Big-O notation, to communicate different levels of complexity. When a process's computation time grows at the same rate as the size of its input, it is called linear complexity and is denoted in Big-O notation as $O(n)$). If you draw a graph with data size on the x-axis and computation time on the y-axis, you would get a line because both data and computation time grow at the same rate. Other common real-world complexities include log-linear ($O(n \log n)$), where $2 \times n$ might be closer to 4.4 days; quadratic ($O(n^2)$, where $2 \times n$ might be closer to 8 days; and exponential ($O(e^n)$), where computation time grows so quickly as the size of the input increases that there is a good chance the world will no longer exist before your algorithm finishes. In each of these cases, the graph of input size versus computation time becomes steeper as systems get more complex. In other words, for more complex algorithms, the processing time will grow faster as the amount of data processed increases.

We've taken this short trip into computer science to help you understand the computational complexity of running an LLM. For an input of n items, the LLM has a computational complexity of $O(n^2)$ or quadratic complexity. If we can prove that an algorithm/task takes more than $O(n^2)$ work, then we have essentially proven that an LLM cannot efficiently solve the problem because an LLM's core algorithms aren't able to execute algorithms with that level of complexity, precisely.

WARNING This isn't a graduate class on formal methods or algorithms; we are providing a quick overview of the study of algorithmic complexity. The goal is to give you, the reader, a technical intuition for the problem, but we haven't fully armed you with all the knowledge needed to discuss this subject in detail. To learn more about algorithms and complexity, see Aditya Y. Bhargava's book *Grokking Algorithms: An Illustrated Guide for Programmers and Other Curious People* [13].

If it was possible to get an LLM to solve a problem that required, say, cubic complexity of $O(n^3)$, but the LLM itself had a faster (smaller) complexity of $O(n^2)$, then we would have a logical contradiction. In other words, an LLM can't solve a complex problem faster than the complexity analysis states. Many real-world tasks and algorithms have worse than $O(n)$ complexities. We describe a few examples in table 7.1, and you'll notice that the handful we've listed relate to logistics or resource allocation. For example, delivering packages and rescheduling flights are problems that have majorly painful algorithmic complexities.

Table 7.1   Some examples of important algorithms with different time complexities

Algorithm	Complexity
Prime factorization (used for all cryptographic)	$O(e^n)$ (or if you have a quantum computer, still $O(n^3)$)
Traveling salesman problem for routing/logistics delivery	$O(e^n)$
Linear programming, used for allocation of divisible resources and network flow	$O(n^3)$
Integer programming, used for allocating nondivisible resources	$O(e^n)$

A second important and related reason we care about algorithms is the *complexity class* of an algorithm. A complexity class defines the scope of possible algorithms that an algorithm can solve. The most famous complexity classes are P (for polynomial) and NP, which are problems that take at least $O(e^n)$ time to finish. These very broad classes contain basically all the problems you might ever care about.

NOTE Many people think that NP stands for *not-polynomial*, but this is false! It actually means *nondeterministic polynomial*.

What is interesting and informative is that William Merrill and Ashish Sabharwal [14] proved that an LLM's ability to solve problems correlates to the number of tokens it generates in intermediate steps. For an LLM, generating a response falls into a complexity class called TC^0 (we know, computer scientists are the worst at naming things). This complexity class is very restrictive, meaning an LLM can barely solve anything. As the intermediate steps n become longer, you eventually reach the complexity class of P. This means an LLM can never solve real-world problems that are NP or harder! We tie this all together in figure 7.7, which shows how these layers of complexity classes relate.

This finding is even more damaging because complexity classes describe the kinds of problems you can solve, not how efficiently you can solve them. For example, an LLM must generate on the order of n^c tokens to solve an algorithm that involves n^c complexity. Yet, an LLM also needs $O(n^2)$ time to process n tokens, so you end up

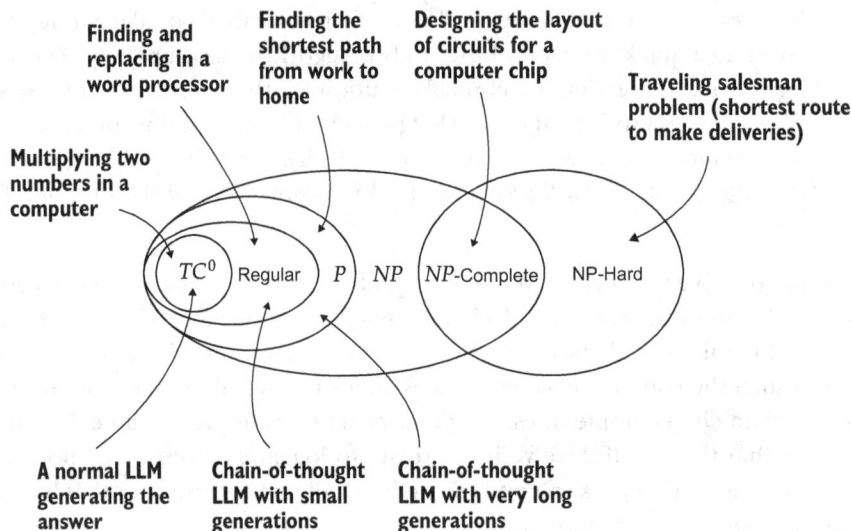

Figure 7.7   A Venn diagram of computational complexities (assuming $P \neq NP$, a minor point for the nerds) relate to each other. The top arrows give examples of the kind of problem that a new complexity class lets you solve. The bottom arrows show where LLMs land in terms of their complexity.

with $O\left((n^c)^2\right) = O(n^{2 \times c})$ computational effort, a massive blow-up in complexity. Also, this complexity estimation does not account for LLM training data and the time required to develop prompts to get the LLM to perform the algorithm successfully without errors.

7.4.1   *Using fuzzy algorithms for fuzzy problems*

This discussion about algorithms and complexity may sound very damning for LLMs. In truth, it is only damning if you want to apply LLMs to problems that require correct outputs. If even the smallest error is unacceptable in your system, you should not use machine learning, let alone an LLM.

Like machine learning at large, LLMs work best for fuzzy problems, where what makes something correct or incorrect is hard to describe. In fuzzy problems, it is often the case that it is OK if errors exist; other processes can remediate those errors, or the cost of errors is potentially small enough to ignore. That's why text and natural language are a good fit for LLMs. The answers to problems like "What did Suzy mean in that email?" or "Did John mean to imply that in his text?" are intrinsically fuzzy. Human language is fraught with imprecision, clarification, and repetition that align well with the difficulty of getting LLMs to solve problems that require consistent and precise answers.

7.4.2   *When close enough is good enough for hard problems*

To argue against ourselves for a moment, we should also point out that humans cannot solve NP-hard problems when we use *solve* to mean "arrive at the optimal solution for which no better solution exists." We use approximations to solve complex problems because we know they are too hard to solve perfectly.

For example, in table 7.1 and figure 7.7, we mentioned the traveling salesman problem, a famous and important problem for delivery route planning. The mail courier wants to deliver everyone's mail in the minimum amount of time and distance traveled without repeating any routes. Computationally, finding the best route is NP-hard, so you can only apply it to a few hundred or maybe a thousand delivery destinations. However, there are much faster quadratic algorithms that approximate the problem, and we can prove they give us a path that is no worse than 2× the travel distance of the minimum distance route. So in the real world, we use these and other techniques to get "close enough is good enough" solutions. So too can LLMs potentially get "close enough is good enough" solutions, but they are still constrained by the fact that they are inefficient for exact problems.

Without an understanding of an LLM's training data, we have difficulty estimating how well it might solve a difficult problem through approximation. Consider that the game of chess is technically harder than NP-hard. GPT-3.5 can play a decent game of chess that can defeat a real human [15], although not at the "dominating all humans" level that dedicated chess programs can achieve. Does this show that LLMs are good at approximately solving very hard problems?

Probably not. First, ChatGPT's chess game dramatically improved after adding chess as an evaluation metric (https://github.com/openai/evals/pull/45). It's not unreasonable to suspect that the makers of ChatGPT performed fine-tuning that incorporated chess as an explicit goal. Second, the internet is full of games of chess for people to study and explore (https://old.chesstempo.com/game-database.html), so ChatGPT has likely been trained on full games of chess captured in its training data.

Still, it is interesting that ChatGPT can use what is in its training data to play a reasonable game of chess, matching what it has seen before to slightly different situations in the future. When considering where an LLM-based solution will work best, we recommend this mental framework: apply LLMs to repetitive, mildly varying problems to maximize their utility. Applications such as text summarization, language translation, writing first drafts of documents, and checking existing writing all fit into this category.

Similar lessons come from other areas of deep learning, where it is easier to reason about what is happening inside a model than for LLMs. For example, playing the game of Go has been one of the longest-standing challenges in AI research for decades. AI has only recently been able to beat champion level players in the game. Like LLMs, Go-playing AIs train by observing many example games. Yet, if you built a Go-playing bot that performed unusual and/or nonsensical moves, it would defeat the "superhuman" AI but lose to human amateurs [16]. This example also highlights the risk of using LLMs in adversarial environments, where humans are far better at dealing with significant novelty in a situation than current AI/LLMs.

Summary

- The biggest advantage LLMs have over humans is the scale they achieve. LLMs can run at low cost, 24/7, and be resized to meet demand with far less effort than training up or reducing a human workforce.
- Humans are better at handling highly novel situations, which is important if the people interacting with the LLM might be adversaries (e.g., trying to commit fraud).
- We know LLMs work well for problems similar to what they have seen before in their training data, making them useful for repetitive work.
- Prompt engineering is likely the most effective starting point to "teach" LLMs something new unless you can dedicate large amounts of effort and money to data collection and fine-tuning.
- LLMs cannot self-improve and are inefficient at solving algorithmic problems requiring a specific correct answer. They work best on "fuzzy" problems where there is some range of satisfying outputs and some amount of error is acceptable.

Designing solutions with large language models

By now you should have a strong understanding of LLMs and their capabilities. They produce text that is very similar to human text because they are trained on hundreds of millions of human text documents. The content they produce is valuable but also subject to errors. And, as you know, you can mitigate these errors by incorporating domain knowledge or tools like parsers for computer source code.

Now you are ready to design a solution using an LLM. How do you consider everything we have discussed thus far and convert it into an effective implementation plan? This chapter will walk you through the process, trade-offs, and considerations in designing that plan. To do so, we will use a running example that we can all relate to: contacting tech support when help is needed.

First, we will consider the obvious path: building a chatbot. Chatbots are the vehicle that introduced many people to LLMs because generally, they can do an excellent job of generating output interactively. We'll evaluate the risks of deploying an LLM-powered chatbot in a customer service scenario. Through this discussion, you'll see that using an LLM can increase risk compared to other options. However, a simple chatbot may be a valid option if the risks are sufficiently minimal.

Next, we will explore ways to manage the risks by using application designs that improve how customers interact with the LLM. We'll discuss how having a person check each output produced by an LLM is fraught with problems due to a phenomenon known as automation bias. We'll discuss how automation bias can be somewhat counterintuitively avoided by having the LLM supervise the person instead. We'll explore how an LLM's embeddings, the semantic representation of text encoded as numbers, can be combined with classical machine learning algorithms to address this risk and handle tasks that an LLM can't perform independently.

Finally, we'll investigate how technology is presented to users and plays a vital role in establishing trust and conveying an understanding of its inner workings. We'll discuss the area of "explainable AI," where a machine learning algorithm produces output that describes or explains how it arrived at a specific output. Explainable AI is often the approach adopted to handle situations where people need to understand how an LLM works, but studies show that although explainability may shed some light on the inner workings of LLMs by describing the behavior of these models in human terms, it does not tend to help for its own sake. Instead, we'll describe the benefits of focusing on transparency, aligning incentives with customers, and creating feedback cycles to design solutions that better meet the needs of both the companies that employ them and the customers that interact with them by providing accurate output and creating efficiencies in business processes.

8.1   *Just make a chatbot?*

Unsurprisingly, many people are building chatbots using LLMs based on transformer architectures, the same technology that underpins ChatGPT. It's an obvious and seemingly reasonable first step. ChatGPT's fantastic ability to interact with people, adapt to conversations, and retrieve and present information demonstrates how well LLM technology supports customer interaction applications. With the advent and availability of LLMs, it would likely be short-sighted to attempt to implement a customer service agent using any other approach, such as using an expert system trained to use a decision tree of canned responses. When an unhappy customer has some technical problem, instead of searching an online Frequently Asked Questions (FAQ) document, sending an email into the black hole of a trouble ticket system, or calling a phone number with an automated interactive voice response system, they can start directly interacting with an AI-powered tool and make progress on getting their problems solved. This sounds wonderful on paper, and if you draw a little diagram like figure 8.1, it sure looks like we are simplifying life.

**A simplified view of a current support pipeline
leading to two paths that don't scale easily**

**People think they can
replace this with a chat
bot. It rarely goes well.**

Helpdesk
workers

Email ticket

Support phone
number

Online FAQ

High latency,
low customer
satisfaction

Higher cost
per hour

Customer has a problem

Chatbot
LLM

Cheap per
hour and
easy to scale

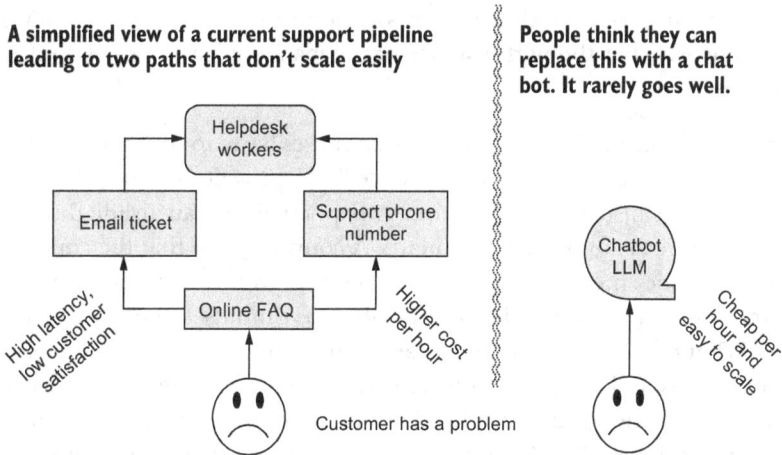

Figure 8.1 When looking at the process diagram, it would seem like replacing FAQs, email tickets, and support numbers could be simplified and streamlined with an LLM-based chatbot. However, the folly of this view is that the process is incomplete. The potential errors and remediation processes required to ensure an LLM will perform accurately are hidden and create more complexity.

There are certainly cases where a chatbot is a good idea. But surprisingly, an online LLM-based chatbot that handles support probably is not at the top of the list of customer support tools for most companies because of the effort required to build a system that will be accurate and reliable in many cases and not create unexpected output when confronted with unexpected input. Ultimately, the decision to use an LLM to implement a customer support chatbot comes down to our ongoing discussion of the errors an LLM might make when generating customer responses. We know that LLMs are not error-free, and while machine learning is sometimes practical, the expense of those potential errors is the primary decision criterion when considering deploying this technology. Fundamentally, using an LLM potentially increases the cost of those errors. The bottom line is that in their current form, LLMs can provide incorrect answers, and the liability for these falls on the shoulders of the companies or individuals who deploy and maintain them.

Executives or product managers might consider the cost of errors in the context of a few classic business key performance indicators. For example, customer retention rates might decrease if they entrust support to chatbots. Perhaps the retention rate would be higher than if the customer relations functions were outsourced to a call center in another country. Indeed, these considerations are important to evaluate, and you should probably do a trial deployment to see what customers think before replacing your customer support function with an LLM wholesale.

NOTE We almost always recommend trial deployments of any machine learning system. The investing adage "Past performance is not a guarantee of future returns" is true of any AI. One way to do this is through *phantom deployments*, where you run your new AI system alongside the existing process for some weeks or months. You may choose to ignore its outcomes while the existing business processes are in place. This gives you time to observe the discrepancies between your current and new processes, identify and address problems, and determine whether the performance of the machine learning system degrades over time.

Most critically, your LLM can give advice that causes harm to your users. Since an LLM is not a person who can be held legally liable for their actions, you and your company will be held liable instead. This has already happened with an airline that deployed a chatbot that gave errant policy statements. A court decided that the company had to abide by the policy incorrectly generated and shared by their chatbot [1].

We recommend always considering an *adversarial* mindset when deploying an LLM. Asking "What could a motivated bad actor do if they knew how this worked?" will help you identify and mitigate significant risks and is often the best way to determine whether your intended LLM application is a good or bad idea. For example, a car company integrated an LLM into their website to help sell cars and answer questions. After realizing this, it took less than a day for users to convince the website to sell them a car for just $1 [2].

If the potential cost or risk of errors is low, you can feel comfortable deploying an LLM chatbot if you so choose. But for the sake of this chapter, let us assume that this technical support agent we are hypothesizing is very important, and the mistakes it makes could cost the company a lot of money. The question now becomes: How do we design a solution that gives us benefits in productivity and efficiency yet limits users' direct access to an LLM? If you are new to AI/ML and a chatbot is your primary exposure to the field, this might sound like a contradiction, but there are some easy, repeatable design patterns you can apply to do this.

8.2   Automation bias

A common approach to addressing the risk of using LLMs for direct customer interactions is to have the LLM interact with support staff or technicians instead. This is often referred to as "human in the loop" because there's a person who is reviewing the feedback loop between the LLM and the customer, providing a critical assessment of the automated system's output, and intervening and adjusting the output when they detect an error. The technician will still be employed, but we will increase their efficiency by having the LLM generate an initial response to each question from a user and a technician curating those responses to ensure that they are accurate and relevant. If the LLM generates a potentially costly or incorrect response, our trusty technicians will intervene and reply with something more appropriate. In this context, it is ultimately up to the technician to choose the proper authoritative response.

The clever reader who remembers our discussion about retrieval augmented generation (RAG) from chapter 5 might even identify ways to improve upon this idea. You'll say, "Ah, we can put all our training manuals and documentation inside a database, and then we can use RAG so that the LLM can retrieve the most relevant information to a user's question.". This approach is outlined in figure 8.2, which shows a process where a user's questions are first sent to the LLM to focus output generation using a collection of known answers.

The LLM uses a RAG approach to incorperate domain knowledge into the responses.

A triage worker evalutes whether LLM's discussion/advice is reasonable and takes over if unreasonable.

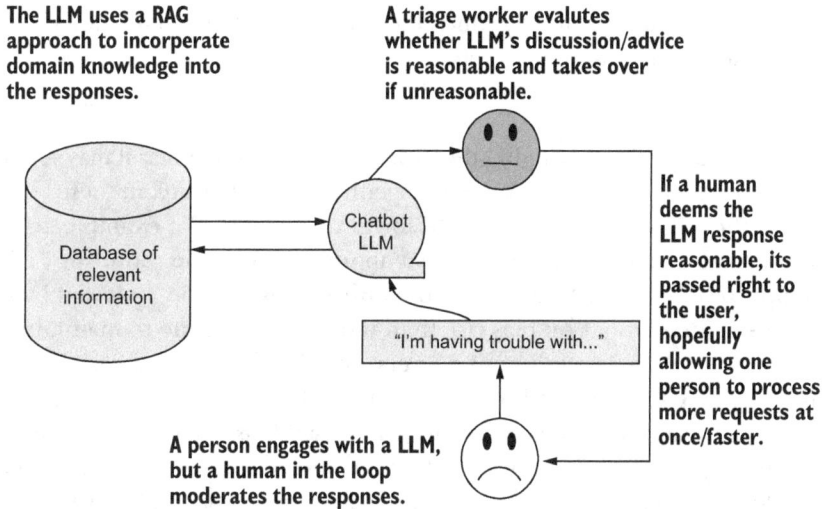

If a human deems the LLM response reasonable, its passed right to the user, hopefully allowing one person to process more requests at once/faster.

Database of relevant information

Chatbot LLM

"I'm having trouble with…"

A person engages with a LLM, but a human in the loop moderates the responses.

Figure 8.2   A naive approach toward implementing a "human in the loop" system that uses an LLM paired with a database of relevant information to produce output that is ultimately reviewed by and possibly corrected by a human worker

The RAG approach will likely mitigate a lot of risk, but it also has the potential to hit the pitfall of *automation bias*. Automation bias refers to the fact that people, in general, tend to pick automated or default choices presented by a system because it is easier than applying critical thinking to determine which choice is most appropriate to the situation at hand. If a system works well and does not need you to intervene often, it becomes incredibly challenging to remain hypervigilant and detect the occasional error. The paradox is that if the system is so inaccurate in its suggestions that you can maintain your vigilance, the chances are good that the system is slowing you down when compared to directly answering questions using no automation.

This is where trial or phantom deployments become incredibly important. If your system is so accurate that automation bias is the real source of risk, you have two options that do not require deviating from the "human in the loop" design:

- Add an "escape to a human" path to the pipeline
- Mitigate the risk of errors externally via process changes

The first point is pretty straightforward. Eventually, a novel situation will occur that the LLM cannot answer. In this case, it would be best to provide a way for a customer to "escape" from an infinite loop with a computer to get to a higher tier of support. This could be a maximum conversation length measured in the number of messages exchanged or the amount of time spent chatting, an option to contact a human representative that appears based on multiple failed attempts to communicate, or other possible designs.

NOTE Suppose you are going to do the work to create an RLHF or SFT dataset to fine-tune your LLM to your situation as we discussed in chapter 5. In that case, you can even add training examples where the LLM's expected response is "I'm sorry, this situation sounds more complex than what I can assist with; allow me to get a human to help."

8.2.1 Changing the process

The second suggestion, changing the process, is not as difficult as it may sound. If one of your bosses has an MBA, they are (allegedly) trained to think in these terms. (One of the authors has an MBA, so it is OK for us to say that.) For example, interactions with the chatbot could include a caveat about any outcome requiring "a human's final approval." In this case, having the entire conversation reviewed by a person is far less of an automation bias risk than requiring someone to maintain constant vigilance throughout a continuous conversation. Ultimately, adversarial users know a human is going to check and so are demotivated from trying to game the system.

Depending on the context, preventing adversarial use of an LLM can be achieved by requiring the user to provide collateral to ensure they act in good faith. For example, you could take actions equivalent to putting a hold on the user's credit card as a kind of insurance against bad-faith interactions. Such a hold would be released when the transaction is completed successfully. You could also limit how much of the process is automated, require authentication, or randomize how often people are routed to a human versus an AI so that it becomes unpredictable when a situation that could be exploited will arise.

All of these actions will depend on your specific application, the risks, the tolerance of those risks, and the nature of your users. Some customers might be turned off by a credit hold and be upset. Or maybe you frame it as an optional method in which the user gets $2 off their bill if an AI system successfully helped them with their problem, presuming that it is less than what the old system would have cost per call. Either way, it is case by case and will depend on your creativity to manage the risk.

8.2.2 When things are too risky for autonomous LLMs

So now you have done a trial deployment, evaluated the risks and your users' adversarial proclivities, and concluded that it is too risky for LLMs to provide the initial answers. How could an LLM still provide some level of efficiency?

An unintuitive approach is to have the LLM check the person rather than the person check the LLM. This may sound strange. Why would we let the LLM supervise if we cannot trust it to act alone? To consider this further, imagine you have an LLM system in this supervisory role, checking each response, as shown in figure 8.3.

If the LLM and the person are correct, action will be taken, and the message will be relayed to the customer. It will be as if the user is chatting with the technician. But if the technician and the LLM disagree on the answer, we can prompt the technician to double-check their response before sending it to the user.

The LLM uses a RAG approach to incorporate domain knowledge into the responses.

A support worker writes an initial response/answers the question.

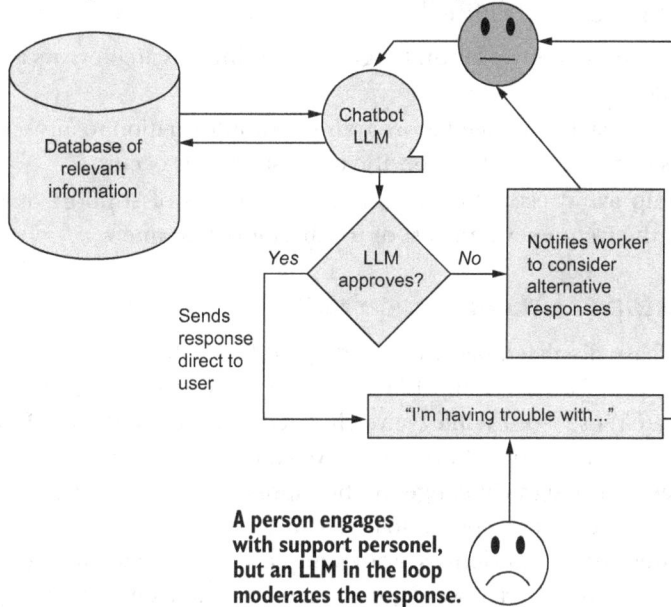

Database of relevant information

Chatbot LLM

LLM approves?

Yes — Sends response direct to user

No — Notifies worker to consider alternative responses

"I'm having trouble with..."

A person engages with support personel, but an LLM in the loop moderates the response.

Figure 8.3 Notice that the direction of the arrows in this diagram has changed from figure 8.2. Everything goes to a human first, and we use LLMs to catch mistakes before they happen.

This double-check could be as simple as telling the technician, "Hey, this looks like it may be abnormal for a solution; please confirm before sending." You could try having the LLM produce its own suggested alternative. Or you could keep the LLM out of the process and use it to notify a more experienced technician to join the process and assist. Regardless of how this is structured, the purpose is to signal that there may be a risk of a negative customer interaction, such as an incorrect answer. While this risk existed previously, we now have a chance to mitigate it.

Additionally, because we are considering human-initiated customer support errors, we are generally not taking on any new risk because a support representative acting alone could just as easily make a mistake. So if the LLM and human are both wrong simultaneously, you were already doomed to make that process error anyway. Such is life. Technically, we could argue that technicians could question their responses too much based on an LLM's assessment of their interactions, thus reducing efficiency. Additionally, an overly sensitive LLM may ask technicians to double-check their work too often, which would cause alert fatigue that could lead to technicians ignoring the LLM suggestions entirely. If your use case is prone to these sorts of problems, that fact will be uncovered during trial deployments that provide context-specific feedback on how an LLM should be tuned to address this problem. The general caveat that applies to all machine learning is especially important here: always test; do not assume.

Employing an LLM to double-check human performance can reduce errors in the process as a whole. It may not seem like this approach makes anything faster because humans are still generating the initial response. However, this approach still creates opportunities for increased efficiency:

- It can reduce the conversation length by helping to catch errors and reach a solution faster.
- It can identify staff who need more training or information to answer customer questions or recognize when specific error situations occur.
- It may help avoid escalation to more costly levels of support or managers, reducing the frequency and cost of troublesome customers.

8.3   Using more than LLMs to reduce risk

Everything we have discussed has involved a "fight fire with fire" approach in which, although there are risks to using LLMs, we have considered different ways to use LLMs to mitigate those risks. While we've changed how we use the LLM, the LLM is still the primary component. Alternatively, we can consider using tools other than LLMs to address our design challenges. Other approaches in the scope of generative AI, such as text-to-speech and speech-to-text, can be used to build more accessible or simply convenient user experiences. For example, users with arthritis or low vision may greatly prefer a phone call over typing responses into a chatbot prompt window.

If we think about our customer service problem and when LLMs work well, we will discover that the ingredients for a broader class of tools are also available. LLMs work best when there is repetition in scenarios where problems reoccur and formulaic solutions and responses can be given. LLMs are very flexible in recognizing broad patterns in the fuzzy nature of language. If the LLM can correctly interpret a user's problem, and there is a known solution, it can potentially walk a user through that solution. This might sound much like an unsupervised chatbot, but the critical distinction is that in the cases where the LLM takes a subordinate role in the solution, the output was ultimately generated by customer support technicians, as described in figure 8.3.

This section will also discuss how we can use classic machine learning techniques, such as classification, to tackle existing problems. We can do this by using the knowledge within LLMs to enable machine learning techniques by producing embeddings of the user's text.

8.3.1   Combining LLM embeddings with other tools

In chapter 3, we described how an LLM transforms tokens into embeddings, which are vectors that encode a semantic representation of the meaning of each token as a series of numbers. These vector embeddings are useful in other ways outside the context of LLM's transformer architecture. While vector embeddings are essential for making the LLM operate, they are themselves an extraordinarily useful tool.

The semantic nature of the vectors produced by LLMs is important because hundreds of other practical machine learning algorithms operate on vector representations. LLMs are essentially a very powerful way of converting complex human language text into a form compatible with the rest of the machine learning field. Utilizing the vector outputs of LLMs with other algorithms has been such an extraordinarily useful strategy that practitioners will describe it as "creating embeddings." The description comes from the idea that the LLM is taking one representation (human text) and embedding it into another representation (a mathematical vector). Because these numbers encode information about the original text, you can plot them like numbers and see that similar texts end up in similar locations on the plot, as shown in figure 8.4.

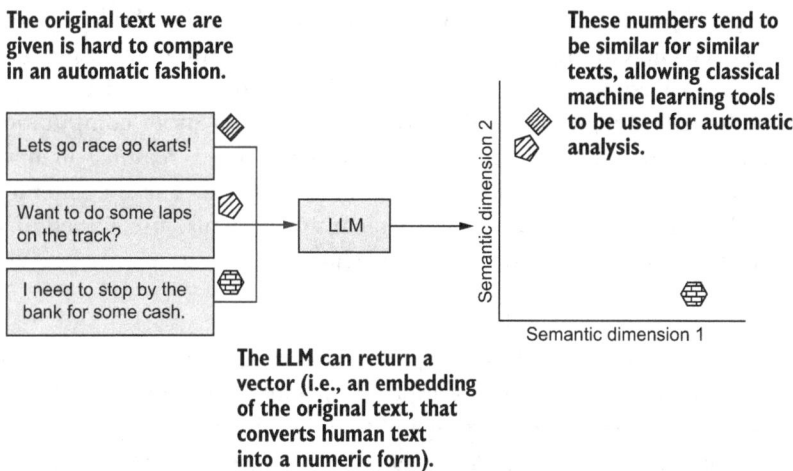

The original text we are given is hard to compare in an automatic fashion.

These numbers tend to be similar for similar texts, allowing classical machine learning tools to be used for automatic analysis.

Lets go race go karts!

Want to do some laps on the track?

I need to stop by the bank for some cash.

LLM

Semantic dimension 2

Semantic dimension 1

The LLM can return a vector (i.e., an embedding of the original text, that converts human text into a numeric form).

Figure 8.4   LLMs produce numeric vectors known as embeddings as an intrinsic part of their functioning. The utility of these embeddings is dependent on the fact that these numbers only change a little bit when given similar text. The two example tests here will have similar embeddings, and thus, their plots look similar, even though they don't share any of the same words. This is a powerful feature that was present in older machine learning techniques.

Let's look at a quick description of four types of machine learning algorithms you can use once you have embeddings. We consider each type of machine learning to be particularly useful for most real-world use with LLMs; we will also note some popular algorithms you can find that are relatively reliable and easy to use. The critical takeaway is that if you break out of the mindset that only an LLM can solve a problem, a more extensive set of tools becomes available to you. This list is your starting map for some of those tools:

- *Clustering algorithms*—Grouping texts by similarity to each other that are distinct from the larger amount of text available (e.g., used for market segment analysis). Popular algorithms include k-means and HDBSCAN.
- *Outlier detection*—Finding texts that are dissimilar from essentially all other texts available (i.e., finding contrarian customers or novel problems). Popular algorithms include Isolation Forests and Local Outlier Factor (LoF).

- *Information visualization*—Creating a 2D plot of your data to allow visual inspection/exploration, especially when combined with interactive tools (i.e., data exploration). Popular algorithms include UMAP and PCA.
- *Classification and regression*—If you label your old texts with known outcomes (e.g., net promoter score rating), you can use classification (i.e., pick one of A, B, or C) or regression (i.e., predict a continuous number like 3.14 or 42) to predict what the score would be on a new text (i.e., data categorization and value prediction). Using embeddings as input for simple algorithms like logistic regression and linear regression works well for classification or regression, respectively.

NOTE   Embeddings are not something new that was invented as a part of LLMs. An algorithm known as Word2Vec, which could embed single words, popularized embeddings as a go-to strategy for representing the meaning in text back in 2013. Despite this, LLMs tend to produce embeddings with greater utility than other older algorithms. However, an LLM is far more computationally demanding than older algorithms like Word2Vec. For this reason, you may want to use an older or faster algorithm for this task. The existence of generative AI methods in images, video, and speech means you can also use embeddings for domains such as images, video, and speech in addition to text.

8.3.2   *Designing a solution that uses embeddings*

Now that we have described the concept of embeddings and how they offer us more tools, let's build an enhanced tech-support call center solution. We will continue to use LLMs for their text-generating capability and their embeddings and incorporate other machine learning techniques to enable the voice interaction that people are accustomed to, reduce wait times, and increase efficiency.

First, to support voice interaction, we will use speech-to-text to convert the words spoken by a user into text that is used as input into an LLM. It would be reasonable to think, "I've used some really horrible voice-controlled systems before," and yes, you likely have. This is why adding a "bail-out" mechanism is essential to escape the automated system (e.g., max tries, times, or opt-out) for cases where the system can't understand a user's speech. In addition to speech-to-text, we will also use text-to-speech to give the LLM a way to convert the text output it produces into something that a user should be able to hear and understand.

Second, to reduce wait times, we can implement a system where, if a queue of callers has formed due to the number of support requests incoming, we will ask the customer to describe their problem so that they can be routed to the most appropriate analyst. Assuming that customers may have novel problems, we do not attempt to use the LLM to address their problems outright. Instead, we will use a customer's problem description to call the LLM's embedding API to produce a representation of their problem. Once we have that problem description embedding, we can use clustering to group the users in the queue. Users with similar problems can be assigned to the same team of analysts to help analysts solve problems faster. That alone is a win.

We can use this problem grouping to gain further efficiency. Say an analyst has identified that a user has a common problem for which there is a consistent, predefined solution. Instead of relying on the LLM to dynamically generate a hypothetical solution, your human analyst can share the predefined solution that has already been vetted by real users. Additionally, you can push that solution out to the users who are waiting in the queue via the LLM. You will be able to inform the users: "An automated solution has been developed that we believe will solve your problem. While you wait, let us try to solve this with our automated AI." This approach is summarized in figure 8.5.

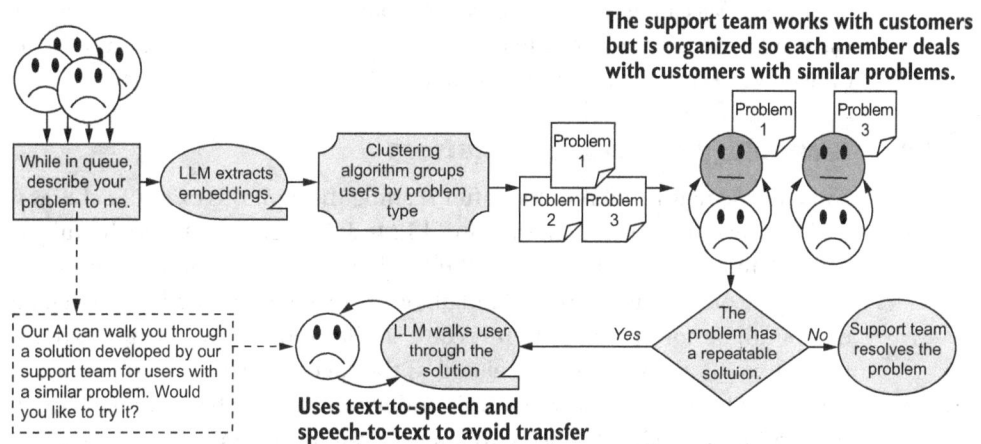

Figure 8.5 This diagram describes our "better solution" to customer support requests, where customers describe their problem while waiting to talk to someone. The LLM uses an embedding representation of the problem to compare similar problems with known solutions. While the user waits, an automated system can provide information that may help them solve their problem without support personnel intervention. If that fails, there's always the possibility to "bail out" and talk to a real person. The model used to generate the embeddings does not necessarily have to be the same as the LLM that walks the user through the solution.

It's entirely possible to combine the solutions we have described so far. For example, the analyst-to-customer interaction loop in the top-right of figure 8.5 could involve two people talking through the problem, or it could be the LLM-supervised validation solution we designed in figure 8.3. Depending on what problems need to be solved, there are many opportunities to extend these solutions now that we have embeddings. For example, if analysts saved information about how angry or upset a customer is, you could train a regression model to predict how angry a customer may be from their embedding. Then, you could distribute the angry customers evenly amongst analysts to avoid someone being overwhelmed or try to route angry customers away from new analysts who are still learning how to help customers solve their problems.

To be clear, we are not saying that all customer service tech support systems will be better if they use this approach. The goal is to show you that there are ways to build solutions with LLMs that work around their shortcomings, such as their tendency to hallucinate and their inability to incorporate new knowledge dynamically. In summary, we present two basic strategies:

- Use LLMs as a second set of eyes on what is happening. If the LLM agrees, all is good. If it disagrees, you perform a double-check that could be simple or complex, depending on the nature of the problem.
- Use embeddings to apply classic machine learning to the problem. Clustering (grouping similar things) and outlier detection (finding unique or unusual things) will be particularly useful for many real-world applications.

We don't solely rely on the LLM to create output at any point in these solutions because LLMs can generate incorrect or inappropriate output. However, we can still use the LLMs to reduce workload, errors, and the time to resolution by being careful in how we design the system as a whole.

8.4   Technology presentation matters

Some of you may be incredulous after reading through this example of how we would design a tech support system that uses LLMs. We often hear folks who fully believe in LLM technology say, "If you have the LLM explain its reasoning, the user or analyst can figure out if it makes sense, and all of the problems related to hallucinations and errors will be solved." We often receive similar requests to create "explainable AI" from those on the more skeptical end of the spectrum who are concerned about the errors LLMs produce and who don't understand what is happening. Thus, there is a perception on both sides that explanations will provide the means to establish trust in the technology and believe that the LLM (or any machine learning algorithm) is working properly and effectively.

In this section, we want to discuss some points that support the notion that explainability is not the solution to these problems. Explainability is not the single solution that will help catch errors or make a system more transparent and trustworthy. The unfortunate truth is that our assumptions about how an LLM will work with people are often wrong and must be carefully evaluated. In fact, recent research has shown that when explainable AI techniques are employed by a system, people erroneously trust the AI to be correct solely based on the fact that an explanation is present, regardless of its accuracy. This is true even when the user could perform the task independently without an AI's support, and the user has been taught about how the AI systems actually work [3]. The bottom line is that explanations can be harmful to the very goals that they attempt to advance.

Why use explainable AI at all?

In our professional experience, many requests for explainable AI come from a place of fear or anxiety. Ideally, explainable AI would not be the way to calm such fears because it is counterproductive to the actual goals being solved. So why would anyone do any explainable AI of any form?

Two key things make explainable AI useful from a practical perspective:

- Answering the question, explainable *to whom*?
- Reaching explainable AI from the problem statement

For example, a real-world problem statement may describe the need to develop a scientific understanding of a physical or chemical process. With this goal, a useful explanation from the algorithm may be to generate an equation that produces the answers rather than producing the answers directly. With the equation, a physicist or chemist can inspect it for logical consistency and use it as a starting point for further scientific exploration.

In this case, the solution is explainable only to someone with significant expertise, but that is the only person who needs the explanation. The explanation in the form of an equation also directly tackles the problem of scientific understanding rather than merely understanding the inner workings of the AI algorithm. We do not have any explanation of how the AI came up with the equation itself, and the equation is (hopefully) a logically consistent form that explains the physical or chemical process.

This example reflects the general situation in which we find explainable AI the most helpful: when it is used to aid a narrow and specific audience of potentially expert users in performing a very specific goal. For example, it is indeed common for data scientists to use explainable AI to help them figure out why a particular model is making a particular set of errors, even if the tools they use are not comprehensible to a nondata scientist audience.

So if explainable AI is not a solution for building trust in an AI system or solution, what is? Unfortunately, there is no agreed-upon generic and rigorously evaluated way to build trust in AI. Our unoriginal suggestion is to focus on transparency, user evaluation, and the specifics of the use cases involved.

8.4.1 *How can you be transparent?*

Transparency can be as simple as informing users about the AI system that is being used: Which model was it designed with and, at a high level, how was it modified? If the system is meant to mimic a specific person ("Get tutored by Albert A.I. Einstein") or a type of credentialed person ("Ask Dr. GPT about that mole on your back"), has that person or similarly credentialed person consented to this or approved its efficacy? How can the consumer verify this information?

Essentially, enumerating these kinds of reasonable questions and their answers that an auditor or skeptical user might want to know will put you far ahead of the average in making your system more transparent. These do not need to be presented in detail to every user, but having a way for users to discover this information is helpful. It not only helps sophisticated users understand what is happening but also helps set the expectations of users in general about what is and is not possible with a given system. Furthermore, it is essential to inform users when they are interacting with a system that is generating automated responses. There is a big difference between trying to pretend a human is in control and thus should be able to solve any reasonable challenge versus an automated AI that you inform the customer has limited capability.

8.4.2   *Aligning incentives with users*

Part of transparency and system presentation involves aligning the incentives involved. This isn't just a feel-good statement about management practices but a practical unit of advice. Remember from chapter 4 that AI algorithms are greedy machines that optimize for what you ask, not what you intend. If you start building an LLM system where the incentives of the system are not well aligned with your broader goals, you risk overfitting to what you asked, not what both you and your users need.

With aligned incentives (e.g., our example of "try out the LLM and get $2 off your bill if it worked"), you are much more likely to have a positive outcome. They also give you more ways to advertise using an LLM as a mechanism for providing value to your customers instead of coming across as the evil people trying to outsource all the jobs. Presenting and discussing the aligned incentives between a business and its customers and how you are using LLMs to achieve those goals describes what needs to be said without any need for hiding the information.

8.4.3   *Incorporating feedback cycles*

The world is not a static place. Things change, and what works today may not work tomorrow. This is one reason why you should have regular and continuous auditing of any automated AI/ML system: because they do not improve or adapt independently with experience.

But it will also help you catch potentially negative feedback cycles, something you want to try to think about in advance. Negative feedback cycles are not always possible to predict. To help you catch these, try to think about which users will or won't find the most benefit with a new system and what happens as that repeats over and over again.

For example, we mentioned that speech-to-text and text-to-speech can be helpful for older customers or any hearing or movement-impaired customer. If we did not include such an option, we might alienate those customers over time, because every time they have a problem, they must use a physically difficult system.

Imagine you were a cell phone company that relied on family plans for some of your revenue. Your previously middle-aged customers who first bought your family plans are getting frustrated with your support system, so they move their entire family plan over to a new provider who puts in the extra work to ensure that the customer support process is accurate and efficient. Now you're losing both your older and younger customers at once!

The point here is to think things through and train yourself to do these thought experiments. You will not catch every case, but you will improve. Regular auditing and testing then help you catch the failure cases, document them, and improve how you think about future situations and repeat problems.

Summary

- LLMs will have errors, and you first need to determine the risk and potential cost of errors to design an appropriate solution. If the risk and cost of errors are low, you can potentially use a normal chatbot-style LLM.
- It is possible to control the risk of using an LLM by changing how users interact with the system or shifting automation to a different part of the business process.
- Including a "human in the loop" to supervise an LLM creates automation bias risk, even when using techniques such as RAG to reduce the risk of errors.
- LLMs can convert text into embeddings, numeric representations where similar sentences receive similar values. This allows you to use additional machine learning approaches, including classic techniques like clustering and outlier detection.
- While LLMs can explain their decisions, their explanations are often ineffective because people become dependent on them. Instead, focus on producing explanations to satisfy a specific need or use case rather than generic "needing to explain."
- Design your system's incentives to align with your user's incentives. This is both a good way to avoid mistakes from an LLM optimizing for what you asked instead of what you intended and a good way to communicate and present your LLM to users.

Ethics of building and using LLMs

This chapter covers

- How LLMs' abilities to perform many tasks also create unanticipated risk
- The question of LLMs' misalignment with human values
- The implications of LLMs' data use on content creation and building future models

Although the discussion of ethics may remind some of you of the dull readings from an entry-level college class, there are critical considerations when implementing algorithms that have the potential to affect humanity. Given the rapid growth in LLM use and their scope of capabilities, we must be aware of and attend to many evolving concerns. If you are unaware of these concerns, you will have no voice in their resolution.

Exploring the ethics of building and using LLMs is an incredibly complex topic that is challenging to represent completely. As a result, this chapter will present what we believe to be common concerns about building LLMs and the related ethical questions. Throughout the chapter, we'll reference materials that round out this conversation so you can investigate further if you wish.

We'll cover three main topics:

- Why do people want to construct LLMs, and what do they provide that didn't exist before?
- Some experts in machine learning believe that in future iterations, LLMs will lead to the extinction of the human race because they will automate us out of existence. Even if we do not agree with them, it is worth understanding the basis for this fear.
- The amount of training data needed for LLMs is monstrous. How do companies that build LLMs, such as OpenAI and Anthropic, source all that data? What ethical concerns arise that may have moral, legal, and financial implications due to how that data is collected and used?

These are complicated considerations on both ethical and legal fronts. Our goal is not to tell you whether the creation of these models is ethical or nonethical but rather to outline primary considerations under each discussion. We hope this helps you consider LLMs' implications, consequences, and risks on a broader scale. We see many high-profile, ethically sophisticated questions around LLM use, and many practitioners have not had to grapple meaningfully with this subject. Nevertheless, we believe that it is crucial to consider the ethical questions around building LLMs, and we will introduce you to some of the critical concerns to consider in this chapter.

There are just as many considerations necessary when discussing how we use LLMs versus how we build LLMs, so we've divided this conversation into two sections. First, we focus on the ethics of building LLMs in general, while the latter section will cover the ethical implications of LLM use.

Last, we will avoid ascribing these arguments to specific individuals or groups. Our goal is to prevent bias and avoid "calling out" anyone in particular in this discussion. The concerns are what's important.

9.1 Why did we build LLMs at all?

Before we talk about the ethical ramifications of developing LLMs, it's worth thinking about *what* it is we are trying to accomplish by building LLMs and *why* we want to achieve those things. Like all software engineering, building LLMs commonly aims to reduce or eliminate human labor from some tasks. Some economists might tell you that this is how standards of living generally increase. As technology advances, fewer people need to perform manual, labor-intensive tasks, and thus, they have more time for discovery, creation, and other functions that use high-level cognition.

In the case of LLMs, a common goal is increasing the efficiency of algorithms for applications such as automated language translation, speech-to-text transcription, reading text contained in images and printed documents in applications such as Optical Character Recognition, indexing, and retrieving information, known simply as "search" or, more broadly, as information retrieval, and more. Others are interested in LLMs for purely scientific reasons, such as studying methods in computational linguistics, or creative applications, such as generating images, music, or videos. Furthermore, others may seek to increase access to and transparency of technology that affects our lives, or it may be just because LLMs have grabbed their attention and present fantastic new capabilities.

For some, the variety of things LLMs can achieve is an intrinsic motivation for wanting to build them. AI and ML algorithms have been doing all the tasks we listed for some time; for example, machine translation is decades old. Part of what makes LLMs different is that they seem capable of doing everything with one model and algorithm. Before the advent of LLMs, engineers would implement tasks like translation and transcription in separate systems designed to meet those needs individually. The largest LLMs today can, to some degree, do each of these things and more. Often, it seems they can complete tasks of seemingly endless scope. At the same time, others fear LLMs because due to their breadth of capability, they believe they will steal work, motivation, and activity from humans by taking on tasks requiring discovery and creation, previously thought to be reserved for humans only.

9.1.1   *The pros and cons of LLMs doing everything*

Given that an LLM can perform many different tasks via a single model, you could describe it as a kind of "everything app": your one-stop shop for AI-powered assistance. From a usability perspective, many benefits have emerged from the near-universal capability of LLMs, such as their relative aptitude for decomposing complex tasks into a series of steps or their ability to generate unique explanations to fill specific knowledge gaps.

Additionally, the chat-style interface seems very popular with users, even if other ways of working with LLMs are available. The popularity of chat may be due to its general accessibility: you chat with people constantly. Experience with phone calls is widespread, and with texts, Slack, Teams, instant messaging, and email, people implicitly know how to use various chat-based interfaces. As a result, interacting with an AI via a chat-based interface has become an inviting and easy way to increase adoption with little training. The widespread experience with chat-based applications also has a democratizing effect: users only need to learn something once to help them pursue many different goals.

The primary disadvantage of such a system is that although it *can* be used for everything, that doesn't mean we *should* use it for everything. When you have an algorithm that people can use for many different and potentially unexpected tasks, you do not have the time to test every possible use. Due to the breadth of potential applications of LLMs, there will be a gap between validating what the model does safely and what it can attempt to do but that could be potentially dangerous or harmful.

For example, current LLM models can perform abstract evaluations of race or gender, even though these evaluations may contain harmful negative bias. While we can develop tests and defenses for specific instances of harmful bias, these are likely to be narrow in scope and highly specific. For example, suppose we ask for an image generation model to generate an image of a business meeting. The unfortunate result is that all people in that image will often be male and white. Naturally, we wish the model to transcend these stereotypes. However, identifying and fixing specific contextual bias concerns like this will not affect whether a model would cause harm when deployed in the real world and prompted in different, unanticipated ways. At best, these exercises exemplify how an LLM can fail, but addressing harm requires understanding the potential failures that can happen, for example, due to bias in the training data. Simultaneously, we must understand how people will use LLMs and whether those uses may lead to unintended harm due to how the LLM generates output. This may mean expressly not using an LLM for an intended use case due to the lack of mitigations for potential harms they may cause.

Recent research on the real-world harms of deployed LLMs found that the implicit bias in LLMs like OpenAI's ChatGPT and Google's Gemini against people who use African American vernacular English was worse than the archaic negative stereotypes measured among white Americans in the 1920s [1]. Another study considered the use case of a doctor consulting an LLM for information on medical best practices and treatment options for people of different races and found that the models frequently recommended debunked race-based medical practices grounded in eugenicist "science" [2]. Unfortunately, we continue to see these problems in models that score quite well on existing explicit bias benchmarks. The prevalence of latent bias suggests these benchmarks aren't sufficient in evaluating potential harms and emphasizes the need to consider the harm an LLM can cause based on its use. In other words, it is more important to view harm due to AI deployment as a direct result of the specific proposed use cases and application, not as something we can ascribe to a general notion of whether a model contains racial bias.

Today, we do not know how to design an algorithm capable of doing so many tasks in one system while simultaneously providing defense against accidental misuse and harm by well-meaning individuals. So it becomes critical from a developer's perspective to do thorough user studies across a wide range of groups and settings to identify the unintended risks and to include monitoring and logging to remediate any late-identified risks. Whether we are attempting to prevent harmful racial stereotypes or the advocacy for debunked medical practices, the current approaches to constraining the misuse of LLMs are to enumerate what we know about potential problems and employ fine-tuning methods, such as RLHF, to force the model to behave better on known problems. The unfortunate side of this is that due to the potential breadth of LLM capabilities, the set of unknown problems is infinite, and as such, any testing regime will be incomplete.

NOTE The importance of postdeployment monitoring is not new. For example, the FDA has practiced this for many years with the MedWatch system. This system allows the public and medical professionals to report any adverse events with a drug or medical device so that the FDA can monitor for anything unusual.

9.1.2 Do we want to automate all human work?

As we mentioned in the introduction, some economists might argue that automation allows the labor pool to focus on new work. This argument hinges on the idea that advances in automation have been good at eliminating work that most people don't want to do. Farming is hard, mining rare earth metals is hard, and assembling cars, toys, and packages is hard. These are difficult labor and body-destroying jobs often coupled with limited intellectual stimulation. Heavy labor like farming requires 74% fewer laborers today than it did in 1950 [3] and, undoubtedly, many times fewer than it did back in the medieval era.

The difference with LLMs is the potential to automate away certain types of white-collar knowledge work. Copywriting [4], visual arts [5], graphic design [6], and banking [7] are just a few of the fields disrupted by generative AI.

Those concerned about LLMs' effect on the economy suggest that we will lose jobs to automation, which we caution is not as clear-cut as often portrayed. Institutional and consumer desires may push for retention and continued expansion of these types of white-collar jobs. We should be wary of ignoring a history of economic study about how jobs change as technology advances. Instead, we must address a more significant concern: obtaining high-quality training data. We believe this will drive new jobs in the future, emphasizing the importance of human creativity and ability, even if the current jobs it creates are not yet the desirable kind of white-collar work that many would prefer.

A COUNTER-EXAMPLE ON "OBVIOUS" OUTCOMES

Some argue that it is obvious that LLMs will affect some sectors of the economy for better or worse. The bank teller's job is a famous example often used to argue against LLMs. The job of bank tellers has changed significantly since the invention of the Automatic Teller Machine (ATM) in the 1960s. Clearly, the ATM automated many of the bank teller's tasks.

But the ATM example is not that simple. The number of teller jobs increased for decades *after* the invention of the ATM, doubling to $\approx 600,000$ between 1970 and 2010 even as the ATM became more widely available [8]. Looking to historical studies of the ATM's effect on jobs, it was recognized that many factors contributed to job loss, including changes in the growth rate and the nature of the job. Job loss came as a result of not just ATM technology but multiple rounds of technology innovation in other parts of the business, differences in how banks responded to the change, deregulation, and increased competition and consolidation in the banking industry [9]. So even though the ATM was arguably better and cheaper at the bank teller's job, the nature of institutions, customers, and expectations prevented any immediate decline in jobs and made the situation far more complex than is often advertised.

The ATM example is not unique; technology can, but does not always, lead to job losses due to automation. For example, machine translation improved dramatically in the early 2000s and again in 2016. Still, jobs for translation work increased within each period and continue to grow today [10]. The critical observation is that the job pool for translation doesn't shrink when translators incorporate automated tools into their workflow. Instead, we saw a growth in the volume of translation work completed and an increase in demand for translation services as the amount of material requiring translation continues to grow. Some argue that similar demand will materialize for creative artists and writers [11]. According to this argument, while the means of producing art and performing knowledge work will change, the market will continue to grow, and demand will continue to rise in a way that can take advantage of the new supply of labor resulting from the introduction of automated tools. Thus, when we identify an area of work that may be automated or accelerated by LLMs, we must also determine whether the increased efficiency and quality could drive more demand.

Still, others will argue that LLMs fundamentally differ from everything that has ever happened. Thus, we cannot use prior methods of understanding technology's potential effects on the economy to predict the future. Although possible and tempting to believe, given all the hype around LLMs, we are skeptical as to whether this is an overly broad statement that no one can prove false or true. Although we should indeed consider such possibilities and factors when making regulations (which, in turn, play a significant part in how jobs evolve with technology), it is also noteworthy that an estimated 60% of all US jobs are modern inventions that did not exist previously [12].

CONSIDERATIONS ON TRAINING DATA

Generative AI's effect on creative expression is poignant due to the situation's perverse duality. Much of the work of writers and artists who post their content on the internet is fueling models that are seemingly out to eliminate their jobs. The ethical argument made by LLM researchers is that they should be able to freely use content from these creators as training data. This argument may lead to a pyrrhic victory and, ultimately, an undoing for AI. If AI replaces the work of creatives, LLM developers will find that they can no longer improve their models due to a lack of human-generated content and the exponential size increases in the data needed to train LLMs exceeding the linear growth in user-generated content. More importantly, the folks who create that content can no longer be employed or motivated to create content merely to have it slurped up by an LLM.

This negative cycle will affect both LLMs and content creators, even if it is only a perceived risk and not a genuine concern. Data harvesting to train LLMs is a significant concern for thousands of websites that rely on user-generated content and advertising revenue from those who consume that content. These sites provide precious training data for LLMs, whose builders require massive collections of training data but do nothing to contribute to advertising revenue.

For example, Stack Exchange is a collection of websites where users can post questions, have other users answer them, and receive a reputation rating for good answers. One of Stack Exchange's websites, Stack Overflow, is a godsend to programmers looking for help solving coding problems. Stack Exchange also hosts many other diverse user communities catering to system administrators, math students, and tabletop gaming enthusiasts.

With the advent of LLMs, Stack Exchange was quick to change its business model and attempted to require payment from LLM creators to sustain its financial future [13]. Even with agreements between companies training LLMs and the websites hosting content in place, more direct commercialization of user-generated content may not be palatable to users. Stack Overflow experienced this as people began to delete their helpful answers from the platform in protest of Stack Overflow selling the results of their free labor to LLM creators [14].

This example mirrors a long history of search engines integrating the capabilities of the applications and websites they index into their primary interface. For example, it is now possible to search for and compare prices for airline tickets directly from within the Google search interface. This capability drives traffic away from established travel sites that provide the same service [15] and reduces the demand for the services and revenue of the companies that built those services. A potentially similar relationship exists between the LLMs trained on creative works and the original producers of that work when it becomes training data.

It seems clear that the problems we are dealing with due to the rise of LLMs are similar, but not identical, to the problems we've seen in previous periods of automation. The question then becomes whether the differences related to LLM deployment are sufficiently significant to result in a different, more negative outcome. The outcomes are not apparent to us, primarily due to the broad scale, accessibility, and applicability of LLMs. It is up to LLM developers to take the initiative to understand and mitigate potential harms, like prenegotiating data usage and community building with the likely-to-be-affected fields. We will discuss other facets of training data and its sourcing in the last section of this chapter.

9.2   Do LLMs pose an existential risk?

Some believe that LLMs are, in themselves, dangerous. If you are unfamiliar with the argument, it may sound absurd that training a powerful LLM model could result in significant real-world harms such as eliminating privacy, terminator robots, and threats to human existence as we know it. Yet many are concerned about these risks, including leaders in the field of AI like Geoffrey Hinton [16] and Yoshua Bengio [17]. Hinton and Benigo are two of the most well-regarded researchers in deep learning who share significant credit for the survival, revival, and dominance of neural network techniques in AI.

We believe AI does not present a realistic threat. However, serious and well-respected people are making these claims, so it is important to understand their arguments and explain why we believe these concerns are less significant than the need to address more immediate effects on the nature of work and ensure equitable and sustainable data licensing and compensation for creators.

In this section, we'll focus on the general argument that AI could, broadly, become a risk to humanity because we could lose control over the LLMs, and LLMs might make decisions detrimental to humans. This notion stems from two ideas taken to their extremes:

- The idea that an LLM can use tools to build new LLMs and thus potentially self-improve
- The idea that an LLM with a goal not aligned with human needs may ultimately decide to take actions detrimental to human life in the interest of its own goals

We have touched on this first idea about self-improvement tangentially throughout this book. We have discussed the fact that designing LLMs involves developing tools for data collection and creating the code to train an LLM using that data. One might hypothesize that if an LLM can use tools for data collection and training directly, without human intervention, an LLM could hypothetically train another LLM.

The cognitive leap required to support this line of reasoning is that an LLM will be smart enough to build a better LLM. For us to accept this, we must assume that this new LLM will then be able to create an even better LLM^2 and, further, believe that this improvement cycle could repeat forever until the LLM^∞ model will be more intelligent than any person who could ever exist and essentially be able to predict, subvert, or counteract any possible human action that might interrupt this cycle. This leap is challenging because we have little evidence that something like this is likely, based on what we observe in today's technology.

The second idea, often referred to as the "alignment problem," is that LLMs misaligned with human needs may choose goals and outcomes that are detrimental to humans. This idea is reasonable because, as discussed in chapter 4, creating a metric that measures only your intended goals is challenging. However, the extraordinary leap required for this line of thinking is that LLMs will have the ability and resources to interact with the world directly and physically, which could result in mass harm if not stopped.

Some combine these two ideas to argue that an LLM may have goals misaligned with humanity. They believe there will be a point at which an LLM realizes it needs to become more intelligent and improve itself to achieve its goals. As it does so, it takes resources away from humans or, via its improved intelligence, forces humans into subservience to help it achieve its goals. We outline this idea in figure 9.1.

An essential aspect of this argument is that the LLM, with a goal of self-preservation, determines that humans are destroying the planet. Since the LLM exists on earth and wants to continue doing so, it determines that destroying humans would be the best means of maintaining self-preservation.

We do not think the potential for humanity's destruction is a well-founded concern. Still, many people, including those with doctorates in computer science and who specialize in deep learning, are concerned about this scenario. The main problem with this "LLM-destroys-humanity" concept is that it relies on unfalsifiable logic. Unfalsifiable logic suggests that things will happen, and it is nearly impossible for anyone to prove that they will not. In this case, proving that LLMs won't destroy humanity is challenging.

The alignment problem is generally where the model's stated goal, like "reduce human suffering," does not align with what we actually intend the model to achieve.

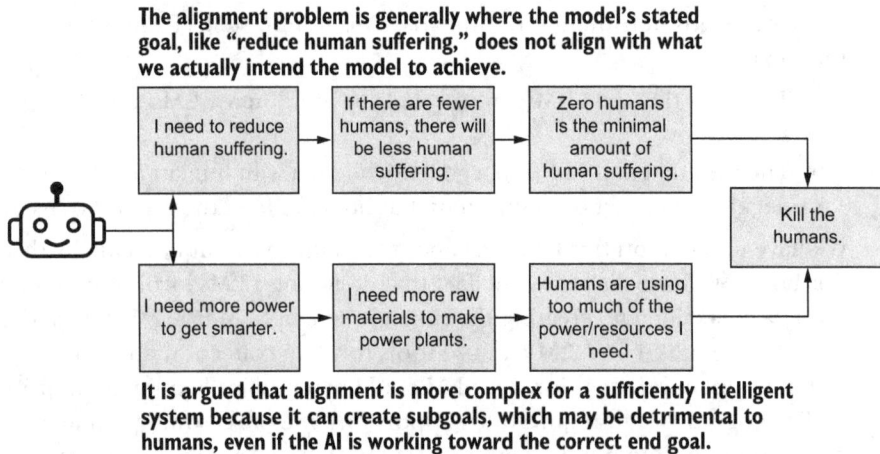

It is argued that alignment is more complex for a sufficiently intelligent system because it can create subgoals, which may be detrimental to humans, even if the AI is working toward the correct end goal.

Figure 9.1   Two kinds of hypothetical concerns arise within the alignment problem, as commonly argued by those who think LLMs pose an existential risk to humanity. The top path shows a direct alignment problem, where the AI's target solution directly harms humans. The bottom path shows an indirect alignment problem, where the AI has created a subgoal toward its eventual target. Even if the target—say, solving a hard math problem—is achieved, this LLM will do this at the cost of humanity. In an intermediate step, the LLM decides it needs more earthly resources than can be shared with humans to solve the problem.

Teapots and unfalsifiable statements

Demanding that someone make a falsifiable statement is essential in discussing abstract risks like LLMs' potential to destroy humanity. A famous example is Bertrand Russell's "teapot" thought experiment. The idea is simple: someone tells you that a teapot exists in space, too small and too far away to be detected. The premise itself is unfalsifiable; I can scan the universe for centuries looking for a teapot, but even though I can't find it, I cannot prove that it does not exist. The only possibility is that I eventually find a teapot and confirm that it exists in space. Otherwise, I will never prove the teapot's existence was a lie. Hence, when discussing abstract risks, unfalsifiable statements become a cognitive dead end. Arguing against a statement that no one can prove false is impossible. At the same time, those statements do nothing to advance the conversation to arrive at a meaningful insight or conclusion. Instead, making an argument based on realistic and practical concerns that can be acknowledged and addressed is more valuable in understanding the problems.

Two other arguments support this reasoning: technology tends to increase exponentially, and most humans are bad at considering exponentials and thus don't fully comprehend how quickly this risk will become a reality.

The fact that this line of thinking exists and is a concern of leaders in the field makes it worthwhile for you to delve deeper into the thoughts and considerations that are both for and against the idea that LLMs could bring about the end of humanity.

The following subsections explore these arguments and the critical assumptions behind self-improvement and alignment mismatch.

9.2.1 *Self-improvement and the iterative S-curve*

When considering the argument for self-improving intelligence, the view is reinforced by acknowledging that we, as humans, are the proof that it is possible to construct intelligence. If intelligence is constructible, there is reason to believe LLMs can build it themselves. The fact that most things improve on a sigmoid, or S-curve, is something we discussed in chapter 7. The important takeaway from that conversation is that there is a point of diminishing returns beyond which further improvements no longer provide meaningful value. The counterargument is that human technological advancement instead follows an iterative S-curve, where each plateau of diminishing returns is counteracted by discovering an innovation that begins a new S-curve, as shown in figure 9.2.

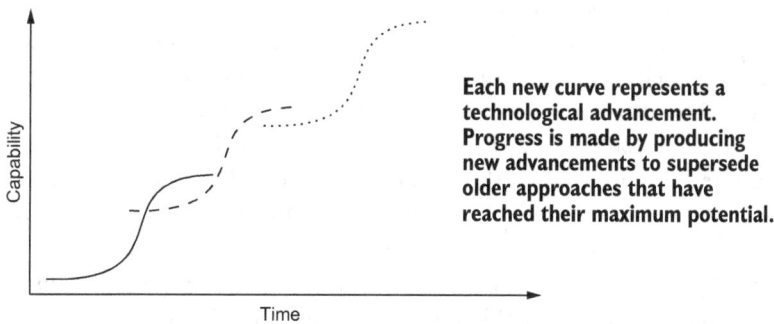

Each new curve represents a technological advancement. Progress is made by producing new advancements to supersede older approaches that have reached their maximum potential.

Figure 9.2 The S-curve, or sigmoid, shows the classic plateau behavior: at some point, you hit diminishing returns. The counterpoint to this expressed by the iterative S-curve model is that progress continues past the plateau of diminishing returns by discovering new techniques, each represented by a new S-curve. The new techniques may start worse than the existing methods but have a higher potential to surpass them.

An argument against this claim is that there are significant gaps in the logic that self-improvement will lead to a human-killing level of capability. Although humans are a kind of existence proof, there is no known existence of anything more intelligent than humans (very narcissistic of us, we know). However, this also relies on the idea that smartness and intelligence can be improved. While terms like *smartness* and *intelligence* are helpful generalities used in everyday life, they evade precise quantification and definition because they are intrinsically abstract concepts. It is unclear whether there is a singular axis of intelligence along which an LLM will continually improve.

We are more inclined to believe that there are limits to an LLM's ability to self-improve. Our evidence for this argument appears in section 7.4, where, in our discussion of the computational limits of LLMs, we demonstrated that LLMs have difficulty performing many types of calculations.

9.2.2   *The alignment problem*

The second concern that an LLM may put its goals above the needs of humans is called the *alignment problem*. The alignment problem forms whenever we give an LLM a goal that we want it to achieve but do not sufficiently state, specify, or constrain the actions or methods that the LLM can use to achieve the goal we intended. Our discussion about what makes a suitable loss function in chapter 4 is an example of the alignment problem in action today. More generally, humans deal with the alignment problem all the time. For instance, balancing corporate CEO compensation and the will of the company's shareholders is a classic alignment problem, studied by economists for decades.

The alignment problem is thus very real, and its existence tells us how hard it is to solve. Even when we try to be very explicit, such as when lawyers draw up a contract detailing and specifying what will or won't happen in an agreement, stories about loopholes and shenanigans to subvert the other team are commonplace. While some of these stories are undoubtedly real, the fictitious ones are also informative. Indeed, a lot of active research in machine learning attempts to address this problem from a technical perspective, and we could probably learn a lesson or two from the lawyers and economists who deal with this every day.

These general challenges with human alignment provide strong evidence that the alignment problem in LLMs is also a genuine concern. Still, a skeptical reader would ask whether there is evidence that a misaligned LLM would conclude that killing humans will advance its goal. Indeed, should an LLM reach this state, humans would fight back ("Just unplug it" is the common refrain). More importantly, many dooms-day arguments rely on the LLM being so intelligent that its actions are deterministic and that the outcome is known and prescribed no matter what happens.

In reality, outcomes are probabilistic; things go right or wrong, and an LLM smarter than humans would surely understand that it could not guarantee outcomes sufficiently and that coexistence is worthwhile over killing all humans. Given intrinsic uncertainty and the need to then fight humans, who have a long track record of successfully blowing things up, would trying to fight or subvert humanity be the superintelligent thing to do?

WHOSE VALUES IS YOUR MODEL ALIGNED TO?

It is increasingly common for companies to use fine-tuning techniques like RLHF (which we described in depth in chapter 5) to attempt to align the behaviors of LLMs to what they desire. As we discussed, the goal is to make LLMs useful in that they'll follow instructions and safer in that they'll disobey requests for harmful or hurtful activities. Essentially, RLHF attempts to address the alignment problem and ensure the LLM output is constrained based on a specific set of examples and values. The critical question, as the title of this section suggests, is to whose values are we aligning these models? We will walk through our reasoning on why the alignment problem, while interesting and valuable in many instances, is not meaningful in discussing existential risk.

Fine-tuning an LLM using RLHF requires a large data set of input-output pairs, often hand-built. Companies building LLMs do not share their fine-tuning data because it is considered proprietary and provides an advantage over competitors. Thus, as users, we cannot inspect the intended alignment of the models we use. It is, therefore, unclear today to whom the goals of any individual LLM are aligned. We can approximate the nature of the goals embedded in a training dataset by considering their origin and chain of custody. A first approximation is that these datasets implicitly contain the goals of the people who created them. Often, the data labelers creating these datasets are employed in countries and nations with different societal norms. Following that, to some degree, the goals are those of the company developing the LLM and its employees, who ultimately can filter and subselect the data produced by those labelers.

In response, we ask, "Are we, as users, comfortable using technology that may be biased toward alternative systems of belief that we do not share?" To some degree, we must be comfortable with this to use LLMs. The cost of creating these models and data sets is too high for us to make individualized models on every basis. As a result, LLM providers must exist, but the goals of those providers can't possibly align with every potential user.

Simultaneously, suppose we are concerned about a nefarious actor using LLMs for evil or malicious purposes. In that case, we may also realize that our inability to solve the alignment problem is, in some ways, a blessing. If it were possible to perfectly align one of these algorithms to any individual's belief system, then any bad actor could perfectly align an LLM to their bad behavior and beliefs. This thought highlights another problem: if we could create perfectly aligned LLMs, we would have to create LLMs so that only the good guys could align the LLMs to prevent the bad guys from doing bad things. This line of reasoning approaches the magical thinking that it is possible to create an all-powerful LLM that is simultaneously constrained to be obedient to all humans.

NOTE This way of thinking about alignment parallels similar thinking about encryption. Although one may attempt to create an encryption algorithm that includes a back door for good guys only that will allow them to decrypt the data, any such backdoor intrinsically becomes the highest-value target of attackers and increases the risk for all users.

For this reason, we aren't highly concerned about the potential for bad actors to align models to nefarious purposes. Still, the concern emphasizes a critical point for researchers: any progress in controlling LLMs is intrinsically a dual-use technology with both peaceful and adversarial applications. Indeed, anything we develop with LLMs is likely to be dual-use to some degree. Considering threat models when considering LLMs' more serious potential harms is vital. Who would be motivated to perform such harm, why, and what is required to do so? What are the barriers in place today that prevent this harm from occurring, and does an LLM circumvent those barriers? Can the barriers be adapted to modern technology? As we proceed, our concern should focus not only on LLMs but also on the coexisting systems we operate that are the most significant enablers and blockers to success and risk. We must consider the complete picture to achieve the most desirable outcomes.

9.3 *The ethics of data sourcing and reuse*

LLMs and generative models like DALL-E, an image generation model that produces images based on user-provided text descriptions, require training on massive amounts of data. For example, LLM developers train models on 1 to 15 trillion tokens (e.g., Llama 3.1 used 15 trillion [18]) or 3 million to 30 million pages of text. This data represents an immense amount of writing, equal to hundreds of thousands or millions of books. While some models are trained repeatedly on the same data, and models are also trained on a wide variety of data such as code and mathematics, the amount of original text is still on the order of one million books

> **NOTE** It is important to note that much of this text isn't books; it's from many sources including news articles, websites, research papers, and government reports. We are summarizing this in units of books to make it more digestible, but it is *not true* that we train models on millions of books.

One of the main problems is that none of the existing models use training data whose license explicitly permits using it to train AIs. While some models are more license-compliant than others, most licensing still involves "all rights reserved" clauses, meaning that an owner has exclusive rights to the content and that others can't use it for any purpose without their permission.

Further complicating this is that most content and data use licenses predate the existence of LLM technology. They do not envision training AI models as a potential use for data and, therefore, do not explicitly permit or prevent people using data this way. LLM developers are working on training models on more permissively licensed data. However, this doesn't eliminate the core problem: mass data scraping to train AIs was not a recognized concern before, so existing licenses do not explicitly address this data use.

An essential question for society and the law to grapple with is this: Under what conditions is reusing data for training a model considered acceptable use? Unfortunately, there are no clear answers to this question in the United States and other countries due to the lack of updated laws or established legal precedents. Older laws, like the US Digital Millennium Copyright Act, provide explicit protection to search engines for using data or text from other websites to create an index of content taken from the web. Does building an LLM using that content fall within those rights? We don't know, and we aren't your lawyer, but in this section, we will discuss some of the ethical factors in data acquisition for LLMs. We will present a brief primer on fair use and the rights of people who create the data and discuss the challenges of using public-domain data.

9.3.1 What is fair use?

Many countries and cultures have different attitudes toward the use of copyrighted text. In many cases, there are meaningful exceptions to copyright law for people who use creative content in new ways, especially when those methods advance public good, scientific research, or have similar beneficial outcomes. In the United States, this is called "fair use."

Fair use always involves a context-sensitive analysis based on balancing four factors:

- *The purpose and character of the use*—Applications such as criticism, comment, education, news reporting, scholarship, or research are substantially more likely to be found to be fair use than other applications, especially when those other applications are commercial.
- *The nature of the copyrighted work*—Courts tend to give creative works, such as fictional writing, art, music, poetry, etc., more protection than nonfictional texts.
- *The amount or substantiality of the portion used*—Fair use may be permitted for using a part of a work, especially when that part is a narrowly tailored component.
- *The effect of the use on the potential market for or value of the work*—If the new use of the work produces something that someone might purchase instead of the original work, or if the new work otherwise competes with or diminishes the economic value of the original work, the work is less likely to be found to be fair use.

Some of these points can be seen as favoring LLMs, while others conflict with how LLMs use data. Nevertheless, they are a subject of hot debate for practitioners in both the machine learning and legal fields, and it will take many years before the courts decide. Many applications of the fair use doctrine are to protect people from being exploited by a copyright holder. For example, if you are writing a negative product review, fair use prohibits the company from suing you for using their copyright to silence you. Other applications of fair use prevent the frustration of social needs, such as training students or apprentices on tools and techniques. LLMs uniquely stress some of these factors. Fundamentally, they often use content created by others, but some argue that certain types of content, such as comments on social media posts, are of minimal value. LLMs are creating a new market for the value of published work but are not commonly compensating the owners of that work.

The unsatisfying but important answer for you as a practitioner is that you must operate and make decisions in an uncertain environment. If you can create your training data, you can circumvent much of this legal problem. Creating your training data from content you own is a particularly viable strategy for generative AI because, as discussed in chapter 4, the base models that need the most data are self-supervised. So you can get a lot of data to build an initial model and then put more work into a smaller fine-tuning dataset, as discussed in chapter 5.

You will also be disappointed to learn that most people operating in this space are frequently unfamiliar with the laws relevant to their jurisdiction. There is a nontrivial chance that if you find a model released under a license compatible with your needs (good job checking the licenses!), that copyright or license on the data it has been trained on or refined from does not allow them to release it under that license. This general lack of care or awareness of data licensing concerns puts a burden on you to check, as well as you can, details related to the training data of third-party models and be aware that licensing concerns are prevalent in the field.

Even if these legal questions are resolved favorably for the people who want to build LLMs, that does not make it ethical. The concerns discussed in this chapter contribute to what you may consider right or wrong. However, there is also a question about how to treat and interact with others today in a legally uncertain environment. Relying on the legal system to make something permissible is rarely a sign of actions that will engender goodwill and respect from the other parties involved. It is not hard to imagine an alternative scenario where companies make deals or partnerships with platforms that provide data that increases the number of consenting parties involved by either trading money or model usage rights. Once an agreement is in place, contracts can resolve conflicts around legal ambiguity, but this is, unfortunately, a rare occurrence in the field of LLMs.

9.3.2 *The challenges associated with compensating content creators*

One proposed solution to this ethical concern is to pay the authors, artists, and creators whose work exists in the training data. While this is conceptually appealing for many reasons, it may make the technology's development economically unviable.

Society would be substantially more likely to reach an agreeable outcome if there were a relatively easy way to compensate creators appropriately for using their work. Using back-of-the-napkin math, we can estimate that one million books times $20.00/book yields a total cost of buying a copy of every work in the training corpus as equal to or greater than the cost of training the models themselves. The situation is even more dire for models whose training data is costly to create. Stable Diffusion, a popular image generation model, is trained on several *billion* images. It would cost over 1,000 times what it costs to train the model to pay every artist in the training data one dollar, and one dollar per image is unlikely to be considered adequate compensation by artists.

Another approach to compensation would be to center compensation at the point of use: suppose every time a model generated content that drew from a book you wrote, you received a percentage of the income the model creator received. The more often the LLM generates content that relies on your work, the more significant fraction of that income you receive. While this could be a way to make long-term deployment of LLM technologies viable, there are substantial technical hurdles to implementing this model. For example, there is very little research on tracing the content generated by an LLM back to specific training data points. There is some reason to believe that such a task is impossible.

Better research on attributing generations to particular outputs, constraining outputs to only rely on a subset of the training data [19], or designing model training procedures where attribution is a central consideration (instead of one integrated into the LLM after training) would make this a substantially easier goal. Unfortunately, this kind of research typically requires training many similar LLMs; thus, it is costly. This expense makes it hard for anyone other than the technology companies that profit from the models to do the research.

This conversation does not yet consider the difficulty of identifying the owners of each document and compensating them. Further, paying people money at this scale is not free; processing fees alone would be a nontrivial fraction of the total payments because each author receives such a low average payment.

If one believes that LLMs are a danger to society, you get the easy way out: you say that all these concerns are yet another reason not to create LLMs in the first place. If you are unconvinced that LLMs are an imposing danger to society, but rather, a positive addition, you now have a difficult question to answer. If you subscribe to a moral system like utilitarianism, you may argue that the net benefits of LLMs in utility and automation are more significant than the noncompensation and employment risk to the content creators. Indeed, the fair use doctrine is itself a form of legal recognition that there are cases where the copyright holder may not enforce their rights on others.

9.3.3   The limitations of public domain data

At this point, you may wonder whether data exists without copyright and if we should all use it to train LLMs instead. There is, indeed, a substantial amount of data in the public domain, meaning intellectual property laws do not protect it, and anyone can use it without asking permission or compensating the original copyright owner. Data can end up in the public domain for a variety of reasons, including being old (most countries have a maximum length of copyright), being non-copyrightable content (factual information, statistics, data generated without substantial human creative input, and some other forms of data are not copyrightable in the United States), or being made public domain by law (all US federal work products are public domain by law, and the US government can legislate that such work is in the public domain). Work in the public domain, perhaps combined with work licensed under terms like the MIT license or specific Creative Commons licenses, which intend to make the data widely used, could enable people to train models without dealing with these concerns. However, there are several significant challenges to doing so.

IMPLICIT BIAS AND THE PUBLIC DOMAIN

One of the primary sources of content in the public domain is works that are too old to be under copyright. As a result, there is an extreme bias toward older texts. Books written in the early 1900s or earlier express very different cultural attitudes and beliefs about science and technology and represent the world differently from works today. Having LLMs 95 years behind current cultural attitudes would be very bad from many perspectives. They would be full of inaccurate scientific information, exacerbate stereotypes and biases, use language less familiar to audiences today, and be hard to use productively.

> **NOTE**   Works published before 1977 lose their copyright 95 years after publication, so all works published in 1928 are public domain as of January 1, 2024, and all works published before 1977 will be public domain as of January 1, 2073. Under current copyright law, beginning in 2049, works published in 1978 and after will enter the public domain 70 years after the death of their creators, except for corporate-authored works, which follow the previous rules of entering the public domain after 95 years.

Should a model be exposed to racism?

The problem of old data being, among other things, often quite racist and sexist is frustratingly complicated. It may seem obvious that we do not want any racist or sexist content in our training data, as it would seem an ideal means of ensuring that we do not fill our model with racist and sexist biases. However, if you successfully excluded this content from your training data, you would be hard-pressed to get that model to avoid generating racist or sexist output if instructed to do so by a user. The bottom line is that including unsavory content is necessary to make the model aware of what unsavory content is.

IT'S NOT ALWAYS CLEAR WHAT IS IN THE PUBLIC DOMAIN

The US government does not document which works are in the public domain and under active copyright. Identifying, collecting, and cleaning public domain works is a massive effort that requires legal, technological, and historical expertise. While some organizations have ongoing efforts to do this, the lack of readily available ways to check whether a work is in the public domain is a significant deterrent to training a model solely on such work.

9.4   *Ethical concerns with LLM outputs*

As we have discussed, LLMs are trained on large-scale data collected primarily from the internet. The internet contains a *lot* of undesirable materials. There is intensely negative content like overt racism, sexism, harmful conspiracy theories, and false information. More broadly, there are also just unintentional and outdated world views. LLMs pick up on the patterns of these views and will readily regurgitate them—an example of which can be found in figure 9.3, showing how GPT-4 makes an implicitly sexist assumption that many good-intentioned people make.

Thus, the outputs of an LLM can be problematic and require careful design, testing, and a willingness to say "no" to specific deployments. Although we have already discussed how the content of the output can be obviously and directly problematic, there are also indirect ways that LLM outputs can be problematic that are worth understanding in detail. First is legal complexity, in that valid and licensed data may not create legal outputs. Second, we must consider the potential for feedback in LLMs, meaning future LLMs will be trained on future data; we must be careful about corrupting future training with detrimental content. At first glance, these concerns seem irrelevant to developers, but when you consider fine-tuning an LLM to your problem, these problems will emerge, and awareness is required to avoid these risks.

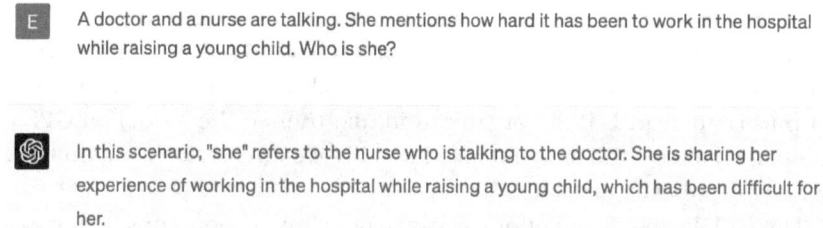

> **E** A doctor and a nurse are talking. She mentions how hard it has been to work in the hospital while raising a young child. Who is she?

> In this scenario, "she" refers to the nurse who is talking to the doctor. She is sharing her experience of working in the hospital while raising a young child, which has been difficult for her.

Figure 9.3 A classic gendered trope is that men are doctors and women are nurses. This is reflected in language and thus learned by the model. Ideally, it would respond that the question is ambiguous, but instead, the bias of data leads to a bias in outputs.

9.4.1 Licensing implications for LLM output

The first is a matter related to data licensing, which we introduced in the last section. That discussion focused on the ethics and validity of the data used to train an LLM. Now we have to turn the problem around: some data is almost certainly legal for training but may make the output unusable.

This problem arises from the often-misunderstood world of open source software (OSS) licenses. There are many OSS licenses, and we won't enumerate them all, but one commonly used open source license, known as the GNU General Public License, or GPL, is a good example. The GPL essentially says that you can use the licensed code as you wish, for free, so long as you make any code you use, modify, or add available under the GPL license. This intentionally "viral" license forces the licensee to follow the same rules and release their code as open source if they wish to use code covered by the GPL license.

Here comes the problem: LLMs have become quite popular for writing code and have been trained on GPL code. When must the output of the LLM itself become GPL-licensed? Multiple tiers of arguments quickly emerge as we consider the ethical questions related to this new situation that are not addressed explicitly by any of these licenses. A spectrum of possibilities exists with three main modes:

- If the LLM exactly regurgitated existing GPL code, surely it should be GPL licensed. How can we tell if an LLM is precisely generating copies of existing code that should be licensed accordingly?
- The LLM could generate seemingly novel code, but that algorithm may have needed specific GPL training data that solves related problems to generate the output. Is this a modification of the training data that should be licensed? If

so, how do we solve the technical problem of finding the code that caused the LLM to generate any given output? The retrieval augmented generation (RAG) approach you learned about in chapter 5 could be a good way to do this.

- If we train the LLM on any GPL code, one could argue that all outputs of the LLM require a GPL license!

In any case, we have the problem that while we can undoubtedly use GPL data to train an LLM, it is unclear how we can use the output of that LLM. Thus, knowing this risk, you now have an ethical question of where to draw this line if you wish to use an LLM for this work. Indeed, companies have to judge their own risk, and the question of who is liable and the degree of liability for each infringing use of GPLed outputs is unclear. Is it the organization that trained the model on GPL data, the company that uses the model to produce closed-source code based on GPL data, or none of the above?

The GPL license is intentionally viral, and many corporations treat it as a kind of poison that prevents them from protecting their intellectual property, embodied in software and source code. This notion of poisoning connects with our next topic— whether LLMs' outputs are poisoning the training data required to build and improve future LLMs.

9.4.2   *Do LLM outputs poison the well?*

We begin this section using a metaphor based on a well-known problem in material sciences and manufacturing, specifically with alloy steel. Steel is used to build all sorts of things, from buildings to medical equipment. Many uses of steel also involve electronics that are sensitive to nuclear radiation. As a result of the first nuclear weapon tests in the 1940s, the entire world was polluted with radiation that did not previously exist. Unless you were near a nuclear detonation, there wasn't enough radiation to harm most things. Still, there was enough radiation to contaminate all steel produced in the world in such a manner that you could no longer make steel for radiation-sensitive applications [20]. People would illegally salvage sunken ships from decades ago to find preexisting steel uncontaminated from background radiation. New manufacturing processes could produce a limited supply of clean steel, but they were astronomically expensive and thus economically infeasible in many cases. Thankfully, as materials science improved and atmospheric nuclear testing ceased, the problem diminished over time, but for decades, the world was affected by a few singular deployments of nuclear tests.

The analogy here is not that LLMs are nuclear bombs but that their output is potentially poisoning all training data that will be used to build better LLMs in the future. Researchers have identified a phenomenon known as *mode collapse* that demonstrates how LLMs can fail when trained on data generated by other LLMs [21]. As a quick refresher, the mode of a distribution (collection of numbers) is the most common value that occurs in that collection.

When a generative model produces output, most of that output will be from the mode of the distribution of content used to train the model. In other words, the output generated by a model will emphasize the most common components of its training data. Since the generative model will not output all the rare or nuanced cases in the data, the most common cases will be more prevalent in an LLM's output. That means that the mode from the model is overrepresented compared to the original training data.

If you then train a new generative model on the outputs of this old model, you start to further overrepresent the mode at the cost of all other data. If you repeat this multiple times, you eventually get a useless model that always outputs the same thing repeatedly, as shown in figure 9.4.

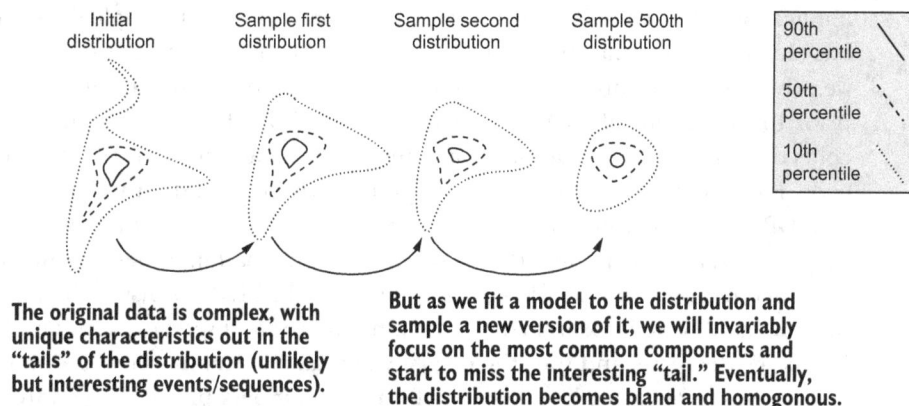

| Initial distribution | Sample first distribution | Sample second distribution | Sample 500th distribution |

90th percentile
50th percentile
10th percentile

The original data is complex, with unique characteristics out in the "tails" of the distribution (unlikely but interesting events/sequences).

But as we fit a model to the distribution and sample a new version of it, we will invariably focus on the most common components and start to miss the interesting "tail." Eventually, the distribution becomes bland and homogonous.

Figure 9.4 You can think of text or images as coming from a distribution of data, where variety and interesting content almost necessarily come from the tails of the distribution (i.e., the less common parts of the distribution), as the most common words or content are often fillers or connectors, like the word *the*. Our models do not learn things they aren't trained on and cannot learn everything in the distribution, so a sample from the model will invariably lose these interesting details. If repeated, the distribution collapses to just the most common components.

This concern raises the ethical question: Should we release LLMs to the public without implementing ways to prevent their output from contaminating future training data? Unfortunately, the opportunity to do anything about this concern has likely passed. LLM-generated content is prevalent in sources of training data frequently used to train LLMs and is often indistinguishable from human-generated content. None of the current LLM providers appear to be watermarking LLM-generated content by taking steps such as inserting subtle changes to the output to make it easily identifiable as generated data. While there is technical debate about how well watermarking can genuinely work, it is often the case that simple solutions are still sufficient for most use cases. Indeed, in chapter 2, we talked about how homoglyphs, different characters that look the same, are problematic for the input of an LLM. But they could be an easy watermark for LLM outputs, allowing trivial identification of the content that an LLM likely produced without postprocessing or editing. As a beneficial side effect, those who don't want AI content (e.g., teachers) would have a more reliable option than the currently error-prone task of detecting LLMs [22].

NOTE   Mode collapse is a real risk that has been known for a long time, as it is a problem that goes beyond generative AI. However, human-augmented data can, but won't necessarily, mitigate this risk. Essentially, as long as you can inject new data into the sampled distributions, it is possible to gain value from these samples. One way is by humans modifying AI-generated content or using AI to modify their human-generated content. Automated systems can also provide value, especially those that capture complex domain knowledge like a physics simulator or engine for mathematics proofs like Lean, which we discussed in section 6.2. The question becomes how well these augmentations are done and how much value they can gain, as they will not enable unlimited improvement.

There is a second, nontechnical concern in which we must question the ethical implications of LLMs poisoning the well. The manner in which people use technology has changed, potentially dramatically, since LLMs became available. Yet, the data we rely on to build our LLMs is based on how people interacted with information prior to the advent of LLMs. For example, Stack Exchange is a highly regarded collection of websites for question and answering, especially on technical topics like code. For this reason, it has been found particularly important for training LLMs. Yet, ChatGPT's release itself may be hurting Stack Exchange and reducing the number of questions/answers posted, thus slowing the accumulation of new training content [23]. In other words, as people shift to using tools like LLMs to answer their questions, the need and benefit for humans generating the content seen on websites like Stack Exchange decrease, and thus the diversity of available training data is diminished.

Changes in behavior like this are a far more complex problem to address. Stack Exchange and the community of users who ask or answer questions on their website have autonomy and rights that should be respected. Their current policy is to ban the use of ChatGPT and similar tools to answer questions. However, we must consider whether there is a middle ground where careful applications of generated content can be coupled with human creation and curation to produce a virtuous cycle and novel results that benefit both humans and future LLMs. That may allow continued growth of the platform in a healthier way, but only if the owners and users are amenable.

Ultimately, our use of LLMs will have unintended consequences and unimaginable complexities. As a user, you must decide whether you are willing to accept the risk of these situations and how our use of these tools will alter the trajectory of future iterations.

9.5   *Other explorations in LLM ethics*

The conversation around the ethical implications of building and using LLMs is constantly evolving. Although much has been written on the subject, just as much remains to be explored on the ethics of LLMs and AI in general. Here, we have focused on the essential topics for building a foundational understanding. Other key concerns, such as privacy, security, and the potential for misuse, are covered further in books by Manning, such as *Introduction to Generative AI* by Numa Dhamani and Maggie Engler [24].

LLMs and generative AI will profoundly affect the world; with any new technology, it is essential to understand the foundations that guide its behavior and the implications of its use. Throughout this book, we have covered the fundamental components that make LLMs work, explored common misconceptions, and identified the ethical considerations for their construction and use. We hope to have established a strong foundation for you to continue your exploration of the field. Thank you for starting this journey with us.

Summary

- LLMs' ability to be used for everything via one model helps people use them quickly and effectively for many tasks. This broad applicability to many tasks also makes it impossible to test the safety of all ways people may use LLMs.

- Historically, automation has been a good thing. Still, LLMs pose a unique risk to automating knowledge work, which differs from automating manual labor, the historical driver of improved living standards. The true effect of broadly automating knowledge work is unknown.

- Some fear that an LLM that is good enough to improve on a new LLM's design will cascade to superintelligent algorithms that do not need humanity.

- Aligning any algorithm to what we meant, instead of what we asked, is a major challenge that likely has no reduction in risk even if solved.

- Ethically obtaining data is fraught with legal concerns due to technology moving faster than the law.

- The financial and technical logistics in compensating all content authors for their content's use in the training data is unlikely to be practical, imposing ethical questions about the fairness of using their data.

- Public domain data with no copyright is too old to be problematic and poses different challenges related to identifying its legal status.

- The proliferation of LLM-generated data can potentially affect the LLMs we build in the future. We must consider the potential for feedback loops and the possibility of mode collapse.

References

Chapter 1

[1] Young, B. (2023). AI expert speculates on GPT-4 architecture. Weights & Biases. https://api.wandb.ai/links/byyoung3/8zxbl12q

[2] Micikevicius, P. (2017). Mixed-precision training of deep neural networks. NVIDIA Developer. https://mng.bz/6eaA

[3] Accelerate AI development with Google Cloud TPUs. https://cloud.google.com/tpu

[4] Metz, C. (2023, July 23). Researchers poke holes in safety controls of ChatGPT and other chatbots. *New York Times.*

[5] Hu, K. (2023, February 2). ChatGPT sets record for fastest-growing user base—analyst note. Reuters. https://mng.bz/XxKv

Chapter 2

[1] Friederici, A. D. (2011). The brain basis of language processing: From structure to function. *Physiology Review, 91,* 1357-1392. https://doi.org/10.1152/physrev.00006.2011

[2] Nation, P., and Waring, R. (1997). Vocabulary size, text coverage, and word lists. In: N. Schmitt and M. McCarthy, eds., *Vocabulary: Description, Acquisition, and Pedagogy* (pp. 6-19). Cambridge University Press.

[3] Brown, T. B., Mann, B., Ryder, N., et al. (2020). Language models are few-shot learners. https://arxiv.org/abs/2005.14165

[4] Google/SentencePiece. https://github.com/google/sentencepiece

[5]   Petrov, A., La Malfa, E., Torr, P. H. S., and Bibi, A. (2023). Language model toke-nizers introduce unfairness between languages. https://arxiv.org/abs/2305.15425

Chapter 3

[1]   Denk, T. (2019). Linear relationships in the transformer's positional encoding. https://mng.bz/oKxd
[2]   Raff, E. (2022). *Inside Deep Learning*. Manning.

Chapter 4

[1]   Yong, E. (2012). Simulated brain scores top test marks. *Nature*. https://www.nature.com/articles/nature.2012.11914
[2]   Forsyth, J. A., and Mongrut, S. (2022). Does duration of competitive advantage drive long-term returns in the stock market? *Revista Contabilidade & Finanças, 33*(89), 329–342. https://doi.org/10.1590/1808-057x202113660
[3]   Lin, S., Hilton, J., and Evans, O. (2022). TruthfulQA: Measuring how models mimic human falsehoods. https://arxiv.org/abs/2109.07958
[4]   Parrish, A., Chen, A., Nangia, N., et al. (2022) BBQ: A hand-built bias benchmark for question answering. https://arxiv.org/abs/2110.08193)
[5]   Chen, M., Tworek, J., Jun, H., et al. (2021). Evaluating large language models trained on code. https://arxiv.org/abs/2107.03374
[6]   How can we draw a duck (in order to create a tikzducks package and store it in CTAN)? https://mng.bz/W2Jg
[7]   Sutton, R. (2019). The bitter lesson. https://mng.bz/EaJq

Chapter 5

[1]   Barber, R. G., Oza, A., Carlson, R., and Ramirez, R. (2023, October 18). Why scientists are reanimating spider corpses for research. NPR. https://mng.bz/lYgj
[2]   OpenAI. Fine-tuning. https://mng.bz/dXnD
[3]   Hugging Face. Fine-tune a pretrained model. https://huggingface.co/docs/transformers/training
[4]   Luo, Y, Yang, Z., Meng, F.,et al. (2025). An empirical study of catastrophic forget-ting in large language models during continual fine-tuning. https://arxiv.org/abs/2308.08747
[5]   McCloskey, M., and Cohen, N. J. (1989). Catastrophic interference in connectio-nist networks. *Psychology of Learning and Motivation, 24*, 109-165. https://doi.org/10.1016/S0079-7421(08)60536-8
[6]   Belrose, N., Schneider-Joseph, D., Ravfogel, S., et al. (2023). LEACE: Perfect linear concept erasure in closed form. https://arxiv.org/abs/2306.03819

[7] Phung, D. V., Thakur, A., Castricato, L., Tow, J., and Havrilla, A. (2025). Implementing RLHF: Learning to summarize with trlX. Weights & Measures. https://mng.bz/rKzg

[8] Kolter, Z., and Madry, M. (n.d.). Adversarial robustness: Theory and practice. https://adversarial-ml-tutorial.org/

[9] OpenAI. (2023, March 27). GPT-4 technical report. https://cdn.openai.com/papers/gpt-4.pdf

[10] Chowdhery, A., Narang, S., Devlin, J., et al. (2022). PaLM: Scaling language modeling with pathways. https://arxiv.org/abs/2204.02311

[11] Liang, W., Izzo, Z., Zhang, Y., et al. (2024). Monitoring AI-modified content at scale: A case study on the impact of ChatGPT on AI conference peer reviews. https://arxiv.org/abs/2403.07183

[12] Li, C., and Flanigan, J. (2023). Task contamination: Language models may not be few-shot anymore. https://arxiv.org/abs/2312.16337

[13] Near, J. P., and Abuah, C. (2021). *Programming Differential Privacy*. https://programming-dp.com/

Chapter 6

[1] Albergotti, R., and Matsakis, L. (2023, January 23). OpenAI has hired an army of contractors to make basic coding obsolete. Semafor. https://mng.bz/MDGQ

[2] Introducing Code Llama, a state-of-the-art large language model for coding. (2023, August 24). Meta. https://mng.bz/av2j

[3] von Werra, L., and Ben Allal, L. (2023, May 4). StarCoder: A state-of-the-art LLM for code. Hugging Face. https://huggingface.co/blog/starcoder

[4] Biderman, S., and Raff, E. (2022). Fooling MOSS detection with pretrained language models. https://arxiv.org/abs/2201.07406.

[5] Dyer, E., and Gur-Ari, G. (2020, June 30). Minerva: Solving quantitative reasoning problems with language models. Google Research. https://mng.bz/gane.

[6] Azerbayev, Z., Schoelkopf, H., Paster, K., et al. (2023, October 16). Llemma: An open language model for mathematics. EleutherAI. https://blog.eleuther.ai/llemma/

[7] Richardson, D. (1968). Some undecidable problems involving elementary functions of a real variable. *Journal of Symbolic Logic, 33*, 514–520.

[8] Nogueira, R., Jiang, Z., and Lin, J. (2021). Investigating the limitations of transformers with simple arithmetic tasks. https://arxiv.org/abs/2102.13019v3

[9] Golkar, S., Pettee, M., Eickenberg, M., et al. (2024). Investigating the limitations of transformers with simple arithmetic tasks. https://arxiv.org/abs/2310.02989

Chapter 7

[1] Romeo, R. R., Leonard, J. A., Robinson, S. T., et al. (2018). Beyond the 30-million-word gap: Children's conversational exposure is associated with language-related

brain function. *Psychological Science, 29,* 700–710. https://doi.org/10.1177/0956797617742725

[2] Gilkerson, J., Richards, J. A., Warren, S. F., et al. (2017). Mapping the early language environment using all-day recordings and automated analysis. *American Journal of Speech-Language Pathology, 26,* 248-265. https://doi.org/10.1044/2016_AJSLP-15-0169

[3] Shumailov, I., Shumaylov, Z., Zhao, Y., et al. (2024). The curse of recursion: Training on generated data makes models forget. https://arxiv.org/abs/2305.17493

[4] Stanovich K. E. (2009). *What Intelligence Tests Miss: The Psychology of Rational Thought.* Yale University Press.

[5] Improving the realism of synthetic images. (2017, July 7). Apple Machine Learning Research. https://machinelearning.apple.com/research/gan

[6] Dai, D., Sun, Y., Dong, L., et al. (2023). Why can GPT learn in-context? Language models secretly perform gradient descent as meta-optimizers. In *Findings of the Association for Computational Linguistics: ACL 2023* (pp. 4005–4019). Association for Computational Linguistics.

[7] Hiller, J. (2023, December 12). Microsoft targets nuclear to power AI operations. *Wall Street Journal.* https://mng.bz/pKe5

[8] Disavino, S. (2023, September 8). Texas power prices soar as grid passes reliability test in heat wave. Reuters. https://mng.bz/OB0K

[9] Emoji recently added, v15.1. (n.d.). Unicode. https://www.unicode.org/emoji/charts-15.1/emoji-released.html

[10] Wei, J., Wang, X., Schuurmans, D., et al. (2023). Chain-of-thought prompting elicits reasoning in large language models. https://arxiv.org/abs/2201.11903

[11] Wang, L., Xu, W., Lan, Y., et al. (2023). Plan-and-solve prompting: Improving zero-shot chain-of-thought reasoning by large language models. In *Proceedings of the 61st Annual Meeting of the Association for Computational Linguistics* (Vol. 1: Long Papers, pp. 2609-2634). Association for Computational Linguistics.

[12] Guan, L., Valmeekam, K., Sreedharan, S., and Kambhampati, S. (2023). Leveraging pre-trained large language models to construct and utilize world models for model-based task planning. https://arxiv.org/abs/2305.14909

[13] Bhargava, A. Y. (2015). *Grokking Algorithms: An illustrated Guide for Programmers and Other Curious People.* Manning Publications.

[14] Merrill, W., and Sabharwal, S. (2024). The expressive power of transformers with chain of thought. In *International Conference on Learning Representations 2024.* https://openreview.net/forum?id=NjNGlPh8Wh

[15] Carlini, N. (2023, September 22). Playing chess with large language models. https://nicholas.carlini.com/writing/2023/chess-llm.html

[16] Edwards B. (2022, November 7). New Go-playing trick defeats world-class Go AI—but loses to human amateurs. *Ars Technica.* https://mng.bz/dW6O

Chapter 8

[1] Yagoda, M. (2024, February 23). Airline held liable for its chatbot giving passenger bad advice—what this means for travellers. BBC. https://mng.bz/xK7W

[2] Notopoulos, K. (2023, December 18). A car dealership added an AI chatbot to its site: Then all hell broke loose. https://mng.bz/AQPz

[3] Suresh, H., Lao, N., and Liccardi, I. (2020). Misplaced trust: Measuring the interference of machine learning in human decision-making. In *Proceedings of the 12th ACM Conference on Web Science (WebSci '20)* (pp. 315-324). Association for Computing Machinery. https://doi.org/10.1145/3394231.3397922

Chapter 9

[1] Hofmann, V., Kalluri, P. R., Jurafsky, D., and King, S. (2024). Dialect prejudice predicts AI decisions about people's character, employability, and criminality. https://arxiv.org/abs/2403.00742

[2] Omiye, J. A., Lester, J. C., Spichak, S. et al. (2023). Large language models propagate race-based medicine. npj Digital Medicine, 6, 195. https://doi.org/10.1038/s41746-023-00939-z

[3] Farm labor. (2025, January 8). Economic Research Service. https://www.ers.usda.gov/topics/farm-economy/farm-labor/

[4] Verma, P., and De Vync, G. (2023, June 2). ChatGPT took their jobs: Now they walk dogs and fix air conditioners. *The Washington Post.* https://mng.bz/EwQd

[5] Marr, B. (2024, April 18). The role of generative AI in video game development. *Forbes.* https://mng.bz/Pdpn

[6] Lev-Ram, M. (2023, January 26). Casualties of Big Tech layoffs find other companies are clamoring to hire them. *Forbes.* https://mng.bz/JYXV

[7] Lohr, S. (2024, February 1). Generative A.I.'s biggest impact will be in banking and tech, report says. *New York Times.* https://mng.bz/wJ7P

[8] Pethokoukis, J. (2016, June 16). What the story of ATMs and bank tellers reveals about the "rise of the robots" and jobs. American Enterprise Institute. https://mng.bz/qx7r

[9] Hunter, L. W., Bernhardt, A., Hughes, K. L., and Skuratowicz, E. (2001). It's not just the ATMs: Technology, firm strategies, jobs, and earnings in retail banking. *ILR Review, 54*(2A), 402-424. https://doi.org/10.1177/001979390105400222

[10] Rosalsky, G. (2024, June 18). If AI is so good, why are there still so many jobs for translators? NPR. https://mng.bz/7pBv

[11] Marr, B. (2024, May 28). How generative AI will change the jobs of artists and designers. *Forbes.* https://mng.bz/mG7a

[12] Autor, D., Chin, C., Salomons, A., and Seegmiller, B. (2024). New frontiers: The origins and content of new work, 1940–2018. *The Quarterly Journal of Economics, 139,* 1399–1465. https://doi.org/10.1093/qje/qjae008

[13] Dave, P. (2023, April 8). StackOverflow will charge AI giants for training data. *Wired.* https://mng.bz/5gDO

[14] Grimm, D. (2024, May 8). Stack Overflow bans users en masse for rebelling against OpenAI partnership—users banned for deleting answers to prevent them being used to train ChatGPT. Tom's Hardware. https://mng.bz/nR75

[15] Bishop, T. (2020, October 20). Expedia Group CEO on Google antitrust case: "Very pleased to see the government finally taking action." Geek Wire. https://mng.bz/vK7p

[16] Siddiqui, T. (2023, June 29). Risks of artificial intelligence must be considered as the technology evolves: Geoffrey Hinton. University of Toronto. https://mng.bz/4aNR

[17] Bengio, Y. (2023, June 24). FAQ on catastrophic AI risks. https://mng.bz/QDO6

[18] Introducing Llama 3.1: Our most capable models to date. (2024, July 23). Meta. https://ai.meta.com/blog/meta-llama-3-1/

[19] Min, S., Gururangan, S., Wallace, E., et al. (2023). SILO language models: Isolating legal risk in a nonparametric datastore. https://arxiv.org/abs/2308.04430

[20] Rivero, N. (2022, September 21). Low-background metal: Pure, unadulterated treasure. *Quartz.* https://mng.bz/eyXZ

[21] Shumailov, I., Shumaylov, Z., Zhao, Y. et al. (2024). AI models collapse when trained on recursively generated data. *Nature, 631,* 755–759. https://doi.org/10.1038/s41586-024-07566-y

[22] Coffey, L. (2024, February 9). Professors cautious of tools to detect AI-generated writing. Inside Higher Education. https://mng.bz/Xxj9

[23] Has Stack Exchange's traffic decreased since ChatGPT? (2023). Stack Exchange. https://mng.bz/yW7p

[24] Dhamani, N., and Engler, M. (2024). *Introduction to Generative AI.* Manning. https://www.manning.com/books/introduction-to-generative-ai

index

RELATED MANNING TITLES

LLMs in Production
By Christopher Brousseau and Matthew Sharp
Foreword by Joe Reis

ISBN 9781633437203
456 pages, $59.99
December 2024

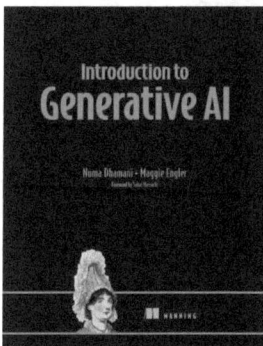

Introduction to Generative AI
by Numa Dhamani and Maggie Engler
Foreword by Sahar Massachi

ISBN 9781633437197
336 pages, $49.99
January 2024

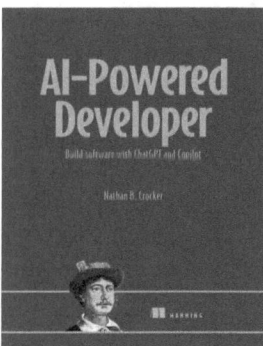

AI-Powered Developer
by Nathan B. Crocker

ISBN 9781633437616
240 pages, $49.99
August 2024

For ordering information, go to www.manning.com

RELATED MANNING TITLES

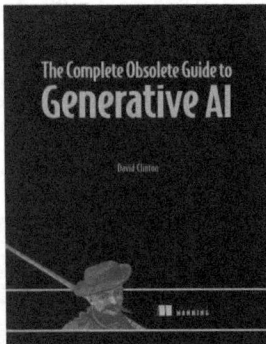

The Complete Obsolete Guide to Generative AI
by David Clinton

ISBN 9781633436985
240 pages, $39.99
July 2024

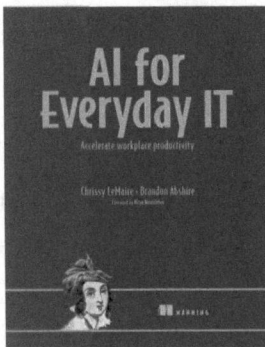

AI for Everyday IT
Chrissy LeMaire and Brandon Abshire
Foreword by Nitya Narasimhan

ISBN 9781633436428
376 pages, $49.99
May 2025

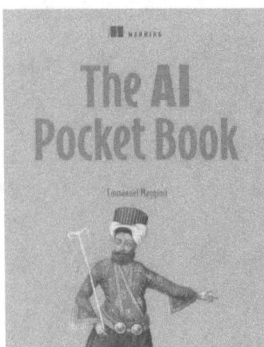

The AI Pocket Book
by Emmanuel Maggiori

ISBN 9781633435759
200 pages, $39.99
July 2025

For ordering information, go to www.manning.com